INDIA CHARM OFFENSIVE

An Expat Pilot Flies The South Asia Jungle

MICHAEL SOBOTTA

Copyright © Michael Sobotta, 2015
All rights reserved

Michael Sobotta has asserted his right under the Copyright, Designs and Patents Act 1988 to be identified as the author of this work.

No part of this publication may be reprinted or reproduced, stored in a retrieval system, or transmitted in any form or by any means, mechanical, electronic, photocopying, recording, or otherwise, without the prior written permission of the publisher.

This paperwork edition published in 2015 by Globerunner Press
15/682 Ramkhamhang Road, Soi 9,
Huamak, Bangkapi, Bangkok, Thailand
Email: information@globerunner.us
www.michaelsobotta.com

This book is a work of non-fiction based on the recollections of the author. Names have been changed to protect the privacy of those who wished to remain anonymous.

Design consultation Phunyanuch Prasantong.

ISBN-10: 0-692-71871-0
ISBN-13: 978-0-692-71871-1

Printed and bound in the United States of America

Many thanks to my parents for years of insistent solicitude—and who took the swearing from this book.* Most of all, thanks to my incomparably beautiful, patient and tolerant wife, Phunyanuch. You took the swearing from my life.

---

*Most of the swearing.

Contents

1. The High Seas — 1
2. Waves of Discontent — 7
3. Mutinous Pilot — 12
4. Delhi Arrival — 18
5. India! — 24
6. Don't Take Tension — 29
7. India Attractions — 35
8. Welcome to the Jungle — 41
9. Don't Take My Kidneys — 47
10. Taking Flight — 53
11. Raipur — 59
12. Morning Black Gold — 64
13. Jagdalpur — 70
14. General Condition, Fair — 78
15. Namaskar Chatterjee — 84
16. Plasmodium Falciparum — 90
17. Red Menace — 98
18. Culture Clubbed — 106
19. Paradise City — 112
20. Security Insecurity — 117
21. Smiley and the Reaper — 123
22. Beereaucracy — 129
23. Bhubaneswar — 136
24. Lock and Load — 144
25. Scandalous Diversion — 149
26. Two-Wheeling — 157
27. Cold Milk — 163
28. Red Planet — 169
29. Spiderman — 174

Contents

30.	Bossus Interruptus	180
31.	Joyriding Rainman	186
32.	Tirathgarh Falls	193
33.	Around the Horn	199
34.	Uneasy Rider	206
35.	Vertical Tsunami	212
36.	The Big Time	218
37.	Old Wicked Ways	224
38.	Middle of Nowhere	230
39.	The Shining	235
40.	Ambushed	240
41.	Carnival of Life	246
42.	Puri Beach	252
43.	One Night in Bangkok	258
44.	The Sky is Crying	264
45.	Happy Diwali	270
46.	Bottle Bass	276
47.	The General	282
48.	King of the Jungle	287
49.	Heart of Glass	293
50.	Chaos at Kistaram	298
51.	Escape India	304
52.	Anika	310
53.	Goat Rodeo	316
54.	Scarred for Life	322
55.	So This Is Christmas	328
56.	New Year	336
57.	Mumbai	343
58.	I.N.D.I.A.	349

The air up there in the clouds is very pure and fine, bracing and delicious. And why shouldn't it be? It is the same the angels breathe.
- Mark Twain

1.

The High Seas

"That bushing is out again, Cager," I said, giving the helicopter its postflight. "Come here and have a look."

The helicopter, a Hughes 369, had been built in the 1970s for use as a wartime scout. We used it for scouting as well, but in a less hostile environment than a battlefield; we were looking for tuna fish in the South Pacific. The old warbird was light, nimble and a blast to fly.

"Well, lemme see it," Cager said, fumbling with his glasses. "S'pose I can press it back in d'ere again. I'll need the ladder and a couple 'a deckhands to help lift the blade… round 'em up for me, yah?"

One eye squinting from cigarette smoke, he glared at me with his un-squinted eye and continued in his impatient, whiny twang, "Or can you help, Your Highness?"

Cager was five foot four and a hundred-twenty pounds, a wiry man about sixty years old with a face sufficiently weathered to have worn out two bodies. Gray, sparse hair and a furrowed brow topped his scowling face and permanently lit cigarette. He had David Bowie eyes, and usually perched on top of his semi-bare cranium at odd angles were smeared reading glasses. What Cager lacked in physical attributes, he made up for with an enviable wit, delivered with such scathing eloquence that verbal sparring was futile. He wasn't shy about sharing his merciless opinion concerning any situation, or me.

I had just landed on the *F/V Universe Kim*, a Korean-owned fishing vessel, after a two-hour flight looking for schools of feeding tuna. We were twelve days and a few hundred miles out of Honiara, Guadalcanal, in the Solomon Islands and had been monitoring the condition of one of the helicopter's pesky rotor blade bushings that did not want to stay put. Cager had been able to press the bushing back into place twice already, but it was becoming an all too troubling reoccurrence. The bushing in question was part of the assembly that held the helicopter's main rotor blades in place, and it was one of two bushings in the root of the rotor blade for which a steel pin went through to attach it to the rotor-head.

According to the maintenance manual, there could be no movement of the bushing, but after this flight it had already moved considerably from where it was meant to be. My fear was that if it came out only partially, spinning around in flight at a few hundred rotor RPM, the rotor-head would become out of balance to the point where I would have to ditch, possibly many miles from the boat. And in the worst case, the helicopter could suffer a catastrophic inflight breakup.

I was halfway through a twelve-month contract working with Cager on a pilot-mechanic team contracted to vessels belonging to this fishing outfit, and in fairness to my homely helicopter mechanic, I'd never won any Mr. Universe titles or modeling contracts either. I had previously worked in Africa, among other places, and when my contract finished there, I had expected to return to the United States and find a job flying helicopters for the oil and gas business in the Gulf of Mexico.

By some stroke of luck, I was invited to interview for a job there in Louisiana and had even been offered a position, but was then unsure that I'd like it. I had also been offered this job on the tuna boat around that time and although I knew it would keep me away from cheeseburgers and apple pie, it sounded like more of an adventure. I declined the offer from the Gulf, waited for my ticket from Guam, and packed my bags for the islands.

But, in my new job, the islands were rarely seen. Home was the boat, a two-hundred-foot-long by forty-foot-wide purse seiner fishing vessel and we cruised the ocean in search of tuna.

At the stern of the vessel sat an immense, neatly piled black net, and perched close by was a large metal skiff. Once within range of a school of tuna, this skiff would be launched with great howling and cheers from the captain and crew. It banged and slid and splashed down into the water, dragging out the net, which it began to deploy for the catch. With black smoke spewing from the stacks and diesel engines roaring, the vessel then powered forward, leaning into the 360-degree turn to encircle the fish. When it reached the skiff again, both ends of the net were secured, closing the loop.

The cable at the bottom of the six-hundred-foot-deep by mile-and-a-half-long net was then winched aboard the vessel, causing the bottom to purse, or close, and the fish to become trapped inside. Most of the net would then be hauled in, making the pursed net smaller and smaller until it became easier to scoop the fish from the shrinking purse by crane. The crane dropped them to the deck, where they slid down a chute into the holding freezer.

That is, if everything went as planned. If, for whatever reason, the fish were wise to us and stopped their surface feeding to dive away and escape from the net, dark clouds and mayhem would descend upon the ship. Misery awaited the deckhand or mate that was so naive or slow as to be within range of the captain's vitriol after such an Earth-ending calamity.

His wrath mainly consisted of spittle-infused, Korean verbal beheadings, but at times he deemed it necessary to include a few backhands, forehands or tight-fisted jabs to the first, second or third mates, or to whoever was within striking distance. He never directed his fury at Cager or me; we always managed to stay away from his blast zone and busy ourselves up on the helideck. Our only punishment would be no Soju liquor that evening at chow, as with the rest of the crew, but we had our own secretly pillaged stash back in the cabin anyway.

The helideck sat toward the bow and on top of the bridge. From there, I would land and take off once or twice a day, depending upon the captain's mood. It sat just forward of too many antennas for my comfort, and of the towering steel mast that held up the crow's nest. Even covered with several coats of paint, it wasn't hard to see scrapes and gouges in the steel, evidence of an unfortunate accident years before; a pilot had hovered too close and his spinning rotor blades struck this small forest of antennas, sending disintegrating shards of metal and fiberglass exploding in every direction.

The area forward to the bow was not used much except during mooring operations; it was mainly for storage of spare nets and other fishing equipment, and rarely would I see anybody there while underway. One person who did make his daily rounds through the bow area was the cook, a militantly superstitious fellow who would take good Soju and sprinkle it on the deck, or over the side railing, in an offering of repentance to the gods of the seas.

The first time I saw him do this was because of me and my good mood. On a lazy afternoon not long after joining the ship, I strolled into the galley whistling a Dwight Yoakam tune. The few of the crew who were there stopped their conversing and stared at me. I detected hostility and stopped my whistling, but not before the cook had heard me, and he stood there, butcher knife in hand, glaring at me with hatred-filled eyes.

I knew something was wrong, but didn't know what until the vessel's chief engineer croaked out a nervous chuckle and explained that what I'd done was considered bad luck. Evidently, to whistle while at sea was to "challenge the wind"— but at the time the wind seemed to be the least of my worries, unless I survived the upcoming knife fight with the cook. It was a superstition I'd never heard of, even back in my Navy days, although more than one senior chief had tried to make me a good sailor.

To the rear of the helideck, we had a big metal cabinet for parts, tools and Cager's marijuana; he had handpicked the weed himself from a hillside on Guadalcanal. Beyond that were the aforementioned antennas and mast, more spare nets and other tackle, then the ladder down to the main deck, where the crew spent most of their time.

Many of the crewmembers were Korean, but there were Malaysians, Indonesians and Filipinos as well. A hard-working bunch, living in tough conditions, with no chance for rest until lights out at night. Not even when the freezer was full and the vessel sailed to port to offload the catch did they get a break. Once in port, the captain headed to the nearest hotel and, if available, golf course while the crew worked day and night to transfer the tuna onto the enormous freezer ship.

While underway, if they were not working the net on fish, they were doing net repair or other sailor work. If it was slow, the paint would be brought out and the boat attacked with brushes and rollers. In the event that the last paint job was holding up, a good scrub down would be ordered, and they were not afraid to suds it up.

On one absent-minded occasion, I was heading down below from the helideck and the instant my flip-flopped feet made contact with the top step of the recently soaped-up ladder, my feet went one way, my butt the other way and my flip-flops went sailing through the air like clay pigeons at a skeet range. By the time I clanged and clattered to the bottom of the ladder, the crew had gathered around to recover any loose change or valuables that might've shaken loose during my descent.

Seeing that I was still alive, they rounded up my flip-flops and helped me and my bruised bum up off the wet deck. From his perch on the helideck, Cager scowled, his face veiled in cigarette smoke. He hollered, "P'urty good! You got a shot at 'dem O-lympics!"

If the crew was lucky enough to net tuna, the main deck was the scene of the major action: the tuna's first stop on the journey to a can in the supermarket. But other hapless creatures which happened to be in the wrong place at the wrong time would end up in the net too, and they would meet their demise on that deck. Stingrays, sailfish—the crew would be overjoyed to catch a shark or two—before being dumped back into the ocean, their fins brutally sliced off and hung to dry. Just to flavor an ignorant man's soup in the Orient.

I am not happy to report that the main deck was large enough to accommodate a humpback whale, and sometimes did so. Of course, killing these and other beautiful beasts was illegal, but being hundreds of miles from any authority made enforcement difficult. Certainly all of the crews out there, who came from Japan, China, Korea and Taiwan, among other countries, were not seeking to net a whale or the like, but more certain was that they would not open their nets to set them free; in doing so, they would be setting free thousands of dollars' worth of tuna.

These purse seiners were built for high-seas fishing, manned by a crew of twenty-five men or so. They held around fifteen hundred to two thousand tons of tuna and could stay out to sea for as long as it took to catch that amount, usually three to four weeks if the fishing was average. There are a lot of those vessels out there, and many of them utilize a helicopter. The captains that I had the opportunity to work with would not leave port without one, and not for just the status the aircraft implied; many considered it a vital tool in their hunt for tuna.

2.

Waves of Discontent

Fanning away Cager's cigarette smoke, I put forth a query. "Wait a second, Cager. How many times has that bushing been pressed back into place?"

I knew the answer, and I knew he knew. I just wanted my chain-smoking master mechanic to stop and consider what he was saying and planning on doing—going the quick-fix, jury-rigged route—given that the consequences of his actions could be hazardous to my health.

The evening before, while pouring Budweiser down our throats, we had also been poring over the helicopter manufacturer's maintenance manual. When we browsed the pages regarding the rotor blade bushings and pins, we found it clearly stated that these bushings could not simply be pressed back into place after each flight. The problem called for more in-depth maintenance to be performed. In other words, the manufacturer didn't authorize the helicopter to be flown in its present condition.

"Fine," Cager growled. "If you don' wanna fly it, let's have a chat with the boss back in Guam."

We may have been hundreds of miles from land, but, through the marvel of satellite communication, the boss could be on the phone in a matter of minutes. The boss was also the company owner, and in exchange for his providing helicopters, pilots and mechanics to the fishing fleets, the fleets provided fuel and food for the helicopter and crews, plus a fat fee back to the owner.

"Hold up, Cager," I said. "You've seen it yourself that the maintenance manual says we can't fly it with a gimpy bushing like this. Don't you think we should fix it the right way?"

Cager had one blue eye and one brown eye. Combined with the cigarette smoke, his mood would determine which one was squinted shut and which one I'd see. Evidently to conserve ocular energy, he only used one at a time, sort of like Popeye. Seeing the blue eye meant that we could perhaps have a beer and be friends, but if his brown peeper was glaring back at me, a quick review of my Last Will and Testament was in order.

The eyelid covering his friendly eye was clamped firmly shut, and he stared at me as if I had insulted his mother.

I continued, "If that bushing works itself out during flight, there'll only be a debris-laden oil patch to mark the spot where I drilled into the ocean, if that."

That may have come out a bit dramatic, but the possibility did exist.

"Hell man," I said, "even if I was fortunate enough to ditch before it came apart, there's a whole lot of water out there while I'm forty miles from the boat. How many sharks are gonna pay a visit before the boat reaches me?"

Forty miles, give or take, was about the furthest I ever flew from the boat. Sometimes the first mate came along, sometimes the captain. The normal routine would be to fly an hour and a half to two hours in the morning and then the same in the afternoon or evening. Unless there was something specific we needed to survey, we would take off and fly in a straight line for forty miles, turn ninety degrees, fly another forty miles, and so on, flying a rough box pattern until we landed back on the vessel, which had been plodding steadily along.

We always flew with the doors off, at five hundred to a thousand feet, on the lookout for "foamers." Tuna feed on small fish like mackerel or sardines, and if these prey fish are near the surface of the water, it becomes white and frothy from all the jumping, swirling, splashing and eating. From several hundred feet in the air, it looks like a white sea of foam. The average foamer was about the size of a football field, but the biggest I ever saw must have covered nearly thirty acres.

During that flight, I had the first mate with me and, upon seeing this massive fish frenzy, he leaned out the door like a

Labrador in a pickup truck, ecstatically pointing and screaming Korean into the radio while the captain screamed back at him. The huge foamer was quite a distance from the boat, and all we could do was circle it until getting low on fuel, and then had to fly back and meet the vessel while it was en route to the spot. They had us on radar and the location dialed in, and were steaming our way posthaste.

The captain was having a spitting conniption over the radio and was in a hurry to get to this apparent great tuna convention. He was in such a hurry that he wouldn't slow his ship to land my helicopter when we returned. Waves were nearly breaking over the bow, and landing on the pitching and rolling helideck was a tad sporty in the rougher-than-usual swells.

Luck was with the tuna that day; by the time our vessel made the location, the ocean was quiet and not a fish was in sight.

Sometimes while we were out scouting, the ship would radio us to check out a specific radar return they had picked up. The quality of electronics on the vessel, including radar and fish-finding sonar, was impressive. Radar could pick up a concentration of a few birds miles away from the boat—an occurrence that potentially signified feeding fish—and direct us to the spot to check it out.

Of course, our helicopter showed up on radar too. I learned that quick enough on my first flight, when the straight line I thought I was flying wasn't as straight as the captain wanted it to be, and he ordered me to quit lollygagging—in the equivalent Korean—and fly an absolute straight heading. They kept a close eye on their helicopter. But that was helpful during rainy weather; the ship could watch both us and the clouds and guide us around them to safety and sunshine via radio.

I never had the chance to check if our helicopter would show up on the ship's sonar—gladly—but when on the bridge, I would stare transfixed at its bright screen, watching the shapes and forms of creatures from the deep, wondering what might be lurking below.

Another common tactic the crew used to find tuna was deploying radio beacon-equipped buoys over, or attached to, drifting flotsam that had the potential to hold fish. The buoys would be dropped from either the vessel or our helicopter and secured with a length of line and a grappling hook. Left alone for several days, weeks or months, the hope was that in the interim, a school of tuna would be attracted to the prey fish congregating around the flotsam raft.

Once while I was hovering over a raft such as this, attempting to deploy a buoy from the bottom of our helicopter, the buoy got caught up in the release mechanism and to no avail could we shake it loose from inside the cockpit. Without consulting me and before I could stop him, the first mate shucked his headset, removed his seat belt and was bouncing, then hanging from the helicopter's float landing gear, trying to set the seized equipment free.

I looked at the size of the swells and knew that if he fell in, it would be a long swim. There was no way I'd be able to land in the water to pick him up without capsizing. After a few tense minutes, he was finally able to dislodge the buoy and send it splashing into the water. He returned with smiles, laughter and relief to his seat beside me. I would guess he was more afraid of facing the captain's wrath for not deploying the buoy than having an unexpected dip with the sharks in the ocean.

The ship's officers were a cold, hard bunch. While I dallied on the bridge one day, a distress call came across the marine radio from someone on a sailing yacht requesting medicine for a family member who had fallen ill. Everyone on the bridge ignored the call. They ignored me as well when I offered to fly the medicine over to the yacht and drop it off. At that time, we were traveling with four other fishing vessels, hot on the trail of the catch, and no one was changing course. At times like these I started to root for the tuna, though the sooner we filled the freezer, the sooner we could return to port and the island honeys.

The first time I met the boat when coming from Guam, via Australia, was in Tarawa, Republic of Kiribati. I was immediately transfixed with the beauty of island women. At that time I was single, and they were dark-haired, lightly tanned and curvaceous young ladies with bright, white smiles. They had me daydreaming about ditching my plans to meet the tuna boat and, instead, spending a few weeks getting more acquainted.

I didn't have a few weeks, but ended up with around a week before going to work, and from my temporary home at the little dance club adjacent to the Otintaai Hotel, I tried to see as much of the historic island as possible. While a youngster, I had read and reread numerous books about the battles of World War Two, including those on Guadalcanal and Tarawa, but not once had the thought entered my mind that I'd set foot in such far-off places.

I was curious to see the beaches where the fighting took place. On Tarawa, the Japanese big beach guns and defenses were still there, the salty ocean air having a hard time corroding away all that cast iron and steel. Along the main road, which was bordered on each side by islanders' huts, I saw pigs and other livestock tied up to, or fenced in with, old military vehicle parts. Near the port, lying half submerged in water was an American tank patiently rusting away.

It was hard to imagine the immense loss of life occurring for such a tiny island.

3.

Mutinous Pilot

Cager belched out a cloud of smoke that darkened the afternoon sun.

"Now listen, I got good 'ndustrial adhesive 'dat I know will hold 'dat bushing in place." His gnarled fist waved a tube of the magical paste through the smoky air. "All I gotta do is take it apart, 'pply this adhesive, reassemble and let the thang cure for twenty-four hours."

He pulled the glasses off the top of his noggin down to his nose and started reading the label on the tube. "She'll be good as the day she came off the fact'ry floor!"

Though I had used it to good effect on model helicopters during childhood, I didn't think glue was what the helicopter manufacturer had in mind when detailing the repair job in the maintenance manual.

"But ain't gonna start on it today," Cager said. "Gittin' late and close to chow time. I'll go talk to the captain and tell 'im there'll be no flyin' for a couple days due to maint'nance."

Giving the dislodged bushing a final glance, I jumped down off the helicopter's float and started to put the doors back on, something we did to protect the interior after nightfall. *You just go do that, Cager,* I thought. *I'll be up here weighing options.*

"I won' tell 'im the nature of the maint'nance," he gave a chuckle that turned into a cringey, vein-popping smoker's cough. Several moments passed while he recovered his breath, then he brought the discussion to a close. "Jus' 'dat it's routine repair. If he knows it's the rotor-head, he might freak out."

With that he lit up another cigarette, glared at me with his brown eye and walked away.

I was not comfortable with his maintenance plan. There were other maintenance discrepancies on the bird already that should've had it grounded. Dented tailboom, rivets missing on the fuselage, unchecked corrosion—the list was getting longer and my faith shorter.

Perhaps it was time for me to move on. When at port in Honiara the previous trip, I had received an email from a pilot friend of mine working in India. He claimed that all manner of great and wondrous things were happening there, and the odds of a pilot position for me were no less than ninety-nine percent.

It seemed like a comely experience: flying over land instead of ocean, with a full team of maintenance support, not to mention the freedom of land-based operations versus living on a tiny boat. My friend was wondering if I'd be interested in leaving the ocean breezes and tuna fish behind to give it a go in India's land of charm.

He did mention that there would be an element of danger, however. Something about Maoist guerrillas. In that region of India, a violent Maoist insurgency had been worsening, and the Indian government was beginning to put more cash and resources toward the problem; that was the main impetus behind the offer of employment. Danger aside, it would be a substantial pay increase, doubling the salary I was then receiving. The potential job involved flying a Eurocopter Astar helicopter in remote parts of East India, transporting police and paramilitary forces along with government VIPs. He explained that his employer was in the midst of negotiating a long-term contract with the government but that the signing of terms was inevitable.

I had never been to India, didn't know what the country was like, or its people, although I'd had the occasion to work with Indians in the past. It sounded like an exotic adventure, and I was intrigued with the offer—besides the salary increase, food and lodging would be paid for, and there were tax advantages for my continued work abroad.

I didn't care to put my current employer in a bind, though. I had a few months remaining on my contract and, for all the rough and spartan living, I was still enjoying the escapade. Just waking up in the morning and looking out at the brilliant South Pacific sunrise beat a lot of other ways I could've been earning a buck. Sure, the food and lodging aboard was not the greatest, but that made the port-of-calls all the more enjoyable once I reached them.

Nonetheless, the opening was there, and the motors and gears were turning in my head. As Cager headed down below deck in his cloud of carcinogens, I began to steel myself for the imminent confrontation with him and the boss. This wasn't the first time that lax maintenance had made me uncomfortable, but perhaps this was the proverbial straw that broke the camel's back.

That evening, we talked the mechanical problems over further, but between the Soju we had at chow and another Budweiser or two watching the sunset on the main deck, the discussion was not of quality. All depositions, arguments and assertions were hereby brought to a halt when Cager declared that he was tired of talking. All he wanted to do from that moment forward was to smoke his Honiara Hillside Hash and contemplate his navel.

I figured that was for the best. While he mumbled and stumbled up the ladder to the helideck, I watched the first stars pop out of their daytime hiding, thinking about India and what better life must await me there.

Morning came and, along with it, clearer heads and subdued small talk, but nothing had changed. Cager could not be persuaded to take a different view, and I had lost all confidence in the suggested arrangement. I wasn't about to give my approval for the maintenance action. The two of us were leaning on the side rail, sipping coffee and watching the ship's waves roll out into the blue water as we chugged along.

Between hacks of his morning cough, he wheezed irritably, "Mike, you wanna fly or not?"

I'd reached the end of his rope. Of course I wanted to fly, but I wanted the problem repaired according to the manufacturer.

There's a reason they compile a detailed maintenance manual. Their repair procedures, I could trust.

We had already checked with the boss, and the boss was behind Cager.

"We don't have time for an in-depth repair job," were the orders from headquarters the previous evening. "Use adhesive on the bushing and get that son of a bitch back in the air!"

In the tame early morning sun, Cager watched me with both eyes—briefly confusing me.

"No," I said. "I won't fly it with that glue."

And that was the end of my tuna fishing days. Without another word, Cager spat out a loogie, flicked his cigarette into the ocean and went to call the boss, who promptly called on me to take a hike. I informed the captain that I would not be flying the helicopter any longer. He took it surprisingly well; his freezer hold was around eighty-percent full, so he decided to head back to Honiara port, offload the catch and get the helicopter sorted out, plus play a round or three of golf.

Again, through the wizardry of satellites, plus the grace of the communications officer, I was able to email my potential new boss in India and then place a call to him twice while en route to port. With my first call, I woke him at four in the morning; guessing at India's time zone, I mistakenly thought it was eight o'clock in the morning, Delhi time, from where we were in the ocean. But he was congenial, understanding and forgiving, and the next time I called we were able to talk contracts, employment visa and starting dates. I knew this decision was destined to work out for the better.

While it bothered me leaving in the middle of a contract like that, my early departure apparently didn't bother the company, as they gave me the full month's salary. There weren't any hard feelings between Cager and me either. After reaching port, I'd see him around the Pacific Hotel, and we had breakfast together a few times, and beers in the evening.

He was usually in the company of one of the prettiest island girls I had ever seen. At first I puzzled over what a cute young lady was doing with him—it wasn't his good looks or sparkly personality. Then I noticed that, every day, she would have a new pair of earrings, a flashy new sundress or, the biggie, a new cell phone. Cager confessed that, with a few thousand bucks in hand after payday, anyone should be able to have a good time, "Even someone like me, who fell out of the ugly tree and hit every branch on the way down!"

Having a few days to sort out and make travel arrangements, I took a bit of time discovering Honiara and the countryside, exploring the beaches and battlefields from World War Two. Far up in the hills above town was the American Battle of Guadalcanal Memorial, made up of brown marble slabs that shone blood red in certain light. Looking north from there, I could see white-capped waves out on Iron Bottom Sound, where the United States had lost over twenty naval ships during the engagement. Thirty to fifty thousand troops died during the battle, and one of the Japanese Generals had said, albeit in his own language, "Guadalcanal is not the name of an island. It is the graveyard of the Japanese Army."

The day before I flew out of Honiara, I rented a skiff and brought Cager a couple cases of beer and cigarettes for being a generally friendly source of frivolity and frustration. My old tuna boat was tied up to the immense factory freezer ship, which was at anchor out in the bay, and the crew was hard at it offloading ton after ton of tuna. The captain, predictably, was at the golf course. Most of them took time to stop and say goodbye, wish me best of luck and take a few pictures.

Except for that hard-bitten old cook, they were good-natured guys. Some were just out of school, others had been around a while and had wives or girlfriends back home, a few showed off pictures of both. It's a hell of a life, being out to sea for so many months, only seeing their families occasionally. I had only planned on doing it for a year; these guys were doing it long term.

Riding the skiff back to the pier, I tied off and climbed the ladder to the top, where all manner of shipping containers and freight were awaiting further movement. There, lying next to a half-dozen oil drums, was the damaged and broken-off float landing gear of a Hughes 369. They were identical to the pair on my recently divorced helicopter. Curious, I searched around the fishing vessels in port, trying to find the story behind those floats, and eventually found an eyewitness to the accident. He said the pilot was close to landing back on the ship when the engine sputtered and quit. The helicopter ended up in the water at a bad angle, shearing off the landing gear and floats. The helicopter, with the pilot and fish spotter inside, immediately sank. Neither were able to get out in time and are still at the bottom of the ocean.

A few years after leaving the South Pacific, I came across a stunning photograph on social media of another Hughes 369 that had ditched in the ocean. The ocean swells were not large, and it appeared that the pilot had brought the helicopter down in one piece. One of the floats was losing air, though, and had begun folding over on itself. The tailrotor was submerged, and the helicopter was listing to one side. The pilot was standing on the float, peering into the water as if scanning for sharks and contemplating a swim.

The photo was in an anonymous post on a page pertaining to helicopters, with no time stamp or information provided, but a thought eased into my head. I zoomed in on the registration number and realized that it was my old helicopter, the same helicopter I flew off the *F/V Universe Kim*.

4.

Delhi Arrival

Out of Honiara on the Air Pacific flight to Nadi, Fiji, we had a scheduled landing at Port Vila, Vanuatu, to board several additional passengers. The stop gave me time to stretch my legs, greet the airport-dwelling cattle population and continue daydreaming about India. After Fiji, I would continue my journey to Los Angeles and Minneapolis, and then to my home in Wisconsin. I had money in my pocket, a pancake breakfast in my belly thanks to Fiona at the Pacific Hotel, and a future that held promise.

Upon reaching the airport in Fiji, a cool little band was set up and playing island music at the gate for all the arriving passengers; airline travel holds no joy—an experience closer to volunteering for the slave trade than to civilized passenger travel—and the music, smiles and grass skirts were refreshing. Perked up by the guitars and ukulele, I found a payphone and, feeding it a credit card, called my eventual new boss, Sami. I wanted to touch base and hear if the government contract had been signed yet. Although I had reassurances from Zach, my friend working in India, doubt would continue to nag at the back of my mind until I knew for sure that it was signed and, more importantly, until I saw my own contract in writing.

"You have nothing to worry about, bro!" said Sami, exaggeratingly optimistic. "Just get yourself home, get your employment visa sorted and we will back you one hundred percent. You are family now, Captaaiin!"

After a marathon homeward journey, I arrived back in the States and began preparing to travel to India. The first item I needed was the requisite travel guide. The one I picked up was the thickest travel guide the bookstore had on its shelves, and I stood between the aisles, paging through stories, travel tips and pictures of this exotic and far away land, sinking deeper and deeper into my musing with each page. Another customer, holding a copy of *Eat, Pray, Love* and bundled up from the cold arctic blast passing through the region, noticed me lost within the pages and brought me back to snowbound Wisconsin. "Are you preparing for an adventure?" she asked.

"I am," I said. "If all goes according to plan, I'll be in India by the end of the month, knee deep in masala instead of knee deep in snow."

Curly blonde locks fell from beneath her L. L. Bean fleece hat, damp from the pre-blizzard outside. "I was there two years ago," she said. "It's chaotic and messy, but I'd love to go back." Then she wrinkled her nose. "So hot, though!"

Gesturing outside to the winter wonderland, I said, "I can't feel my toes right now. A little heat sounds like an upgrade."

Due to the time difference, I was getting out of bed in the small hours of the morning to stay in contact with my new friends in Delhi. They had indeed acquired the new contract with the Indian government and, in turn, had sent an employment contract for me to sign.

Obtaining the employment visa was not without frustration or delay, but my time in the United States eventually drew to a close, and I found myself sitting on the tarmac in Minneapolis on a connecting flight to Chicago. A nasty weather delay meant that catching my flight from O'Hare to Delhi was going to be close; after we belatedly landed in the Windy City, while making my first step off the gate into the bustling terminal, I heard the announcement, "Last boarding call, Flight 292 to Delhi..."

I had always pitied the tardy souls I'd seen in the past sprinting through airports, their eyes searching out clues to guide them to their distant gate, backpacks bouncing on their backsides, dodging the other more relaxed and fortunate passengers who had two-hour layovers and were holding overpriced Starbucks lattes. Smugly, I'd be thinking, *Those poor waifs, if they would only plan better and be on time, they wouldn't be knocking over six year olds and tripping over pet carriers. They could be relaxed, like me...*

Now it was my turn to be pitied. Still, no one was hurt during my Olympic-style sprint through the airport, and I reached my boarding gate in time. Quite a few security personnel were there to check me, wondering where I'd been, why I was sweaty and red-faced, why there was latte on my hiking boots. My ID and travel documents checked out, and I was allowed to board the plane, where I received impatient looks from the already settled-in passengers. Finding my seat, I buried my nose in an issue of Newsweek and caught my breath.

In something that has become quite rare, the seats on the Boeing 777 were only filled to three-quarters capacity. The airlines usually have their marketing and sales strategy down to an exact science, knowing just what it takes to have all seats occupied. The vacancies could have been attributed to the fierce storm that had me doing sprints through the terminal; perhaps the unfortunate passengers were delayed or stuck around the country. Another possibility was that they had gone down with medical injuries during their own run through the O'Hare obstacle course.

Their bad luck would turn out to be my good luck during the fourteen hour flight—I had an entire row of four seats to myself. Greedily guarding access to any of "my" seats with loose clothing, pillows, a memoir by Michael Perry and paperbacks from Christopher Robbins, I planned to fold up the armrests and get cozily comfortable after a gin and tonic. In the back of the plane, where I was, whole sections were empty. Soon after the captain turned off the seat belt sign, other travelers began taking over their own multiple seats.

The flight went by quickly. We were fed a couple of times, and I watched a movie or two, but I snoozed away much of the flight. With bleary eyes and a blurry mind, I heard the captain announce our descent into Delhi International Airport.

"It's close to midnight local time, folks," he said, "but the temperature is still one hundred degrees Fahrenheit..."

Delhi Arrival

When I'd left Wisconsin twenty-four hours earlier, it was zero Fahrenheit.

After landing, I could feel the heat soaking through the jet bridge where I walked with my fellow pilgrims, most of them Indians returning to their homeland. It was hard not to notice the extraordinary beauty of Indian women, whether wearing Western-style clothes or their traditional sarees. With their long black hair, dark eyes and mostly fit and trim bodies, it seemed natural to stare with my jaw dropped, although I resisted the impulse. I also noticed the machine-gun carrying security personnel. There had been recent terrorist attacks in Mumbai, and the authorities were on high alert across the country.

I stampeded with the rest of the herd through the airport and down the steps to Immigration where light chaos and all manner of regressive, ill-tempered behavior was taking place. It seemed that politeness and standing in line had not yet been embraced in this strange land. If there was space for a poker card between me and the person in front, it was promptly filled by an elbowing and overeager Indian globetrotter.

In spite of the queue cutting, after a time I was able to amble up to the bored, disinterested and half-asleep immigration officer to offer my passport and virgin employment visa. His eyebrows raised a fraction and he perked up when he saw me approach his glass. He peered first at my face, then my documents and alternated three times between the two. My passport was halfway through its lifespan, and when my picture was taken for it five years before, I'd had the high and tight crew cut, embracing the neat and trim look. Lately, I had been in more of a Bohemian stage, looking hippyish and rough; perhaps confusion had arisen behind his bushy eyebrows. He gave me a meager smile, revealing red paan-stained teeth, and his stamp of approval. Then he handed back my passport, saying, "Welcome to India, Mr. Mee-shell," mispronouncing my given name and briefly making me a Frenchman.

As a youngster, I never gave a thought to the idea that a backwoods country boy like me would ever set foot in India to fly helicopters. I'm sure there were teachers during my reckless school days who would have been surprised if I even found the country on a map. Goes to show that with the right inspiration and hard work, plus knowing the right people, a guy can get around.

After changing a few dollars to Indian rupees, I found my beat-up and over-traveled suitcase at baggage claim and walked out of the terminal to locate the company driver who was supposedly standing by. There were dozens of drivers waiting for passengers lined up at the railing adjacent the door, and they were all holding up signs with names. I walked through the platoon of outstretched arms and mustaches twice before finding my guy, half asleep and snoozing. His sign had drooped down, hiding my name.

Though it was late in the night, there was still a lot of action and general pandemonium on the roads. The driver careened through the streets, dodging all species of motor vehicles and transport. Cattle, bicycle rickshaws, scooters, motorbikes, buses, oxcarts, pedestrians, farm tractors, dump trucks, Tata sedans and still more cattle. The chap hauling the most weight of all, though, was riding his old bicycle, having somehow strapped on a couple hundred pounds of steel rebar destined for a construction site. All the while, a relentless, cacophonous din rose off the streets from the apparent and insane necessity for everyone to lean on their horns.

Sami called while en route via the driver's phone and told me to sleep in the next morning. He said he'd stop by in the afternoon to see me at the company guesthouse where we were heading. This was a small surprise, as I had been told to expect a hotel. I wasn't anticipating a five star, but at least a domicile with adequate comfort, amenities and services. My new accommodations would turn out to be a slight downgrade compared to when I was bunking with Cager back on the tuna boat.

The guesthouse was basic and a tad shabby but, figuring it was standard for my new company's way of doing things, I was content just to be shown my bed. Travel weary and in great need of stretching out, I ignored the few smudges on the bed sheets and plowed headfirst into the dingy pillows of suspect cleanliness.

The time difference between America and India is about ten or eleven hours, so I expected a few rough nights of jet lag, and the first night's sleep was indeed poor. While the house itself seemed to be of robust construction—there are earthquakes in Delhi from time to time—the windows were poorly fitted and ill-maintained. Hence a lot of outside noise became inside noise, including distant traffic and occasional shouting. Plus, we were below the busy approach path to Delhi International.

I had learned long ago that quality ear plugs were an absolute necessity. They are survival gear for a road warrior, and I am much saner for having them. Little sounds still get through, however, and the sound frequency of pigeons cooing tickled my ear drums too easily after what seemed only an hour of sleep that first morning. I woke up when the over-amorous fowl began scrabbling around on the window ledge. The feathered love makers could have been on the pillow next to me for all the commotion.

No problem, I thought. I'd simply go downstairs and rustle up a cup of coffee.

But in India, I would find, nothing could be simple.

5.

India!

Except for a dimly lit image of the Hindu god Shiva, it was dark throughout the house, and although the sun was on its way up outside, all the windows were closed and the inside remained inky black. From my upper-floor room, I carefully maneuvered down the steps to the rug at the bottom.

But it was more than just a rug—it was a human embedded in a rug. The company-hired houseboy was wrapped from head to toe like a pig-in-the-blanket from a man-eating giant's hors d'oeuvres tray. Before realizing the pile of cloth contained a living organism, I clumsily grazed it with my foot, and the innocuous mound of textile erupted into a flurry of wild hair, grunting and elbows. He came scrambling out of the rug crazy-eyed, with ninja speed, and I stumbled and scrambled back up the stairs, fearing an early departure from India, or from this life. Why he preferred the floor to a couch only a couple feet away, I could not ascertain.

After a reality- and eye-adjusting moment or two, his heaving chest slowed. With a venomous gaze, he wondered aloud, in Hindi, just what the hell I wanted and what the hell I was doing.

"Coffee," I said. "I need coffee."

"Kofi?" His furrowed brow and tone implied that this was an absurd request.

"Yes, coffee." I was plenty prepared to make my own and, knowing his English was minimal, I tapped my chest for clarity and added, "I'll make it, no worries, my friend."

When I made that announcement, his dark eyes narrowed even further, and he eased into a position between me and the kitchen door signifying that I, apparently, was not welcome in there. He told me to wait and relax, a difficult thing for an early-morning coffee addict to do until the hot mug was delivered.

India!

But catching the drift and feeling that I'd had enough of the indoors, undid the front door locks and walked outside. Perhaps I'd thin out the number of pigeons living so noisily on my window ledge while I waited for him to make the brew.

The rest of the morning and into the afternoon was unremarkable and lazy. The boss didn't show up during that first day like he said he would, and I was feeling a bit isolated. There was no phone or internet at the guesthouse, and I had to venture out into the late-afternoon swarming masses to find an internet café. Using my Delhi guidebook, I figured out where I was and where the closest shop would be and started walking. In Delhi, the summertime temperatures can reach above a hundred degrees Fahrenheit routinely, and I was baked by the time I reached the scruffy shack with an internet connection.

I found a computer and wrote an email to friends and family, letting them know I had arrived safely, answered a few others and then checked BBC news for the latest. After getting my news and information update, I paid the forty-rupee charge and walked to a neighboring bookshop. Both the internet café and bookshop were located within this open-air plaza, and a Pizza Hut, along with other Western fast food joints, were also lined up within; after perusing the bookstore, I could not resist a greasy slice of pizza and went to see their offerings. Surprised to find pepperoni on the menu, I made my order, though I doubted that it was actually pepperoni. The availability of beef or pork seemed unlikely due to the prevalence of Hindus and Muslims.

With my belly pleasantly full of tomato, cheese and mystery meat, I wandered in fading light through the smell of urine, feces and other nastiness along the crowded street back to the guesthouse. A letdown after the gastronomic pleasure taken at the pizza parlor. Along the way, I stumbled upon two little beggar kids that looked to be around four years old. One was sickly looking and lay asleep next to an old, nonfunctioning water fountain and the other little creature tapped me on the elbow and, in the most weak, dejected and heartbroken voice I'd heard, held out his grimy little hand and asked, "Dolla' p'ease? Dolla'?" He gave up on his efforts so despairingly quick as I walked by that my conscience screamed, and I turned back to give him a few rupees.

By the time I reached my quarters and swung open the screen door, it was well into the evening, and the houseboy's face was a mask of concern; perhaps worried that I'd been run over by an oxcart. Seemingly annoyed at me for being away for so long, he had taken it upon himself to fetch chicken tikka for my dinner and looked hurt when I started to decline the meal. Although my belly was full it seemed impolite not to accept, so I downed most of the bird anyway. That wouldn't be the last time my stomach would get abused. Months and months of that were coming.

In an ill-advised attempt to sleep the whole night through, I later popped two Tylenol PM before hitting the sack, having read or heard somewhere that the drug would help me sleep. What a pile of baloney. When I got up to answer nature's call after midnight, the combination of jet lag, an overstuffed belly, and the medicine gave me an out-of-body experience. While standing over the porcelain, it seemed I was hallucinating, hovering behind and above myself. It was a creepy feeling and, hurriedly finishing my business, I dove back under the sheets.

Early the next morning, with the pigeons on my window ledge cooing and scuffling ever louder on the metal eave, I gave up on sleep again. Determined to make my own coffee, I cautiously tip-toed around the houseboy, who was wrapped up tight in his usual spot on the floor. I opened the kitchen door, flipped the light switch and watched with dread as rats scampered away from my intrusion through various holes in windows and doors. From the looks of the disaster they'd left in the kitchen, they were full-bellied and satisfied. But the lure of roasted coffee beans was too powerful of a force, and I wasn't about to let the bug-eyed little vermin dissuade my mission.

Enjoying my morning cup and after an outside weather check, I started up the stairs for the morning bath. The houseboy had awakened but was moving slowly. Both eyelids struggled to stay open as he tracked me blankly with eyes like two pee-holes in a snow bank, one hand scratching his spiky straight hairdo and one hand scratching his backside, only a loose towel wrapped around his torso. He mumbled incoherently in what I assumed was a breakfast inquiry, and hoping he'd wash his hands first, I replied in the affirmative. The breakfast special, day after day, was to become onion omelet, toast, banana and coffee, at least until I begged him to leave out the onions. Gesturing toward his Nokia phone on the table, he continued with his vague dialogue and I deduced that Sami had called and that he or one of the company associates would be coming to see me soon. "Okay, got it," I said, and continued up the stairs.

There was no shower; the morning bath was a bucket and dump-it system. Fill a bucket of water, dump it on your head, lather up, fill another bucket and dump that on your head. Repeat as necessary to obtain the desired sheen. The risk of injury on the slick floor was not insignificant with all the bending, dumping and splashing. Sudsing safely was vital. And an eye opener in the morning when there was no hot water.

Breakfast consumed, I pestered the houseboy for yet another coffee and, with banana in hand, went back outside for a short stroll. The guesthouse was located in a neighborhood block of three- and four-story concrete apartment buildings and, across the small side street from the dwellings, was about an acre of trees that ran amok with rhesus monkeys. A short distance down this dead-end side street, there was a half-acre park also overrun by the monkeys; they had the run of the entire area. I'd already witnessed their thieving and pestilent ways, climbing up the sides of buildings to steal food out of an open window or patio and then scurrying away into the treetops while raucous squeals from their partners in crime echoed down the street. They were nasty, vile creatures without fear.

Turning to the right from our door and walking toward the little park, I didn't get ten yards before being blindsided by a brown flash of fur. The little bastard gave me a surprisingly strong push on the butt, startling me, and in an instant, the scoundrel had stolen the banana right out of my hand.

I turned to give pursuit, but he was already up in the trees, his buddies—his posse—all cheering him on as he devoured his pilfered prize. The glare this banana burglar gave me as I peered up into his tree was unsettling and, upon seeing his teeth, a little frightening.

Leaving the scene of the crime to the sound of monkey taunts and squeals, and cursing the little felon under my breath, I continued into the park, where more monkey fun awaited. It was tree lined and held a faint green hue compared to the dust and gray of the grimy surrounding buildings. There were even a few birds flitting about. Around the perimeter of the park lay a cement walkway for strolling, and in the middle was enough space to kick a ball around or just relax on the few blades of grass that had stubbornly chosen to grow.

With coffee in hand and sunshine on my shoulder, I began my first lap of introspection around the walkway. But, when I was nearly halfway around and getting deeper in thought, I became distracted as something fell from the thick trees onto my head. Brushing off my hair it appeared to be a shell from a nut. Curious, I stopped and looked straight up—straight into the eyes of hostility and hatred. Another gangster monkey was not more than two feet above me in the branches and leaves, eating nuts. When our eyes locked, he seemed to lunge for what I thought might be my carotid artery.

Taken by surprise again, I had no time to react. It was like that scene from *Alien* when Sigourney Weaver comes face to face with that hideous and moist devil creature, its only goal to rip people apart from limb to limb. At that moment, it seemed plain that this sharp-toothed beast of the trees had the same in store for me. Making no quick movements, I slowly lowered my gaze and, with butt cheeks puckered, walked away.

6.

Don't Take Tension

Later that morning, I was to meet Sami and travel to the offices of the DGCA, the Indian Directorate General of Civil Aviation, for the process of validating my FAA pilot's license. This would allow me the authority to fly for hire within India and for Indian companies without having to obtain an Indian DGCA commercial pilot license. Once they checked my records and logbooks and made sure I was the qualified pilot I claimed to be, I would receive a Foreign Aircrew Temporary Authorization, or FATA, certificate. Together with the FATA, my American FAA license would then allow me to pilot helicopters in India.

Indian commercial pilots were not happy to see foreign pilots come and possibly take their jobs, but the industry, especially the booming Indian airlines, demanded experienced pilots, which the country lacked. While there may have been a number of Indian commercial pilots in need of a job, their limited experience was not acceptable to the airlines or private air services and the companies that insured them. Aviation can be a tough field to break into; the industry says the pilot needs experience in order to be hired, but to build experience someone has to hire him or her. For Indians, gaining experience was made more difficult by the lack of low-time, entry-level pilot positions within the country.

After my morning of monkey mischief, I returned to the safety of the guesthouse and read a book on the doorstep, waiting and watching the side street until Sami and his associate arrived. Initially, they rolled in on a motorbike and for a moment, I thought we'd be riding treble to the DGCA building with me cozily sandwiched in the middle. Groups of three or four people on a bike were not uncommon, and it was routine to see entire families on bikes. Pulling in behind them, however, was a white Tata sedan that the company had hired to haul us there.

"Good morning, Captaaiin, I'm Sami!" With a gleaming white smile and bursting with energy, he reached out to shake my hand, "Great to finally meet you face to face, is everything well?"

"Good to see you, Sami," I replied, shaking his hand and that of Sanjay, his assistant. "I'm doing alright, ready to get to work."

Sami was a self-assured man of about forty-five. He dressed well, had a neatly trimmed goatee and hairstyle and spoke good English. He could've skipped a portion or two at meal time, but I'd say he was handsome if any judge, which I'm not. Troubling, though, was his disconcerting way of cleaning out his nose with his fingers. Upon first meeting him, I took notice of which hand he was using to execute this operation, but then saw he could be ambidextrous when excavating his nasal cavities. I vowed never to offer a handshake again.

Sanjay was a happy chap of about thirty who had hands and fingers so filth-encrusted that I could not imagine them being unintentionally that dirty. The brown residue was layered so thick that it appeared wax-like. The quality of hygiene was poor in India and a frustrating aspect of day to day life. I could probably count on the boogered fingers of one hand how many chaps took it seriously.

There were a number of foreign pilots waiting for their validation interviews by the time we stormed into the office. Most were headed to the airlines, and they all came from Europe, the guys I talked to anyway. There were no helicopter pilots other than me.

Sami, Sanjay and I were prepared for battle when the DGCA officers called us in; we had duplicate or triplicate copies of all required paperwork, including pilot logbook pages, passport, visa, flight medical certificate and other necessary documents. Every company is required to have a DGCA-approved booklet of what's known as an Operations Manual; this covers standard operating procedures and other rules, plus regulations and guidelines set forth by the company. I'd been studying ours since arriving. Most of their questions concerned this manual, but they also delved into my experience and background, plus specific rules pertaining to flying in Indian airspace.

Everything went smoothly. Although we had a long wait beforehand, it was only a matter of minutes from when we entered the office until we were set free with my license validation, the FATA, in hand.

In the different countries I have experience with, this was the usual procedure to have my FAA license validated: an interview and then a written Air Law exam followed by a check flight at some point. In the other countries, though, the Air Law exam had to be passed before the validation could be received. Not so with the Indian DGCA—I was allowed to fly with just this interview under my belt, and the exam could be written at a later date. Foreign pilots had that additional time to study while working and, more importantly, getting paid.

That was an important milestone to obtain since, in our contract agreement, it was stated that I would not be on the payroll until the day of validation. Now that I was, that pressure was off. It didn't matter if I was sitting in a shop eating tandoori chicken or flying, I was on the payroll. And since my housing, food and—as I was to learn—a dangerous hodgepodge of ground transportation were company provided, I looked forward to socking away nearly my entire salary.

Having received the FATA, I was prepared to relocate to our area of operations and get to flying as soon as possible, next day if need be; the walls around the Delhi guesthouse were closing in, and I loathe wasting time, idle. My new employers did not share this passion, though, as it would be days before I would board the airliner and meet up with my crew and helicopter, which was already flying in the jungles of East India, in the state of Chhattisgarh.

Growing up and working in America, I was used to a certain operations tempo and work ethic that encouraged getting the job done, accomplishing one task and quickly moving on to the next. Over the course of my time spent working in India that was just not the way it would be; time and time again I would become exceedingly frustrated with the pace of straightforward tasks or decision-making.

"Don't take tension, Captain, don't take tension!"

I would hear this often when my impatience and annoyance peaked. Eventually, I would learn somewhat to live on "India Time" and plan accordingly, but those first few weeks were an adjustment for me and my blood pressure.

Waiting for my travel orders as the days ticked off the calendar with aching slowness, I was determined to make the most of it by seeing what I could see. I checked out parks and monuments, and took early morning walks along the boulevard outside the housing complex. A lot of time was spent at the nearby plaza. Here were the Western restaurants, like the aforementioned Pizza Hut, but also Sbarro, Subway, Ruby Tuesday's and McDonalds. I could not expect a cheeseburger, though—no beef on the menu anywhere. At the Bennigan's Pub, there was some kind of beefless cheeseburger on the menu—India mystery meat again—possibly domestic water buffalo and they did not taste the same. But the beer was always cold enough and delicious.

On a late morning at the plaza, I was relaxing underneath a great-smelling, beautiful and tall tree in full bloom; the smell from the pink blossoms reminded me of lilacs and seemed to neutralize the hideous smells that were otherwise prevalent. I was having a snack of Pepsi and potato chips when two beggar girls, about seven or eight years of age, came slinking shyly along. They were dusty but wore bright pink Indian outfits, smiling and giggling with an aura that belied their position in life.

They acted cute and shy, but they weren't too shy to look me in the eye and hold their hands out. I gave them my chips and Pepsi—an unhealthy choice for me anyway—and their smiles and giggles became bigger and louder. They took turns with the chips and soft drink, milling around the tree, chatting and giggling until both the bag and can were empty. An overstuffed garbage bin was not so far off, but they carelessly dropped the trash at their feet. Then planted themselves in front of me again, held out their hands and pleaded in unison, "Mista? Mista?"

Giving them the snacks was the most charitable I was feeling at the moment, yet they continued their bubbly begging. They weren't disheartened by my stinginess, but kept on giggling like they hadn't a care in the world. This was brought to an end when a policeman came along and chased them off. If anything, that just made them laugh harder while they skipped away through the crowd.

Walking back to the guesthouse, I stopped alongside the road where a chap was selling a type of sweet lemon fizzy-drink. I was only mildly surprised when the customer in front of me finished his drink, handed back the glass, and it wasn't even rinsed before my order was placed in the same receptacle. I was hot and thirsty and had planned on gulping it down with avidity, but the suspected Ebola on the rim of the glass made me hesitate. Nonetheless, I slammed it down my throat and except for the body-odor aftertaste it wasn't bad.

The guesthouse was a zoo. The neighborhood dogs were chasing the monkeys from tree to tree and from car-roof to car-roof, barking and snarling while the monkeys screeched and squealed back at them. Out in our little neighborhood park, I watched a family of squirrels foraging for nuts and seeds off the ground when, from the corner of my eye, saw a mongoose streak across the ground and ambush one. The sleek little beast took half a second to give the squirrel a good brain-bashing shake and then disappeared as fast as it came. The remaining squirrels screamed and chattered in horror at the murderous crime. One went over to sniff the scene and start an investigation.

Adjacent to the housing block and only thirty yards from my quite permeable room window was the site for the neighborhood laundry activities. A group of ladies would gather every day to scrub and clean. Laundry was an outside job, done in big, permanent concrete tubs where all the neighbors' clothes were washed together, in the same water, by hand. The quality of cleanliness was debatable, but being that it was the way laundry had been done in India for centuries, the technique was perfected and not to be questioned.

One of these ladies was the mother of a disabled child about ten years old, and it was unfortunate that poverty kept the lad from being given professional care or the chance for school. It was also unfortunate that he liked to wander, and with work of her own to do, she was left with little choice but to tie him to a pole with an eight-foot line. All he could do was sit there all day long until she was finished. But he did not sit quietly. I would be in the middle of a book after lunchtime, or dozing in the quiet of early afternoon, when he'd let out a bloodcurdling shriek. Sometimes the yelling and shrieking would last for quite some time until she was able to console him.

A call to Sami inquiring about my travel date, "Sami, I'm ready to get to work, should I pack my bags?"

"Captaaiin!" he said, habitually prolonging the last syllable. "Bear with us a couple more days, just a few more administrative items to clear up on our end."

He didn't mention specifically what those were, but I guessed they had something to do with the government contract or, thinking more cynically, a general slowness having taken root in the company after receiving the agreement.

"You gotta get me outta here, my friend, I'm climbing the walls!"

"Yes, yes, I know you're a man of action!" he chuckled. "Don't take tension, Captaaiin, don't take tension!"

7.

India Attractions

During those endless days of waiting to climb in the helicopter and get to work, my sanity was saved by meeting the girl next door. Her retired father, who lived in an apartment near our company guesthouse, at times would have his meals prepared by our houseboy through some vague affiliation with the company. I wasn't clear what that was and didn't care to investigate; it was her that I was vastly more interested in.

After returning from Bennigan's Pub one evening, I heard the gentle sound of female laughter while approaching the guesthouse's screen door. Upon my entry, this goddess turned from the two people she'd been talking with and aimed a brilliant white smile at me and said, "Good evening. You must be Captain Michael."

Through glistening, plump, pink lips, her accent trilled words off a tongue that was surrounded by a contagious smile. I attempted to replicate it with a smile of my own and then the room became much warmer.

"You're correct, Miss," I said, stunned from her smile's afterglow. "A good evening to you as well."

Then, not knowing what else to do with my greeting, extended my hand like a clowny politician looking for votes.

"I'm Anika," she said, then went on to introduce the others she was talking with, one of them her father. "I heard that an American pilot was staying here and just had to come and meet him."

Anika was a business professor in Bhubaneswar, Odisha, one of India's eastern states that cradles the Bay of Bengal. She had traveled to Delhi to visit her Dad and help with his medical appointments. Saying the least, she was exquisite.

Thirtyish, big dark eyes, jet black hair, light mocha skin and a knock-me-out body of Venus.

Her English was accented with that unique South Asian intonation, but it was quite understandable and, after a few fits and starts, our conversation stretched into the evening. Over the next several days, we managed to spend more time together, becoming acquainted and enjoying each other's company. Sami and the others at the office seemed to be dragging their feet and to have all but forgotten about me, holed up in their guesthouse. But, for the time being, my travel delay was working out favorably. Anika was keen to see me, and we were able to explore a bit of India, taking advantage of her father's car and driver.

Beginning one day with a leisurely breakfast from our guesthouse kitchen, *The Ratatouille*, we set out to see two of India's most iconic tourist destinations, the Lotus Temple and Taj Mahal. The Lotus Temple, a place of worship for the Bahá'í faithful, is a prodigious concrete and marble structure built to resemble a floating lotus flower. Twenty-seven marble "flower petals" were erected amongst nine pools of water, the entire site covering twenty-six acres. It was hard to imagine, but a tour guide said that as many as a 150 thousand people could visit it in one day and that, during certain years, the number of visitors exceeded those who visit the highly touted, world-renowned Taj Mahal.

We had to take our shoes off and shove them in a bin before we could walk around the place, and Anika's dainty feet and red polished toenails contrasted sharply with my near-blinding white feet and furry toes. If I had known we'd be barefoot, I might've trimmed my toenails. While we made our way along the path to the temple, Anika giggled and said, "You know, Michael, you can take your socks off, too."

"I did, they're back there stuffed inside my shoes."

Giggling louder, she teased, "Those are your feet? They're white as athletic socks."

"Ha, ha..." I said. "They won't be white long with this microwaving sun."

The day's growing heat and blasting sunshine were indeed becoming intense; my eyes squinted so hard behind my sunglasses that I was near to facial cramps. The heat didn't bother Anika, though. She was dressed in a light-green and white saree that offered ample ventilation and showed part of a bare midriff. When stealing a glance just right, I could catch a glimpse of a belly-button surrounded by her toned tummy. Ravishing. Wearing my simple polo shirt and cargo pants, I was a hobo walking next to her.

Finished with our Lotus Temple sojourn and wishing to escape the heat, me more than Anika, we climbed into the back seat of the cool, air-conditioned car. The driver, who had been waiting in the shade underneath a tree, had seen us making our way back to the parking lot and had the cold air on full blast by the time we reached the vehicle. We briefly reconsidered the three- or four-hour drive to the Taj Mahal, which would make for a long day, but in the end we decided to go. Her time was short as she needed to get back to her professorial duties, and soon my company would wake up and send me to the jungle. I was expecting a call at any time.

As a kid growing up, I had heard about the Taj Mahal, how it was one of the Seven Wonders of the World, and I remember knowing simply that it was way over in some foreign land called India. I didn't give much thought of ever going there; I didn't think that it would ever happen, or that I would care to go. Now, years later, not only was I at the Taj Mahal, but I was accompanied by a drop-dead gorgeous native woman of the land.

We took too many pictures and, after an exhausting final photo session around the pools, we moved on to admire the work of local marble engravers. A large staff was kept on duty whose purpose was to replace the many marble inlays and decorations of the monument when they were found to be corroded or crumbling. We visited their workshop and watched them toiling away, cross-legged on the ground, with their traditional tools. In a nearby room, they sold trinkets and souvenir items, like coasters and cups, made from the marble. I was tempted by a marble inlaid chess board but demurred, wanting to avoid having my chess game's butt kicked on such a pretty board. Anika came away with a gift of matching plates for her sister in Bhubaneswar.

By that time, the sun was on a downward track toward the horizon. Having baked India enough for one day, it was moving on to torch Pakistan and Iran. Our stomachs were grumbling, and we found a roadside snack of spicy curry and rice; then, with a full belly and burning mouth, I crawled into the back seat with Anika once again and headed back to Delhi. It was going to be past ten by the time we reached there, so she called her Dad to tell him not to worry. She and I chatted for a while, but both of us started dozing off from full bellies and the comfort of the cool air.

Sometime later, I awoke and groggily gazed out of the car at the fading day and rushing traffic. Anika was curled up next to me with her legs tucked and head tilted back. Her little snoring sounds resembled attempts to start a flooded McCulloch chainsaw. She seemed to be out for the duration, and I let her sleep. Then, while lost in thought watching the trees, fields and concrete flicker past the window, I happened to notice the fuel gauge, and it was reading close to nil.

My first thought was that the thing must be broken. But, just in case, I pointed it out to the driver. Since he spoke no English, I reached across and tapped the gauge, drawing his attention to what I perceived as a potential problem. He replied with something in Hindi and didn't seem alarmed; in fact, he kept the throttle pinned to the floor while we passed yet another gas station. I assumed then that the gauge was indeed broken and that he had our next gas stop all planned out.

Not quite the case. A few more miles down the road, the engine sputtered, coughed and died. We ran out of gas. The driver cranked the starter anyway, nearly to the point of killing the battery, and I pointed at the gas gauge again, saying emphatically, "Petrol? Petrol!"

Looking at my tapping finger, but apparently ignoring the gas gauge behind it, he flung open his door, jumped out and popped open the hood in an attempt to appear in control of the situation. Perhaps he figured that if he stared long and hard enough at the damned engine it would fix itself, but I'd tried that once or twice in my younger days and knew the strategy would not work.

By this time, Anika had woken up and was able to tell him that we needed to find gas. It was fortunate for us that we were not too far from the go-juice, but unfortunate for me since I was the only source of horsepower until we reached there. She had a streak of diva in her and wasn't about to get out of the car, and the driver, like a captain of his sinking ship, refused to leave the helm. I pushed and heaved and hoed, until a few of the lads working at the nearest gas station could be summoned for assistance.

We'd made the correct decision to go road tripping when we did, as Anika's departure for Bhubaneswar came all too quick. She was catching the train late one morning for the twenty-four hour journey and asked me to see her off from the station. After a light breakfast at the guesthouse with her and her dad, I helped to carry their luggage from his apartment to the car; he would be accompanying her during the train ride. With her black mane of hair in a thick ponytail, she was again dressed in an enthralling saree, pink and white. This traditional style of dress, while meant to conceal conservatively, left latitudes of imagination for a young man.

Her dad sat in front with the driver and, at each turn and braking decision, an argument ensued between the two for the proper execution of such; Anika and I were in back, giggling like chaperoned teenagers. While cruising along through the noisy traffic, out of the blue came a song by Deep Purple on the Hindi radio channel. My ears were orgasmic, having heard nothing but Bollywood music since I'd arrived, and I sang along to "Perfect Stranger" until Anika gave me a look like she had eaten a sour strawberry.

Reaching the train station, I found it as expected. A statistic I had gleaned from the travel guide stated that over 200 thousand people could be crowded into Delhi's station at any given time; and there seemed to be twice that number pushing, yelling and jostling for tickets and space.

After walking with them through the station to their train, Anika and I traded gifts: books. I gave her a John Grisham bought at the bookshop by Bennigan's Pub, and she gave me a William Dalrymple. She wanted me to write something fresh and witty inside the cover, and I obliged her, but Shakespeare I am not. Certainly, my scribbled thoughts left her underwhelmed, though she thanked me and gushed like an actress clutching an Oscar.

She insisted we stay in touch and predicted that we'd meet again—"that destiny will bring you to Bhubaneswar someday, Michael"—since the company had an office there. I didn't know how realistic that was, working in the jungle was all my company had ever talked about, but I hoped we'd meet again.

We waved goodbye, and the surging crowd swallowed first her, then the train while I jostled through the swarming masses back to the car.

8.

Welcome to the Jungle

"Captain Michael, this is Air Marshal Singh, the man in charge," Sami said, beaming with nervous energy.

The man behind the desk stood up, spread his arms wide and pointed into the air as if preparing to give a lecture. He smiled through a bushy beard and said, "Ah yes! But God is truly in charge!"

The air marshal was a Sikh; he wore an oversized navy-blue turban and had eyes that twinkled with cheer, or perhaps mischief, when he spoke. His English was quite articulate as he told me, among other things, that he'd been involved in aviation for over fifty years and had flown both airplanes and helicopters. A veteran of the Indo-Pakistani conflicts, he had once been wounded in the leg while out on a mission; keen to show me the battle damage, he hiked up his trouser and propped the scarred leg on his desk. I guessed he was about seventy years old, but nimble and sharp; neither the wound nor age had slowed him down much.

His office was decorated better than any I'd seen in India, with sculptures and paintings, military citations and awards, plus a number of family photos. While we sat and chatted, the office tea maker and chai wallah brought us cups of the hot brew and a package of biscuits. Revealing a cranky side, the air marshal became upset and appeared close to throwing him out the third story window when the boy left the room without properly offering the biscuits on a plate. The presentation of biscuits was strict business.

They hadn't mentioned a date yet, but I knew the day was drawing nearer when I would take my flight from Delhi to Raipur, the capital city of Chhattisgarh state just north of the jungles and hills where our flying operations would be. In fact, the operations had already started: a Captain Chatterjee had been flying the company's Eurocopter Astar there, but they were planning on moving him to one of their other helicopter operations in the north of the country.

It had been decided that Chatterjee would stay for ten to fourteen days, helping me become familiar with the area and then leaving me on my own. My duties would consist of flying in support of the IPS, the Indian Police Service, and CRPF, the Central Reserve Police Force, along with other paramilitary organizations called in for the fight against Maoist rebels. The air marshal and Sami also felt there would be charter flights requested from state government VIPs. I was looking forward to it all. Being in charge of a one-pilot, one-helicopter operation was appealing to this independent individualist with admittedly woeful and deficient social skills.

There would be traveling first, though, by air and by road: once I landed in Raipur, they said, "just a few hours" of driving would be required to get to our base in Jagdalpur, "mere miles" to the south. Sami and the air marshal debated about the travel arrangements. Sami suggested that traveling at night through the countryside would be dangerous, especially for a foreigner, but the air marshal had a more liberal take on my journey to the jungle. Having become more worked up after the biscuit incident, he raised his voice and said, "I've taken trips cross-country plenty times at night, there is no harm in it!"

"But, sir," Sami said, speaking with less gusto than usual, "It is quite a long distance... at night... plus a foreigner?"

"Listen, you," the air marshal said, shaking a long, boney finger at Sami. "Make arrangements for a driver to pick up Captain Michael at Raipur Airport!"

I just wanted out of Delhi, and if a road journey at night was part of the plan, then so be it. I would have been less enthusiastic knowing what was to come, but I imagined only a rollicking road trip through the countryside.

Relaxing in the air marshal's office, munching on our plate of biscuits, I thought that this was just a visit, a social call with my new mates. I still had no idea when the travel date was to be; no one had mentioned anything. Sanjay then entered the office and enlightened me by asking, "Captain, are you packed for your flight?"

Up to this stage in my working life, I'd been called Michael, or Mike—among, perhaps, other epithets—but India was big on titles, and I was getting used to being addressed as *Captain* or *sir*.

"Ah... what flight?"

"Your flight to Raipur, sir," he laughed. "You don't expect to stay in Delhi, do you?"

"Of course not, I'm ready to get to work... Wait, I'm leaving today? My flight is leaving this afternoon?"

"Yes Captain, I booked you on a flight just now. We'll hafta' hurry and get your luggage from the guesthouse. Looks like we only have a couple hours before takeoff."

"Oh." I was mildly shocked by the swiftness and apparent secrecy with which the travel arrangements had been made. "You could've told me yesterday, or this morning, yes?"

To that, I received a blank stare from Sanjay. Sami was studying something on the floor, and the air marshal grinned back at me like he'd been told a good joke.

I only had a vague idea of what I was getting into at this point. If I had known better, I would've demanded an airline flight the next morning, a daytime road trip being much safer. Eventually, I learned what to avoid and to question the head office when required. Their motives, at times, were not geared toward the comfort, needs, or most importantly, the safety of employees. At that moment, however, I was excited simply to be on the move out of Delhi and getting to the jungle, getting to work.

We had a quick round of handshakes and smiles. Sami regained his enthusiasm and pumped my arm until his second chin jiggled. The air marshal grabbed my hand and, eyes twinkling once again, said, "Good luck, Michael, I know you will perform your duties well." Clapping me on the shoulder, he guided me to the door, "Now, Captain, go with God!"

Sanjay and I dashed out of the office and dodged the hectic traffic back to the guesthouse. It didn't take long to pack all my worldly possessions, one smallish suitcase and a couple of carry-ons, including my headset bag. Meanwhile, Sanjay hired a car and driver to take me to the airport.

The houseboy's usual sour expression changed to one of relief as I headed out the door, and it seemed that even the gang of monkeys stopped their thievery for a few moments to salute the banana-man taking his leave. I took a brief look around the neighborhood and decided it would not be missed.

"Here, Captain," Sanjay handed me a worn Nokia phone and charger. "All of our numbers and office contacts are entered."

Then he held out his grimy hand, and I reluctantly gave it a light shake. "A driver is waiting in Raipur to take you to Jagdalpur. He knows you're coming."

"Okay good," I said. "Thanks, Sanjay. See ya when I see ya."

"If you have any problems, call me!" he shouted, as I shut the door, giving me the fingers-to-the-ear sign language for the same.

Arriving at the departure terminal, there was a massive amount of security. The Mumbai Attacks had recently occurred, in which radical Pakistanis had landed on a beach in inflatable boats and massacred over 160 people, and the country was on edge. Security teams were posted at regular intervals on the route leading to and around the airport; troops were stationed behind sandbags and barbed wire while others patrolled on foot with AK47s and Sterling submachine guns.

I checked in to my flight with little time to spare. Having a quick look around while rushing through the domestic terminal, I noticed it had been recently opened and was still shiny and clean, which was in contrast to the average scene in India. My flight was called while I hurried to the gate and upon reaching it discovered there were no sky bridges yet for this particular airline, Kingfisher, so passengers were boarding buses to get to the airplane. They crammed us into the bus cattle-herd style, with passengers pushing in close to each other, but most abuse was kept to a minimum. The outside temperature had read forty-four Celsius on the inside terminal wall and the air conditioning on the bus was trying, but having a hard time keeping the overexerted and stressed passengers even marginally cool.

Reaching our gleaming red and white airplane, I stepped off the bus and was nearly wiped out when walking into the path of a Sky Chef truck bringing our dinners. The driver braked hard and impatiently waved me across with one hand, the other hand losing a finger so far up his nose he might've been scratching his frontal lobe. Once aboard, though, the plane held refreshing beauty. The air hostesses were all smiling brightly and looked to be supermodels promoting the latest style in red form-fitting miniskirts, tailored white blouses and red blazers.

It was an hour-and-a-half flight from Delhi to Raipur and once settled into the cruise, I went about studying information I'd printed off at the internet café and giving more thought to what lay ahead. Having been given a little background of the area by my buddy Zach and the guys at the office in Delhi, I knew that where I was headed was not a nice place, but I was to learn much more.

The area was primitive, vast and had few roads. The roads that did exist were not well maintained and, at times, were too dangerous to drive due to a group of radical communists, referred to in that part of the world as Maoists, or Naxalites. The origin of the group and their moniker was a peasant rebellion in the eastern Indian village of Naxalbari, West Bengal, located on a jut of land between Nepal and Bhutan. The Research and Analysis Wing of India's intelligence agency estimated that between twenty and fifty thousand armed Maoist-Naxalites were operating in East India, and the Indian Prime Minister had declared them the most serious internal threat to India's national security.

The Indian government had been struggling with the group for well over thirty years, and thousands of people had been killed, including police and paramilitary, innocent civilians and the insurgents themselves. The Maoist-Naxalites claimed that they supported the poor rural population and frequently targeted police and government personnel in what they said was a fight for improved land rights and more jobs.

Just prior to my arrival, when I was still riding the waves in the South Pacific, the Indian government had planned an initiative for affected states aimed at dealing with the Maoist-Naxalite problem. India's media would come to call the general offensive against the Naxalites "Operation Green Hunt," though this was somewhat erroneous as only one specific ground action by the police in Chhattisgarh had been officially given that name.

The states included Chhattisgarh, Odisha, Andhra Pradesh, Maharashtra, Jharkhand, Bihar, Uttar Pradesh, and West Bengal, and the operation involved funding for road building, electric power distribution, telephone service and schools. This, in a region that had little, if any, economic development for many years.

The program also included special funding for better law enforcement and reduction of Maoist-Naxalite influence in the area. That was the reason my company received a contract with the IPS and, subsequently, the reason I found myself in India, burping quietly from the chicken samosa that Kingfisher Airlines had fed their passengers.

It was a heady and potentially dangerous assignment. But from talks with my new company, I was assured that, in coordination with the IPS, CRPF and other paramilitary organizations, we could do the job safely and effectively.

9.

Don't Take My Kidneys

The broiling sun was calling it quits for another day and hiding behind the terminal when we piled out of the Airbus and onto the ground at Raipur. Although it was cooler than Delhi in the waning light, the daytime heat absorbed by the airport apron radiated up like it was just-hardened volcanic lava.

Peering down on the city as we flew over, Raipur didn't seem large from the air and I was surprised to find out that it held over one million people. But I had to reckon that the population was a condensed twelve thousand head per square mile—spacious, with elbow room to spare compared to Delhi, which shoehorned in more than sixty-six thousand people per square mile on average. In a country with a population of over a billion—well on its way to two billion—the citizens appeared used to a bit of overcrowding.

My fellow passengers and I didn't dally on the tarmac and obediently let the rifle-toting security guards herd us into the terminal to wrestle with our luggage. After collecting my meager belongings, out the front doors of the little airport I went, not knowing who or what to expect, having only been given Sanjay's word that an agent would meet me and get me to Jagdalpur. Notably, no promises had been made regarding getting me there in one piece, however.

The only foreigner in a sea of sarees and polyester dress shirts, I wasn't hard to spot and was quickly approached by a shady-looking kid wearing a cubic zirconia earring and a cheap designer t-shirt. Holding a sign with my name, I assumed he was my Raipur rendezvous and connection. The chap wasn't much for English, though, and my Hindi vocabulary was still in its infancy.

They say don't judge a book by the cover, but he had nervous eyes and the look of an unprincipled fugitive from justice. To check his bona fides and be on the safe side, I gave Sami a call, which he ignored. Giving Sanjay a ring, I had more success. He confirmed this chap was the driver I was looking for and not some rogue in the employ of a nefarious villain.

Stowing my suitcase amongst the dirt and clutter in the trunk, I squeezed into the back of this, another white Tata, and settled in for the ride. Strange land, strange people and a strange journey ahead; at that point, just off the plane and on the move, I didn't want to trade places with anyone. The future held mystery and adventure.

My Indian gangster driver sat down at the steering wheel, started up the car and, in a cloud of reddish-orange dust, we barreled out of the crowded parking lot to the soundtrack of howling engines and screeching tires, everyone leaning on their horns as if that would magically clear the road for them. We went screaming down the tree-lined lane outside the airport, dodging pedestrians, bicycles, motorcycles, oxcarts, cars and trucks—all forms of ground transportation being put to toil—along with hundreds of wandering cattle, and they always had the right of way.

He kept the hammer down for five minutes until we pulled into a gas station. I figured it was only logical to gas up before the journey, but wait: gangster driver was having a serious chat with one of his confederates parked nearby. There seemed to be planning in progress, with much arm waving and what sounded like insults being exchanged. When they popped the lid on the trunk, I deduced that wheeling and dealing had gone down.

Indeed it had, and they played charades for me, trying to explain that I needed to switch cars. I hated to be a bother, but I thought another phone call to my mates for verification wouldn't hurt. Only this time, no one answered from the office in Delhi. Gangster Driver and his collaborator both let off a vibe of potential organ smugglers. One of them appeared to be studying my rib cage for where best to start the incisions.

They stood staring at me as if daring me to run. Sizing up the second driver, I calculated the odds of having to kick his butt later if he made a go for my kidneys and guessed it would be at least a draw. They already had my suitcase in the other car and were getting impatient and twitchy. With a few more moments of hesitation I finally transferred cars, instinctively covering my abdomen with my arms for self-defense while doing so.

We left Raipur at six in the evening, which gave me about an hour's worth of daylight to take in the surroundings and grab a few photos. Jagdalpur, our destination to the south, was 170 miles by road from Raipur and, from Sami and Sanjay's sugar-coated claims, only a two- or three-hour drive. They had never been there. In reality, the journey was a night-long Le Mans endurance event on poor roads through rural countryside, with landscapes varying from flat land and rice paddies, to lowland and steep hills, to rivers and sharp curves. I would never take that journey again at night.

Traveling at night on the roads was a death wish. India is consistently ranked one of the most dangerous places to drive in the world, and it is no wonder. All manner of transport, with vastly differing speeds, was trying to share the same route. Combine the narrow and ill-maintained roads with an oxcart traveling at three miles per hour and a forty-passenger bus traveling at fifty miles per hour, and the results range from dangerous to deadly.

Add cattle. Vagabond cattle roamed freely in India, from the urban sprawl of Delhi to rural dirt tracks and everywhere in between. The beasts are not concerned that a fifty-mile-per-hour steel and rubber death machine may be barreling down the very same road they intend to cross at their own slow pace. Having a head-on collision with one of these revered bovines would seem bad enough, but if you do accidently hit one and survive, don't expect sympathy from the locals. There were many cases where villagers ganged up and beat the driver of a vehicle involved in a car versus cow smash-up.

Then add *night* to the cattle conundrum. The patchy pavement had been soaking up the warm sunshine all day, making it comfortable bedding for the beasts. Never mind that it was the only road connecting growing and developing cities, the animals preferred to relax in the fast lane. No one bothered to disturb them, either; not even the work-shy traffic police would clear them from the road. My driver/executioner had the brakes locked and tires squealing every twenty or thirty miles over the course of the drive because of unperturbed cattle stretched out over the dark, broken blacktop, chewing their cud. Many times the driver was forced to detour around them using the ditch, or shoulder, if there was one.

It was a white-knuckle ride, and on the far side of midnight when we swung off the main road and puttered around the first shacks of Jagdalpur. Only then was I slowly able to unclench my butt-cheeks.

My new crew was waiting up for me when we found the company guesthouse a half-hour later, and they welcomed me graciously. After I bailed out of the car, grabbed my belongings and told the driver and part-time organ smuggler thank you, I never looked back; I was grateful that my kidneys were where they should be and that the son of a bitch hadn't got me killed.

A couple of the guys spoke English, and we chatted over Kingfisher beers and cigarettes, soothing after my journey through the gauntlet, though what I really needed after that frightening hell ride was a shower and a bed. The crew and houseboy/cook showed me my digs and then faded off to their own, satisfied that their new pilot had reached them safely; perhaps losing bets between themselves as to whether I would arrive intact. I settled into my room, clicked on the air conditioning, found what I needed in my suitcase and had a good splishy-splash in the shower.

That accomplished, I looked forward to stretching out on the bed, but the mosquitoes needed my attention first. They were ravenous, and the windows were again half-assed and shoddily built, letting them pass into my new domain freely.

We had all been thoroughly abused by them while standing outside during the introductions, and now they were in the mood for second servings of my B negative. I had no mosquito net, so while muttering curses, I turned the air conditioner down even cooler and, hoping for the best, wrapped up head-to-toe in a bed sheet, killed the light and hit the sack.

Not more than fifteen minutes later the power failed. That, or the mosquitoes had chewed through the electrical wiring. I assumed it had affected the whole neighborhood, but when peeking out of my burrito-like mosquito wrap, saw that a dim streetlight was still lit and no unusual sounds were coming from within the house. I listened intently, hoping to hear someone scurrying around checking breakers and fuses. But all was quiet, too quiet, now that my air conditioning and ceiling fan had gone silent. I could hear the buzzing mosquitoes, though. It sounded like reinforcements were showing up, that they were gleefully expecting victory, and their bellies would soon be full.

The temperature was still above ninety degrees, and I was hoping of all hopes that, whatever the problem was, it would fix itself. Laying there in my expanding pool of sweat, I only wanted sleep, but it was not to be. Surrendering to the heat and the mosquitoes, I fumbled around for my clothes and went in search of assistance, but of course everyone was crashed out. And having just arrived in the dark, I had no idea where the hell anybody was.

It seemed that the only electrical power outage had occurred in my room. I could hear other air conditioning units purring away and blowing out that blessed cool air. Even the ceiling fan in the living room was twirling around steadily. There was no air conditioning there but, putting the fan on high tornado speed, I hoped that the mosquitoes and their damned little devil wings would be blown away. After several failed attempts at trying to find someone, anyone, I grabbed my bed sheet, wrapped up the best I could, and, with hungry squadrons of vampire mosquitoes in pursuit, flung myself onto the living room couch.

Around two hours later, with the new dawn approaching, the cook woke up and discovered his new houseguest half-dead at the mercy of innumerable mosquitoes and cowering beneath a ceiling-fan-induced windstorm. Alerts went out to all sectors. Frenzied investigations ensued, fuses were checked, switches clicked on and off, volunteers were enlisted and a fix was acquired in the form of a heavy-duty, high-speed, gale-force pedestal fan placed into my room with an extension cord run to a hot outlet elsewhere. The mosquitoes didn't stand a chance against this machine. My hopes of sleep didn't stand a chance, either, as the high-powered fan came close to peeling paint off the walls.

The other pilot, Captain Chatterjee, who had been attempting to sleep when I arrived the night before, also lost power in his room. He looked a little worn out and ragged the next morning, but I felt close to lukewarm death and was surely no font of beauty either. After arguing with Sami about the cost, we were driven to a hotel in town where we were able to cool off and snooze in air-conditioned and mosquito-free comfort. Good for us, explained Chatterjee, because we had a flight coming up in the afternoon.

10.

Taking Flight

Captain Chatterjee was a smiling but serious ex-Indian Air Force pilot that had been flying with the company for two years, the past three months of which he'd spent working with the IPS and CRPF in Chhattisgarh, flying the Astar. Middle-aged, six feet tall, balding and with a slightly protruding belly, he had thick glasses, and his eyes fluctuated bigger and wider depending on the level of excitement and tension present.

He was married with children. When describing his family, he told me in heavily accented English, "...and I have a son in the Martian Navy."

I wondered what I had missed. The USA was still struggling with interplanetary travel and here the Indians were already preparing a naval fleet for Mars. It took me a moment to decipher the pronunciation and that he meant "Merchant Navy." As with many of his countrymen, the more buzz in the vicinity, the faster the speech patterns became and, as a result, syllables and a consonant or two were sacrificed. Still, Chatterjee was thorough, professional and courteous, a genuinely good person and an asset to humankind. If someone or something began cloning people, Chatterjee would have been a good one to start with.

Due to his military time, he had experience with the monstrous, Russian-built Mi17 thirty passenger helicopter, one of which the company owned and had based in Shimla, the state capital of Himachal Pradesh in northern India. It was the company's intention to get me settled in the Jagdalpur area and rotate Chatterjee to the Mi17.

During discussions at the office, we planned a week or two of dual-pilot jungle flying out of our base at Jagdalpur in order to get familiar with the area and operation. Chatterjee had remarked that the flying was constant. He was logging five, six or seven hours a day and figured with that amount of flying, I would see most of the more important landing zones in short order. The others were well documented and had their coordinates referenced in the helicopter's GPS. In several days, Chatterjee could cut my cord and be on his way to the cooler hill country of Shimla.

After our sleepless ordeal at the guesthouse the night before, Chatterjee and I spent most of the day in our rooms at the Hotel Devansh. I showered and snoozed, then gambled on vegetarian room service, twice.

In the mid-afternoon, we had a Jagdalpur-to-Raipur flight and, in my newbie enthusiasm to see the airport and helicopter, I asked Chatterjee one too many times when we'd go. He was in no rush, relaxing in the lobby and reading a newspaper.

He chuckled and said, "Relax, Captain, we're in no hurry here... Don't take tension."

I paced around and gazed out the lobby door at my new "hometown" and all the strange and bizarre new sights along its dusty streets. "Mike," he said, "we won't miss anything by waiting another few minutes."

When the time was right, we left the cool confines of the hotel and walking outside, I realized why he had been taking his time. It was bloody, skin-singeing hot, and there was no air conditioning in the company's little Suzuki Maruti. By the time we drove the five minutes to steamy Jagdalpur Airport, sweat was vacating my every pore.

Built during World War Two, a period when many airports were constructed in India, Jagdalpur Airport had a small apron, no air traffic control tower and only a common radio frequency provided two-way communication between aircraft. The nearest air traffic control was in Visakhapatnam, over 100 miles away, or Raipur, 130 miles away. Field elevation was eighteen hundred feet, and the paved, brush-lined runway was about a mile long with no taxiway; airplanes would simply back-taxi, then use the runway dumbbells to get lined up for takeoff. Not many aircraft landed there, but occasionally the state owned Beechcraft King Air or, rarely, an airplane belonging to a mining company.

Only our Astar was on the ramp when the car dropped us off; we had the whole airport to ourselves. Not that there was much there. No hangars or buildings, just a rundown stucco shack that served as a barracks of sorts for the IPS forces guarding the airport. The company had finagled one room in this shack to keep a few spare parts and lubricants for the helicopter and, by default, held an impressive collection of cricket bats for the crew; any leisure time came to be dominated by the game of cricket. Fuel was stocked in fifty-gallon drums outdoors, the promise of an actual fuel truck had been mentioned but was many months away from existing on the premises.

I arrived in the jungle at the hottest time of year. There wasn't a cloud in the sky, and the sun was white hot, scorching the countryside in a 110 degree blast furnace, pushing the density altitude up to nearly six thousand feet. Density altitude is a measurement used to determine what an aircraft's takeoff performance may be, based on the day's temperature and field elevation. The higher the temperature and elevation, the less efficient engines and wings become. This was not a problem for the Astar, though, as it had plenty of power in the hot temperatures to takeoff at its maximum gross weight. Meaning, I could top off the fuel tank, fill the seats with passengers, take a bit of cargo and still be able to get airborne underneath the relentless sun.

This was the first I'd been able to see my helicopter and I was anxious to look it over and give it a good preflight. I was thrilled to be flying again after too much time off. Forgotten was the excruciating wait for the employment visa, the long journey to India, another mind-numbing wait in Delhi for the red tape and paperwork to pass, and the recent treacherous ride down the Indian autobahn.

The engine panels were open on the helicopter when we walked onto the ramp, but it still looked menacing, and when the panels were closed, the aircraft looked like it could fly away itself. It was in better than average condition for being close to fifteen years old, the airframe only in the mid-three-thousand-hour range. Except for a few chips in the paint, it was a beautiful aircraft. No air conditioning, but I was assured there was a unit on order, and that sounded like a cool idea.

Pre-flight complete, Chatterjee put away the phone that hadn't left his ear since we'd left the hotel. We strapped in, cranked up and took off north over Jagdalpur on our way to Raipur. Even with sweat streaming down my face, I was delighted to be in the air at speed again and watching the scenery slip beneath my feet. The world is fascinating from a helicopter, whether flying over backcountry mountains or through big city skyscrapers.

At a helicopter's low cruising altitude, the Earth's features are seen in better detail; the scope and breadth of a mountain valley reveals its true scale, as does the complexity of the engineering feat that it was to build a highway through said valley. The world seems more in order when viewed from above, where the sight of mankind's garbage and junk gets filtered out. A good example of that was Jagdalpur. It appeared well planned and orderly as we choppered overhead, but from what I had seen of the broken streets and littered paths so far, knew it was just as chaotic and gritty as any of the other burgs spread around the country.

Chatterjee, sitting in the right seat, spoke loudly over the helicopter noise on the intercom. "We'll climb to a cruising altitude of four or five thousand feet."

"Do you normally fly that high?" I asked.

"Yep, to avoid gunfire from the bad guys below in the jungle." He pointed down with his left hand, the hair on his furry arm buffeting from the open air vent.

Recently, there had been an incident in Chhattisgarh where a low-flying Air Force Mi17 was hit with gunfire. The pilots were able to avoid a catastrophic crash, but an engineer aboard was shot in the head and killed; he had stood up and leaned forward to monitor an engine gauge between the pilots just as several rifle rounds were shot through the cockpit. The rounds missed the two pilots by inches and would have missed the engineer, too, if he'd been in his seat.

Chatterjee went on, "You do know the company's other Astar was hit by gunfire when flying here a while ago?"

"No, I don't. No one told me anything about that." I imagined how bullets might sound when hitting the fuselage. "Neither the air marshal nor Sami, they didn't say a word."

Chatterjee chuckled. "Oh? Did they leave that little piece of information out?"

The company pilot and engineer on that flight had, upon landing, discovered a bullet hole through one of the main rotor blades and another through the horizontal stabilizer. No other damage was found, and the pilot hadn't even realized he was being shot at.

Chatterjee made it clear that the higher the better, especially when crossing hills or a ridgeline, "Besides," he said, "the outside air temperature is cooler and more comfortable the higher you are."

"Got it," I said. "It's nice to have the Astar and its fast climb rate." Giving him a cheesy thumbs-up, I felt confident about avoiding any rifle fire and didn't plan on taking any foolish chances.

On the way to Raipur, I took in the view of the type of topography I'd be flying over. There were few roads, sparsely scattered and tiny primitive villages, rice paddies and a whole lot of jungle and trees. The land was not flat, except for the rice paddies, and almost resembled the rolling farmland and forests of my home turf in Wisconsin—albeit without the red barns, Holsteins and women with large, hay-bale-tossing hands.

Chatterjee was flying a straight-line direct course from Jagdalpur and occasionally our flight path would parallel or cross a road, but the majority of time we were quite a few miles from any human development. Mostly, we were flying over extensive stretches of jungle with no open space or clearing for miles, where if we had to land due to an engine failure or other trouble, the result would probably be chopped wood and a barbeque. This was a quite remote region, and even if we survived the landing, there was no cellular service, no satellite phone provided, and due to the vast and forested landscape, there was little hope of being found if it came to an aerial search.

In just the two-year period prior to my arrival, two helicopters had been lost in Chhattisgarh. From what information I had found about the crashes, they were likely due to bad weather, but it had taken months to find the wreckage. In one case, it had been almost a year before a goat herder stumbled across the burned and mangled flying machine. The first aircraft downed was a Chhattisgarh state government-owned Eurocopter EC135 flying Bhopal to Raipur, and the second was a helicopter the state had chartered to replace it, a Bell 430 that went missing between Hyderabad and Raipur around a year later. Both of these were twin-engine helicopters; our Astar only had one lone donkey pulling the cart.

Silently, I questioned the wisdom of flying over large tracts of thick jungle. Looking at the area chart, I could see that the hell's highway I had been on the night before shot a fairly straight course from Jagdalpur to Raipur. If we followed that, our safety margin would improve substantially while only adding perhaps ten to fifteen minutes to the trip. A negligible amount for safety's sake. Our customer, the Indian Government, paid for the fuel, and I assumed they were more concerned with their politicians and paramilitaries being safe than with the use of a few extra gallons of jet fuel.

I realized there would be occasions when flying over stretches of inhospitable land could not be avoided, but when it made good, practical sense, my inclination was to give myself and the passengers a better chance of survival in case the unfortunate did occur. We fly modern, well-engineered aircraft with phenomenal safety records, but machines do break, fuel can become contaminated, and a pilot cannot assume that his engine will never fail. Nonetheless, I was not in charge at that point, but taking notes of what to do when I would be.

11.

Raipur

Our flight to Raipur would be a little over an hour. Cruise speed in the Astar was 120 knots and, depending a great deal on what routing instructions we would receive from Raipur ATC (Air Traffic Control), the flight distance was 130 nautical miles. If there was any landing or departing traffic, however, the controllers would become overcautious. They seemed to prefer a twenty-mile separation between aircraft, making the flight longer. Our eventual landing would be six miles from the airport at the Raipur IPS-secured, Chhattisgarh state government heliport, a place I would be operating out of frequently.

There were many rivers flowing through Chhattisgarh on their meandering way to drain in the Bay of Bengal to the east. Of them, the Indravati in Jagdalpur and the Mahanadi near Raipur would become important landmarks. These natural water supplies were not sufficient, it seemed, or else Mother Nature had not located them optimally for farming, as there were massive canal projects to redirect the flow being established throughout the region. These became more evident the closer we flew to Raipur.

The Mahanadi Canal System of Chhattisgarh had been in operation about a hundred years, with many dams and canals added since then. As Chatterjee and I flew north, the extent and size of these canals was revealed. There were smaller canals and drainage ditches connecting rice paddies and such, then there were broad, cement lined canals that diverted vast amounts of water from the rivers. These larger canals measured over 150 feet wide and tens, if not hundreds, of miles long. The reach of the project would have been impressive in a country like the United States, but in India, the lack of modern earth-moving machinery made it remarkable. With a population hundreds of millions larger than that of the USA, cheap labor was probably the key to success of ambitious projects such as this.

Forty miles from Raipur, we established contact with ATC and, shortly after, they directed us to descend to twenty-five hundred feet. By this point, we had mainly put behind the area influenced by Maoist-Naxalite insurgents, and flying at lower altitudes was safe from their target practice. Being in Raipur's control zone and having contact with the controllers, we had to follow their instructions anyway.

Thirty miles from Raipur, we crossed the Mahanadi and this being the apex of the dry season, the mighty river was just a trickle flowing through sandbars on each side. In places, the bare, sandy white riverbed stretched to three-quarters of a mile, and the tiny ribbon of water in between looked narrow enough to jump across. Chatterjee remarked that during the monsoon season, seeing the river full and running bank to bank would be impressive, though, at the time, with the riverbed nearly empty, the river was a mere creek. The huge canal system was flowing full of water, however, and trying to imagine what the area looked like before man's intervention, I visualized a healthy river teeming with fish year-round. The land, instead of cleared for rice paddies, covered with jungle and roamed by tigers and elephants.

Twenty miles inbound, ATC had us maintain our altitude and hold in a clockwise orbit due to departing traffic from runway 24. Chatterjee and I both agreed that holding twenty miles out while at our low altitude was excessive, but we offered no argument to the controller and, after ten minutes of plowing invisible circles in the sky, were cleared inbound to the airport.

The closer we came to Raipur, the more the ground elevation dropped off, and the terrain changed from mostly hills and forests to flat land, most of it being used for agriculture: rice paddies, sugar cane and the rare corn crop. The ground we flew over was an immense puzzle, the individual paddies and cropland quite small compared to the sprawling industrial agricultural fields of North America, and it was an eye-catching mosaic of polygon-shaped greens and browns. The land nearest the canals and rivers was greenest, the green fading into brown the further away from the water source, irrigation becoming untenable.

Chatterjee and I continued our flight inbound, dropping to fifteen hundred feet MSL (Mean Sea Level), which was around five hundred feet AGL (Above Ground Level), and crossed the airport's only runway to turn left in the direction of the Raipur Heliport. The heliport wasn't difficult to locate once we were close enough to minimize the smoggy haze. It was nestled between a couple of ponds and the reddish-brown rectangular IPS parade ground, and sat well within the city and its thousands of three and four story, grime-covered concrete buildings.

Positioned at the west end of the parade ground, the heliport was in front of Chhattisgarh government's two-helicopter-sized hangar and aviation offices. The pad was concrete, but we generated a huge swirling dust storm over the Roland Garros-colored patch of sun-blasted dirt; we flew in on the safest approach path available through the buildings and radio towers, and then landed on the oversized yellow "H" painted on the cement.

Once on the ground and shut down, Chatterjee's phone became attached to his ear once again as he checked in, reporting landing times and receiving any updates on our mission the next day. I peeled my sweaty self from the seat and, in the testy afternoon sunshine, did a post-flight walk around. An engineer named BK had flown with us, and I helped him with peeking under the hot cowlings, tying down rotor blades and digging out the windscreen cover from the cargo compartment.

The sight and sound of the helicopter attracted a large crowd of onlookers. We were on the IPS base, so the hundred or more civilians that watched could only come as far as the ring of security personnel. The IPS themselves were a curious bunch, and excited chatter developed from both groups when they spotted the overheated foreign helicopter pilot trying to find shade underneath the aircraft's tailboom. I didn't think Raipur, Chhattisgarh, was on many tourists' bucket lists, and seeing a real live foreigner may have been a once-in-a-lifetime event for some folks. I went about my business, but the amount of eyeballs following my every move was a tad unnerving.

The helicopter secured, a vehicle was summoned and we were driven to the Hotel Grand for the evening. I thought I had seen the limits of chaos and congestion in the streets of Delhi, but the sights, smells and sounds encountered on that short drive blasted my senses with even more troubling effects. It is not much of an exaggeration to say that a vehicle, person, cow or dog was on every square yard of flat ground. Small piles of rubbish scattered along the road had been set alight and smoldering, the only apparent form of solid waste management. That, combined with the diesel and gas fumes being released out of thousands of exhaust pipes, plus the suffocating heat, made for a toxic gas chamber effect. Every now and then, I spotted a tree clinging to life, trying to urge its little green leaves out into the pernicious air, but there was no room for proper landscaping; and, as usual, above it all was the torturous screams of every horn in every car and motorcycle on the road in Raipur being blown.

We reached our hotel unscathed and after brake-squealing to a stop the bellboy, wearing a threadbare uniform and brimless bellboy hat, opened my door for me and grabbed my bag. Not satisfied with only one bag, he started tugging on the laptop bag already on my shoulder. I politely refused four times before he let out a "HUFF" in frustration and released his grip, glaring at me.

Once inside, I was first met with stares and goggle eyes from about twenty chaps in the lobby. Then, in contrast, I approached the front desk, where the two young ladies on duty wouldn't look at my face or bother to return my greeting of "Namaste!"

Chatterjee was able to negotiate for a couple of rooms with them, but the women never once made eye contact with me. I realized I may have been a little ripe and sweat stained, but hey, I'd been on the receiving end of foul odiferous whiffs from many of their countrymen and was not any worse than them.

Later, once settled, I accepted the offer of a Kingfisher beer from the hotel manager at their bar and, when my throat was properly rinsed, enjoyed a meal of buttered fish. The manager was an outgoing chap who, in telling me a bit of his life story, said that, years before, he had run away from his family and India to the Philippines. He had fallen for a Filipina through an online dating service and was madly in love. His dream to escape India was short lived, though; he'd spent only a couple of weeks there before his family pressured him into returning and getting into the hotel business. With both their hearts breaking, he told the Filipina goodbye and returned per his family's wishes.

"Mista Mike, now I have two wives and four childs," he said, holding up four fingers, his English so-so, "and my family wants me to marry again!" He rolled his eyes in frustration.

"How can you marry all these women," I asked. "Is polygamy legal?"

"Yes, for Muslims it is." He looked down, slowly shaking his head. "Bad for me... I don't know how to keep all these wives happy."

Before retiring for the evening, Chatterjee and I talked about the next day's flight, a three-legged mission. We would takeoff from Raipur with VIPs, land in Jagdalpur, wait, and then return the passengers to Raipur in the afternoon. If there was daylight left, we planned to return to Jagdalpur empty. The passengers were IPS officers headed to the Jagdalpur headquarters for meetings. Takeoff was set for eight o'clock, but we planned to leave the hotel plenty early to verify the fuel and sort out the flight planning.

After my first day's flying in Chhattisgarh, it felt good to get back in the cockpit. The helicopter was solid and the crew seemed dedicated and competent; I was eager for my future in India and looking forward to flying off the hours with Chatterjee and being left on my own.

12.

Morning Black Gold

Zero dark thirty the next morning, and deeming it a good sign my cell phone alarm had woken me up on time, I alternated prying open first my left eye, then my right eye long enough to dial the number for hotel room service and order the morning nectar of the gods, coffee. Indians drink tea—chai, they call it—but the taste did not appeal to me. I had been a diehard coffee enthusiast for years and wasn't about to give it up. Indian coffee seemed mostly sugar and milk, with just a little actual coffee, and that syrup-like extra caloric kick made it even more addictive.

The night's sleep had been interrupted two or three times, the other guests having two voice volume settings, one, labeled where I'm from as your "outside voice" and the other setting a few decibels louder. Whispering or talking quietly at two in the morning in an empty hotel hallway wasn't considered necessary, and it seemed that Indians had the power to sleep through a train wreck. Lucky them. I'm a light sleeper, but I had come equipped with my trusty ear plugs, and ninety-nine percent of auditory intrusions were effectively blocked.

Traveling light, I slept in my birthday suit and enjoyed the freedom, but at times this caused difficulties. When I got up, I had thrown off the bed sheet in the dim light, wrapping a towel around my waist and shuffling over to the desk to fire up my laptop, going about the process of waking up. Suddenly, the towel vacated its spot above my hips as a violent twisting and pushing of the door handle, followed by a loud, staccato knocking made me jump out of my skin and sent my heart racing into boost-mode well before it was ready.

"Room sa'vice," a muffled shout came. "Coffee, saa!"

I readjusted my towel while the knocking continued, then the door pushing again, so hard that the cheap wood was straining, making small splintering sounds against the hinges and doorjamb. Preferring to wake up at my own pace and belligerently cranky if not allowed to do so, I yelled, "Coming, you son-of-a-bitch!"

I opened the door to find a nervous and sweaty-looking bellboy carrying a jittering tray of the morning black gold. No greeting, no smile, he brusquely walked past me and then, a little too carelessly, plopped down the steaming, sloshing coffee right next to my booting-up laptop. Without a word or glance in my direction, he rushed past me once again, trailing his all-night body odor and slamming the door behind him.

Good morning, sir.

I quickly noticed there wasn't enough coffee there to choke a sparrow, certainly not the quantity required to satisfy my dire needs. I dialed room service again and ordered a second, reserve carafe. The chap on the phone seemed cheery for five in the morning, in contrast to his colleague the bellboy, who must have missed the latest hospitality training.

Ten minutes later, again to my shock and surprise, the bellboy flung open the door without so much as a tap. I had forgotten to lock it behind him, and knocking before entering was for losers in this part of the world. But that may have been the epiphany moment when all things would change for him; the towel had slipped to my ankles once again and the glare from my backside probably caused him flashbacks for years.

After a breakfast of hard-boiled eggs and toast choked down with orange juice, I met Chatterjee down in the lobby. He was pacing around like an expectant father; there was confusion regarding our vehicular transport, and we were in danger of running late. The hotel had sent all their cars to the airport with guests and had forgotten about our shuttle request to the heliport the night before. But judging from the number of landline phones and cellphones being shouted into behind the front desk, they were acquiring substitute transport for us.

Chatterjee used the delay to explain the intricacies involved with filing a flight plan with the authorities in India; I had filed plenty of flight plans, but India's process was to become a patience-trying new exercise. He explained that two flight clearances were required before a flight could leave the ground, a Flight Information Clearance, FIC, received from Airports Authority of India, AAI; and the Air Defense Clearance, ADC, received from the military authority.

If the flight plan was filled out correctly and raised no questions from AAI or suspicions from the military, the pilot could expect to receive the FIC within two hours before takeoff and the ADC about an hour before takeoff. It seemed simple enough, explained that way, but then he continued.

Since we were a non-scheduled operator, the worker bees at AAI were reluctant to do the extra bit of work in filing our flight plan. We were a helicopter landing at a point other than an airport, and those points could only be defined by latitude and longitude coordinates; thus requiring them to plot that point on a wall map.

It was much easier for them to file a scheduled airline flight plan—for example, a plan that showed Air India flying a 737 from Delhi to Kolkata—than a small, non-scheduled helicopter flying from a nondescript little heliport in Raipur to an even more nondescript police-cleared helipad in the jungle defined only by coordinates. They simply had to do more work for operations like us.

Chatterjee explained, "First, Captain, the night before the mission, receive the flight request from IPS, including takeoff times, destinations, passengers and their weights, and how much fuel is to be prepositioned at the destination, if possible."

"Okay, got it," I said.

"Second, you need to fill out the AAI flight plan form."

"That can be expected," I said. "Piece 'a cake so far."

He held up a finger. "Ah, but your work is only beginning. You then fax the plan to FIC. That's the only way. They will not take dictation over the phone."

"I see. What if I have no fax machine available?"

"No excuse to them... They're evil," he said, only half joking. "And there are only certain times you should fax. If faxed too early, the risk of it getting lost in the system multiplies, I'm afraid. Faxed too close to departure time, and the proper clearances might not be ready for your requested takeoff time, especially the ADC from the military."

"Uh-huh. Should I be taking notes?"

"Now," he continued, "once faxed, it is of utmost importance to immediately redial AAI and get someone on the phone to confirm receipt of the faxed plan. No confirmation, and it's likely you'll call back later, just before takeoff, to receive clearance, and the scoundrel will say he never received it." He paused for a quick gulp of air, "And in the eyes of the VIP who is already boarding your helicopter, Mike, you—the pilot—are the scoundrel causing his delay." He poked me in the chest with his finger.

"Are my eyes glazed over?"

"Finally, about a half-hour before takeoff, while also taking calls from the IPS, or the passengers, the company, or engineers—the phone calls are endless—you start the process of extricating the clearance numbers from AAI."

His eyes were big, hands gesticulating wildly as if retelling a horrible experience, which this seemed to qualify as. He continued, "And there are only three phone lines that they make available to get through. A busy signal should be expected." His chest heaved slightly as he breathed through his nose.

"Sometimes you'll be lucky and receive both FIC and ADC clearance numbers from AAI with the first office called, but there'll be many more times when you have to call the military yourself and go through the same dial and redial business until you are able to talk to someone, probably repeating much information, until receiving the ADC."

"This sounds ludicrous, Chatterjee. I've never heard of such a preposterous procedure. Why couldn't someone do this at our company operations department in Delhi?" I asked.

He smiled, shook his head and asked, "Did you see any operations department in Delhi?"

It occurred to me that I had not. "My time was rushed at the head office with Sami and the air marshal," I said. "I didn't see much of the building."

"There's not much to see. Really, if you want the job done right, do it yourself, Mike."

I was surprised the pilots were even bothering with that part of the flight operations process; I hadn't filed my own flight plan since working as a flight instructor. That was something left to the ops departments I've worked with in the past, in the US and other countries. Now I understood why Chatterjee's phone was usually seen affixed to his ear.

A suitable replacement for our transportation needs was finally provided and, through the morning hubbub of a mid-sized Indian city waking up, out to the heliport we went. BK, the senior engineer and crew chief, had secured transport via earlier channels and was already there, doing his preflight and finishing up the refueling. Scurrying about were several other younger engineering technicians or apprentices fetching rags, wrenches, ladders—anything in an attempt to look busy and important.

In India, an engineer flew with the helicopter wherever it went; this was something new to me and, at first, I thought it an unnecessary waste of a seat that could otherwise be offered to a passenger. As time went on, though, I found this a welcome requirement and quite helpful when flying in the bush; whether it was refueling from drums in a remote corner of the forest or hot-loading passengers and maintaining crowd control, the engineer/crew chief was vital to have aboard. For that first day of flying passengers, however, BK stayed in Raipur. There would be technicians along our route to receive us, and the extra seat was indeed needed for a passenger. On our final leg to Jagdalpur, BK would join us for the return.

Chatterjee and I finished our day in the late afternoon at Hotel Devansh. Other than my first fragments of frustration with AAI, the flights had felt routine. I learned that when VIPs gave a desired takeoff time, it was spoken of in vague terms, and we had to be prepared to revise the departure and arrival times with AAI, resulting in more phone work and the tension of trying to get through and be understood.

With the electrical power still out and no air conditioning at the guesthouse, Hotel Devansh was a cool and clean alternative. Having missed lunch earlier, I was famished and determined to find a winner off their vegetarian-only room service menu. The waiter offered me the menu, and on the cover was a glossy photo of a Margherita pizza. Anything resembling a pizza made me rabid. I stabbed the picture with my finger and queried him for a beer. There was none available on the premises, but through charades and grunts we struck a deal where he'd run to the beer shop across the road and fetch two for me.

I had him grab a pack of Gold Flake cigarettes as well, and after he returned with two bottles of Haywards 5000, I gave him a grin-inducing tip. Then feeling stuffy in my room, I ventured forth, looking for a way up to the roof. The Devansh was a four-story hotel, and there was nothing taller in Jagdalpur. It had a decent view when I found the top—I even caught the hazy sunset while relaxing before dinner.

The roof seemed to be the domain of the laundry department, and hanging in the open spaces were dozens of white bed sheets fluttering in the early-evening breeze. While the sun was setting, two housekeeping women appeared and began taking them down and folding. They were dressed in what looked to be expensive and elaborate sarees, but from what I'd seen so far, rich or poor, women dressed in traditional styles always looked elaborate. I'm sure there were variations in the quality of cloth, but to tell the difference was well beyond my fashion sense.

They were a tad startled to see someone up in their realm, a foreigner no less, and one enjoying firewater and smoke. After a few seconds of wide-eyed surprise and chattering consultation amongst themselves, they continued with their work, casting a glance in my direction from time to time, making sure I wasn't up to any no-good tomfoolery.

13.

Jagdalpur

I didn't learn my lesson about locking the hotel door. By habit, I expected it to automatically lock after closing. The happenings at Raipur a few mornings prior should have impressed upon me that, in this land, doors and doorways were made to walk through as one wishes—nobody was to be bothered with politely knocking and sedately waiting for permission to enter. But there I was again, walking across the room *al fresco*, when the door suddenly rattled and was flung open by the room service waiter, carrying my tray of coffee-flavored sugar.

Startled he was, but if the wide-eyed native was blinded by my great white posterior, he didn't miss a step. While I hastily wrapped my belongings in a towel, he placed the tray on the desk and dashed out. It was my fault, I suppose, leaving the door unlocked when returning from my search through the hotel lobby for early morning satisfaction. The desk manager there had assured me that coffee would be brought to my room posthaste, and he had not exaggerated. Like in Raipur, that's just how they rolled in the Jagdalpur part of the world. Door knocking wasn't part of the program.

Jagdalpur, like many Indian communities, had a human history stretching back many centuries. At one time, it was the capital of the kingdom known as Bastar; a royal family still lived in the fifteenth-century palace built between the Indravati River and one of the town's small lakes. Jagdalpur was deceiving in size; by looking at where the buildings stopped and the rice paddies began during my first flight out of its airport, I had guessed that the population was no more than fifteen or twenty thousand; it just didn't look that big from above. I was quite surprised to find out the number was deep into the six figures; but being surprised in India was a matter of course.

We had been at the Hotel Devansh for a couple of days and between flights, Chatterjee and I were going over information on India's airports—seemingly every one of them. He felt compelled to share with me all the information he had accumulated over years of flying and had thoroughly detailed in a stack of binders and notepads. He was relentless.

"The DGCA publishes this info preprinted, or online, yes?" I asked.

"It's possible, but I wouldn't trust it," he said. "This information I'm giving you is firsthand knowledge. Plus, I have useful contact numbers for each city I've been to, pilots I know in the area, engineers, nice hotels. Be a sport, Mike, and write this down. It might benefit you someday."

As it turned out, there was plenty of information available online. At the time, though, he was insistent on sharing every airport's radio frequencies, runways and their orientation, phone numbers for ATC personnel, weather offices, fuel offices and any other contacts that had a vague connection to the airport that he thought were relevant. I filled up a notebook with my chicken-scratch writing while he rattled on for hours, sometimes getting sidetracked in lengthy recollections of missions long past.

I was to the point of thrusting an ink pen into my abdomen when his stack of papers finally dwindled off and the room became peacefully quiet. Instead of my spleen, I thrust the pen into the air and, startling Chatterjee, who was lost in foggy reminiscence, shouted, "Success through perseverance!"

He smiled and said, "See, Mike? There's nothing to it but to do it."

Professional and thorough, he went into great detail explaining procedures or approaches into certain airports, even airports on the other side of the country that he thought I might fly into someday. I appreciated his efforts and hoped to remember the information he had given me or, at least, make sense of my written notes when the time came.

Later, after being convinced that electricity had been restored to the Jagdalpur guesthouse, we checked out of the hotel and shifted back to the company digs. The good news with that was the availability of Wi-Fi throughout the house. I was able to log on and fire off a few emails. The bad news was someone else's good news. A neighbor had just taken ownership of their new house a few doors down, and it appeared they were gearing up for a festive house-warming shindig. Countless laborers wearing the Jagdalpur equivalent of hard hats—turbans—were setting up scaffolding and rigging for a gigantic pink and white tent that, when finished, cloaked the entire road.

A truly ominous sign was a large truck reversing its way down to the gaping mouth of this tent and the laborers starting to unload speaker after speaker for the sound system. We had been made aware of a mission for the next day, but any sleep during the night seemed unlikely when the microphone switch was thrown on and a prematurely tipsy, tone-deaf Elvis wannabe started making unbeautiful and unnatural sounds, singing to some housewarming Hindu god through the maxed-out distortion of those jumbo speakers.

In the evening, we ventured forth to mingle with the new neighbors even though the horrendous music made my eardrums pound—I was fearful they'd simply break off and roll out my ear canal. Women dressed in bright and colorful sarees were shouting and gossiping together on one side of the tent, and men in button-down dress shirts and large mustaches were grouped together on the other side, bottles of whiskey being tipped at regular intervals. Kids ran wild, screaming, and the pre-teens stared at me like I was an alien.

The night ended up being a long one. Even with the earplugs jammed in tightly, the noise still penetrated my skull when it became time to attempt sleep. My fluffy pillows and bed sheets vibrated with the drum beat. When dawn broke the next morning, a wounded animal was still singing down the street. The guy had stamina, but that was all. As Chatterjee and I tiredly said our good mornings, he said that the louder and longer the singing and chanting went on, the greater was the chance that the gods would hear it and, in turn, give greater blessings to our new mortgage-holding neighbors. Then he dryly observed that the gods this chap chose to sing for perhaps had their ears covered. Halfway to the airport, we could still hear this miserably drunk and tortured soul bellowing off-key chants through our open car windows.

Our flight was to the IPS district headquarters in Dantewada, southwest of Jagdalpur by forty miles. The town had a population of thirteen thousand and, along with Raipur and Jagdalpur, would become one of my most frequented landing zones. From the helipads there, we would load up troopers and fly them to the IPS or CRPF camps scattered throughout the jungle, where they'd relieve other troopers who were returning to Dantewada on transfer or leave orders.

With infinite hiding spots for Maoist-Naxalites in the jungle, Chatterjee had shown me previously how he made a spiraling descent to the waiting troopers. Directly over the landing zone, we began the descent from our four-thousand-foot cruising altitude, and the object was to offer a difficult target to anyone hiding in the bush as we neared the ground. We set pitch and engine power for sixty-five knots airspeed, then banked the helicopter steeply and funneled downward, keeping in mind the direction of wind, locations of radio antenna and trees, and the razor-wire topped perimeter fence. Then, by timing the spiral just right, we would level the helicopter on the last tight turn below tree line and rapidly reduce speed on short approach to the helipad before landing.

This type of landing approach was aggressive and sporty but within the capabilities of the aircraft; and it might've even been fun if the potential danger of gunfire from behind every tree or rock could have been eliminated.

The helipads at Dantewada were bordered by a road, the headquarter buildings and, on the other two sides, thick jungle. We did not shut down to load passengers; as soon as we were on the ground, BK jumped out and directed nervous-looking troopers aboard with their rifles and an assortment of bags, blankets and personal effects. We spent less than sixty seconds on the ground and then were airborne again, making a spiraling climb to our safe altitude in the sky. Although it was just after eight in the morning, the temperature was pushing well into the nineties. The Astar, a powerful, robust machine and a good climber, didn't climb as fast as I would have liked while fully loaded, but it climbed faster than most single-engine helicopters.

Heading south several miles, Chatterjee pointed out the Kirandul iron ore mine, an enormous strip mine that was removing a mountaintop one dump truck at a time. Beyond that, we were deep into the wild country where if we had any mechanical trouble and had to land—or crash land—the chances of being taken prisoner, if not shot outright, were high. The country had beauty, however, in a wild and isolated way. Now and then we'd spot extraordinary cascading waterfalls coming down the hillsides, or a delicious patch of open green meadow within thick jungle, plus captivating, sun-blasted rock formations: remote treasures for the eyes that few humans had ever seen.

The destination on this leg was an IPS camp and village named Chintagufa, my first time landing there. It was just over fifty miles from Dantewada and one of the more remote camps, though they were all quite remote. There were dirt roads to these camps, but they were considered too dangerous for the troopers to travel on. If their vehicle was stopped by a group of the Maoist-Naxalites who controlled those areas, death was inevitable.

The Maoists had it in their heads that roads were bad and bridges were worse; if they had explosives available, they would blast them apart and make them impassable. If explosives were scarce, they would dismantle a bridge by hand before the IPS or CRPF could do anything about it. Troopers traveling by roads at that time in those high-risk areas were in danger. Thus, we were called upon to deliver both personnel and vital supplies, and the number of flights was expected to increase.

As we approached Chintagufa, which looked to consist of only trees and rice paddies, a trooper lit off a smoke canister. Only then was I able to see our intended landing zone. We had an arrangement with the IPS and CRPF that, before we landed, a signal smoke was to be activated to let us know that all was clear, safe, and that bad guys had not overrun the camp.

Setting up for descent and landing, I leaned the helicopter over in a steep bank and entered a tight, spiraling dive. As we neared the ground, an increased tension and adrenaline within the cockpit became palpable. Chatterjee's eyes were wide, and his head was on a swivel, as was mine. Our view out the windscreen went through multiple 360 degree rotations as the circles we flew became tighter. The scene grew strange and suspicious. Even the troopers on the ground, who were supposedly protecting the landing zone, looked like they were ready to blast us out of the sky. They were all armed, but none of them wore a uniform. A few were shirtless and didn't wear trousers but, instead, the loosely tied traditional sarong, or dhoti, that rural Indian men preferred. Their headgear was the fashionable and versatile turban, resplendent in the latest spring colors. The only way I could identify them as good guys was that they weren't shooting at us.

After landing on the cattle and goat-grazed grass next to the barbed wire-covered compound, BK wasted no time offloading the fresh troops and loading the guys rotating out of camp. Six skinny, weary looking and bedraggled troopers had come rushing to the helicopter with their backpacks and bags, but we only had room for three; BK did a quick job of sorting out who was coming and who was staying. The three who were turned away glared at Chatterjee and me with hostility, the rifles in their hands shifting about.

Total time on the ground was no more than thirty or forty seconds and while BK closed and latched the door, I was raising the collective lever and getting us on the move. We accelerated in ground effect over a rice paddy until we had about forty knots of airspeed, and then started our spiraling climb once again up to four thousand feet.

"The tighter the spiral, the better," Chatterjee explained. "The troopers are under orders to provide a secure perimeter one and a half kilometers around the landing zone. In theory, the closer we fly to the center of that perimeter, the further from the potential threat lurking in the jungle."

I asked Chatterjee over the intercom, "Are they really providing a kilometer and a half safe zone?"

He shrugged and waved a hand through the air. "Some of them, but who knows for sure? The jungle is too thick to see anybody down there."

We returned to Dantewada, a thirty-five- to forty-minute flight, shut down, took fuel, had biscuits and chai with the base helipad commander, Rabinesh, and fired up again for a flight to the village of Gollapalli. It was in the same general direction as Chintagufa, only further south and over a steep ridge. Returning again, we refueled and made a final flight to Bheji, a dozen miles from Chhattisgarh's riverine and forested state border with Odisha in the east and Andhra Pradesh to the south.

Our first attempt into Bheji, we had to go-around due to stampeding cattle across the landing zone. During our spiraling descent, we had the cattle so confused and nervous that they didn't know which way to run and ended up in the middle of our windscreen on final approach. It was quite a large, organized herd for India, and I wondered if way out there, away from any semblance of services, but a perceived lack of food, if those cattle were meal-worthy or were given the same immunity as the rest of the beefers in India.

After the three flights from Dantewada, we finished up at two o'clock, shutting down at Jagdalpur in the blazing sunshine with the thermometer nearly maxed out. The crew had been talking about the monsoon season coming up in June or July, when rain can be expected every day. During the postflight walk-around of the aircraft, sweat drenching my clothes, a little rain sounded refreshing.

The driver was waiting to give us a lift back to the guesthouse, and we were about to climb in the car when Chatterjee

Jagdalpur

received a phone call. I could tell by how big his eyes were that something was not going right for someone somewhere.

After we had left Dantewada, there was a mine blast on one of the roads nearby and troopers were hurt badly. We were being asked to return for medevac.

A bit of rushed tension ensued. Technicians scrambled with fuel drums, cowlings were closed and secured, and everyone but me seemed to have a phone stuck to their ear, including Chatterjee, who was arguing with AAI about receiving an expedited FIC and ADC clearance. About the time we had the aircraft refueled, we received another call and were told to stand down. The flight was not deemed necessary, as the critical trooper had died from his wounds. The others were receiving medical care but were expected to live. There was nothing else we could do.

We returned to the guesthouse at three-thirty in the afternoon, right on India time for lunch.

14.

General Condition, Fair

India had a skewed approach to meal times, or maybe I did. They were skewed compared to what I was used to, anyway. They took breakfast way into mid-morning, for example. I'm useless if I don't have a meal in my belly soon after daybreak. Although there are those who'd argue that I am just as useless, full belly or not.

Breakfast about ten, lunch at three, and dinner was nine to ten in the evening everywhere in India that I'd been, including the Jagdalpur guesthouse. If we had a flight in the morning at our normal takeoff time of eight, I was given a gracious giftbag of egg roti while walking out the door; the engineers and technicians would not have anything to eat until after the helicopter was gone. I never saw Chatterjee eat, but his rotund belly implied he did not miss out.

I hoped to get on the good side of the cook at the guesthouse and receive my meals sooner, especially in the morning—holy blood-sugar, Batman. As far as cooking my own meals, that seemed to be out of the question. The kitchen was not meant to be my area of operation, nor did I care to set foot in that steamy, filth-ridden room.

Someone had once told me that an Indian diet and all the spices that it contained were a natural deterrent to mosquitoes. That person had to be full of malarkey because I had been eating my share of spicy Indian dishes and the mozzies still considered my blood a delicacy worth dying for. During a bit of down time, I decided to put an end to my bloodletting and collared one of the technicians to be my guide while on the hunt through town looking for mosquito netting. It didn't take long to find a suitable model and, with a length of cheap plastic rope and bowline knots, I had a decent mosquito stopper installed over my bed.

A person may wonder why there was all the problems with mosquitoes *inside* the house when they should all be outside. One reason was that closing the guesthouse's front door behind oneself wasn't a cultivated habit amongst my comrades, nighttime or any time. Another reason was that doors and windows were not precisely engineered, which let any number of worldly effects through, from the neighbor's blasting Bollywood music, to a soft rain, or my constant companions, the bloodthirsty mosquitoes. In fairness to the builders, the windows did seem impermeable to large birds.

Relative paradise was found behind that net. One night, when we had another one of those pesky power cuts, Chatterjee asked me if I wanted to stay at the hotel again. I declined and slept like a log. Without air conditioning, it did become a little warm, but not being at the mercy of those little rascals had me feeling content.

Before coming to India and its reputation for mosquito-borne diseases like malaria, dengue and encephalitis, I had considered this potential problem and checked into prevention and pills. To me, the side effects from the anti-malarial pills sounded as bad as the disease itself, and their effectiveness was also in question. I decided against them. Even with the poor sanitation and drainage around Jagdalpur, I was assured by Chatterjee not to worry much. Out deep in the jungle was a different story, during monsoon season, with the abundance of water and mosquito breeding sites, villagers could have a hard time of it.

We didn't have to contend with mosquitoes inside our helicopter, though. We stayed busy with Dantewada, Kistaram, Gollapalli and Bheji being the most requested flights, but there were many others. Jagdalpur airport was our second home. As Chatterjee had promised, we were usually flying from five to six hours a day or more, with some days approaching the DGCA daily legal limit of seven hours. Afternoons were becoming more and more weather active, however, and cumulonimbus clouds could be seen building most days, accompanied with occasional distant, grumbling thunder and a few large raindrops splattering on the baked pavement to let us know that monsoon season was coming. We were generally on the ground by no later than two or three in the afternoon, resting and relaxing back at the guesthouse. The weather from morning to early afternoon didn't pose any problems—yet.

We received a request one evening for a flight to Raipur in order to assist the Chhattisgarh government with VIP transport. A politician from the village of Aundhi had been gunned down by Maoist-Naxalites, and the VIPs, including Chhattisgarh's chief minister, desired to be flown to the village to pay their last respects at the funeral. The chief minister had his own helicopter, a twin-engine Agusta AW109, but for maintenance reasons it wasn't available for the flight.

A chief minister's request took priority over any other, unless there was an emergency medevac, so I started the flight planning to the Raipur and Aundhi areas. It was then decided by the company that this would be Chatterjee's last mission in Chhattisgarh state; once finished in Aundhi and upon returning the chief minister to Raipur, the helicopter would be converted back to single-pilot operation, the dual-pilot controls would be removed, and Chatterjee would catch the next flight out of town. This was convenient for him as he could avoid the jungle trail enduro-run from Jagdalpur to Raipur, and it was good for me as we could now free up one additional seat in the helicopter and carry more passengers. There was also the matter of a minor maintenance inspection that needed to be completed in conjunction with the removal of the dual controls at Raipur, and Sami was sending an additional engineer to assist BK there.

We had a relatively cool early morning start the next day, which helped me recover from dinner the evening before. The spicy dish had burned as if chili peppers were the main ingredient and the bits of chicken floating around were just included for texture. My stomach fought the good fight, but there had been too many trips to the bathroom throughout the night, and breathing deep of the cool morning air had a soothing effect.

There was still a low bank of fog hanging over the end of the runway that the morning sun hadn't burned off, and I brushed it with our downwash as we took off and climbed north to Raipur. I reveled in the fresh breeze from the air vent while sitting in the left seat, but Chatterjee, sitting on the right, would get baked as the sun rose higher.

Any time is a good time to fly, but early morning the best. Winds are lighter, and having to deal with the vexatious updrafts, downdrafts or bumpy thermals comes about later when the day warms. There's no need for sunglasses at that time and watching the world wake up while cruising low level and in excess of a hundred knots puts me on top of the world, figuratively as well as literally. Then, late in the day, as the sun is setting and the lights from humanity start to twinkle on, dusk-time flight can be quite beautiful just the same. I'm privileged to be a witness; those sights never get old.

We reached Raipur in plenty of time to refuel and sort out FIC and ADC clearances. Chhattisgarh's top VIP was coming along with his entourage, so there were more troopers around the heliport providing additional security. Also, there was a disproportionately higher number of their superior officers, all pressed and polished, pacing briskly about, looking serious and important with cell phones to their ears.

As I clicked off the phone with AAI, a young technician walked up and grunted, "You. Docta'. Heeya." And, with a twitchy glare, he waited for me to respond.

Those first weeks, I occasionally misinterpreted the lack of English skills for rudeness, something I eventually adjusted to, but the glaring, shameless gawking and staring was vexing and harder to ignore.

A bit confused, I asked the lad, "Sorry, who... what?"

But he simply pointed inside the hangar and returned his gaze to the study of my face.

Walking inside and to the back of the hangar, where the state's Agusta 109 sat disassembled, was an office and lounge area, and there on the sofa was Chatterjee, getting his blood pressure checked. At first sight, I thought, *Oh no! The stress was too much for Chatterjee! He's having a heart attack!*

Then the Velcro band was ripped off my colleague's arm, and the old man sitting on the coffee table in front of him smiled at me and said, "Come, please sit down. Just a few checks before you fly with the chief minister."

The gray-haired, fragile-looking chap indeed turned out to be a doctor, and with shaky hands he wrapped the blood pressure cuff around my arm and checked my pulse. He wrote down on his lengthy checklist that my vital signs were normal. That seemed optimistic, considering all the nervous tension seeping through the heliport, but I was not to argue.

With his job finished and the medical form filled out, he asked me to sign on the bottom line. Glancing it over, I saw that he had written:

"The pilot had not been drinking."

—and also—

"The pilot's general condition, fair."

Both true statements, although a drink was not a bad idea and I really felt much better than fair.

Chatterjee and I stood inside the hangar, making small talk and seeking protection from the climbing sun, waiting for the honorable chief minister to show up. His scheduled takeoff time came and went, and at close to half an hour past departure time, I tried to get AAI on the line for a departure revision. Just after hitting redial for the fifth time, we began hearing sirens wailing in the distance.

Slowly making my way to the side of the aircraft, I wondered where laid the prudence in announcing for miles around that the chief minister was on the move. If a would-be assassin was lying in ambush, wondering when he should load his rifle or arm his IED, the blaring sirens would be a hint, I'd guess.

As the sirens became louder, an air of urgency gripped the heliport. Security personnel and troopers scurried about, their superiors shouting and pointing. Civilians, who were lining up and jamming the perimeter hoping for a glimpse of the great man, were told to back away, only to push in closer still as the troopers moved along down the line. The scene reached its climax as the VIPs arrived in a reckless, speeding caravan of Tata SUVs and Hindustan Ambassadors about a city block long.

With dust swirling, bodyguards swung their doors open simultaneously. Big dudes with assault rifles on shoulder straps, dressed in black and wearing dark shades, encircled the ministers and scanned the crowd for anything or anyone out of place; they seemed to focus their attention on the foreigner slouching near the helicopter.

What was once a peaceful heliport scene became a shouting tangle of legs, elbows, guns and mustaches as junior officers scrambled for best position to give their practiced salute to the passing politicians. I had intended to offer my own hand and introduce myself, thinking it was the polite thing to do. It was an idea I quickly discarded, though, and retreated to the safe confines of my helicopter.

15.

Namaskar Chatterjee

Newspapers, drinks and snacks were brought aboard for the inflight entertainment while the hoard slowly made its way across Raipur Heliport to the aircraft doors, and with a brief wave to the adoring crowd, the VIPs climbed into their seats. I was glad there were enough hands and helpers to assist those in back with their seat belts; most were somewhat portly and had a bit of a grunting struggle clicking them shut.

After asking the technicians to clear the tailrotor, I fired up, did my after-start checks, asked Chatterjee to handle the radios, lifted to a hover, then checked my power and we took off climbing to 500 feet. Raipur Tower had landing airline traffic, and it was their habit to route us to the airport in a situation like that. It didn't make much sense as we were flying so low and out of the way, but perhaps they thought it was better to keep an eye on us, lest we get into mischief, or so it seemed. By the time we reached the airport, the Air India airliner was already on the ground and back-taxiing to the terminal. We were cleared to cross the runway and turn right, climb to three thousand feet and proceed on a direct track to Aundhi, ninety miles away. We had a light headwind, but I figured we would be there in forty-five minutes.

Our new friends in the back seats attempted a conversation amongst themselves over the noise, but soon gave up and settled in with their newspapers and snacks. Glancing back a few times over the course of the flight, I noticed a lot of mopping of sweat and general uncomfortableness. Perhaps this flight would be an excuse to motivate the company into installing air conditioning more promptly. The warming temperatures didn't help us outside the helicopter, either, as we were gently jostled by the rising thermals.

When we flew over Aundhi, someone from the mass of troopers below lit off the smoke signal and we started our descent, keeping the turns wide and shallow—not wanting the VIPs to experience more unpleasantness than they had to. We could risk the wider turns with the idea that the biggest Big Man in Chhattisgarh was coming to town, the landing zone and all the surrounding area was crawling with troops and security and we could never be safer.

The landing zone was a dry-cracked, dusty patch of dirt, and a slight brownout was inevitable. As I switched on the sand filter, Chatterjee said, "Keep a rapid descent rate through the dust and land quickly. Don't worry about a rough landing... just get us on the ground before we're totally blind."

"Got it," I said. "I'll use that for an excuse if I knock someone's tooth loose with my landing." Then, with a slight bump, we were down and engulfed within a massive dust cloud.

The whole village and residents from miles around came to see the chief minister and his helicopter. The place was overrun with well-wishers. While he went off to pay respects to his murdered colleague, Chatterjee and I were given plastic chairs and a table for relaxing in the shade of a massive old tree. It was still over one hundred degrees in the shade, but a breeze was blowing, bottled water and biscuits were provided and, an hour later, plates with spicy chicken and sabjee were prepared for us.

I didn't think meals could be any spicier than what my mouth and throat had been enduring back at the guesthouse, but struggling through the taste-bud-boiling specimens given to us in Aundhi made me realize that Indian cooks were all trained in torture. After taking a little bite of chicken, I'd drain half a bottle of water down my throat, trying to extinguish the inferno.

Chatterjee glanced at me, smacked his lips and said, "Mmm, they made it a little spicy, didn't they?"

"Yeh, 'ittle spicy," I managed to croak. Avoiding his look, I stayed focused on a piece of chicken in my fingertips, trying to hide my teary eyes.

Finishing the meal, Chatterjee picked at his teeth while I tried to find the best position to hold my mouth and tongue to relieve the lingering burn without drooling on my shirt. Flicking his toothpick at a lizard by the tree trunk, Chatterjee took a phone call and, while listening, stared at me with ever-expanding eyes. Speaking and acknowledging in Hindi, he then clicked off the line and explained that there had been a large explosion near Konta, the southernmost IPS/CRPF camp in the state. They reported many casualties and were requesting a medevac.

Konta was a long journey, closer to the Bay of Bengal than to Raipur. Fuel and weather were going to be a concern. Then there was the problem of what to do with the chief minister; first, it was decided to leave him in Aundhi and head straight for the nearest fueling stop on our way south. Our frustration in asking AAI for expedited FIC/ADC clearances to perform the medical evacuation reached new heights. Their complete inability to understand the situation had Chatterjee pleading breathlessly into his phone. Not helping was the spotty, poor-quality cellular coverage out in the rural sticks.

Then, about the time we had the emergency flight plan accepted, word came through that the chief minister would not stay in Aundhi and that he needed to return to Raipur. "He'll be coming in five minutes," the senior trooper at the helipad said, or rather, lied.

Back to square one with AAI. At that point, we were only confusing them more. We decided to fly back to Raipur and take our chances with ATC using our old FIC and ADC clearances. While waiting for the VIPs, I wondered how soon I could divest myself of this phone-calling headache and entrust it to someone in an office with a proper phone line and fax. What I needed was an operations liaison between the IPS, AAI, the company and me, something that every operator would normally have.

The five-minute wait turned into twenty, then thirty. I was empathetic for the man—he only wanted to pay final respects to his friend and the family—but men in Konta who were not dead yet were counting on our medevac, and weather in the afternoon was nothing to take lightly. The longer we waited, the more chance the afternoon heat would produce convective activity, creating rain and thunderstorms. If we were going to make it to Konta that day, the chief minister would have to rush things along a bit. As the minutes ticked by, the flight seemed more and more unlikely.

We finally bundled him back into the helicopter and took off for Raipur. ATC let us fly direct to the Raipur Heliport, and we weren't even asked to hold and orbit at some ridiculous distance while inbound. Arriving overhead, the same swarming crowd watched us land and before I even had the rotor blades stopped, bodyguards and security personnel whisked the VIPs into their long line of waiting SUVs. With sirens blaring, they disappeared down the street the same way they had arrived, in quite a conspicuous hurry.

At the helicopter, technicians and engineers were hustling. Some were rolling fuel barrels or peering under the hot cowlings while others were wiping down the fuselage and tailrotor. BK and another engineer, Chandru, were working on removing the dual-pilot controls, but time was running short, as they still had that minor inspection to perform on the aircraft.

My immediate concern was the weather and what it was doing to the south toward Konta. The only way to know was to have a reliable source in the area walk outside and take a weather check; no weather radar around those parts. And *reliable* would be the operative word; I didn't know who to trust. I called our contact in Dantewada, Rabinesh, who was likely biased in having us fly no matter what the weather—he would not want to be the guy held responsible for holding the helicopter on the ground. After getting him on the line, he said the weather was sunny and clear, which I found difficult to believe. In Raipur, it was overcast and getting worse. Not threatening yet, but the weather was changing rapidly.

Then I called one of our company lads in Jagdalpur. His bias was against work. If I flew south, I undoubtedly would end up back in Jagdalpur, where he would be put to task that evening. He claimed tall, ominous clouds were forming and that there was thunder in the distance, but getting louder.

"Prob'bly not good to fly, Cap'n," he said, in an exaggerated tone of grave concern.

Although hating to do it, I chose to be conservative and canceled the flight. Time was an issue also, as nightfall would be fast upon us and the India DGCA did not allow flight after dark for Visual Flight Rules (VFR)-only helicopters like ours, even in an emergency such as this. The medics would have to treat the wounded the best they could, and I would get there as quickly as possible in the morning.

I did not make any friends with the IPS or CRPF with that decision, but it was better than trying to pacify them and kill myself doing it.

Chatterjee and I retired to the Hotel Grand at sunset and, after getting our room keys, we jabbered on for a while, relaxing in the lobby's armchairs. He asked me how it felt to be in charge. I replied confidently, but had much to learn and a lot to coordinate, especially with no operations department to help. Having made up in my mind to at least have one or two chaps to help out with AAI phone work and the FIC/ADC, I mentioned that to Chatterjee in a bid for his opinion. He shrugged and smiled, put a fatherly arm on my shoulder and said, "Do it... if you can."

He was happy to be moving north. Flying the Mi17 in Shimla, the cooler and scenic hill country where he was headed, would be an enviable experience for any helicopter pilot, and we talked on about it at length.

Then, holding out his hand, he smiled and said, "Good luck, Mike. Stay in touch, and if you have any questions—please—do not hesitate to call."

"Alright, my friend," I said. "I appreciate it. Namaskar, Chatterjee. Good flying with you and thanks for all your help."

He was not a drinker, so we shared no toasts or salutations. On the other hand, I was thirsty after a hectic day. I called the bellboy, gave him a handful of rupees and told him not to return until he had secured a couple of Kingfishers and a pack of Gold Flakes. Once the cold frosties were in my hands, I trekked up to the night-shrouded roof of the hotel, lit a smoke, sipped a beer and thought over the day's events.

I considered all the politicians, all the phone calls and all the tension that made up the day. And I considered my friend, Chatterjee, off to new adventures in the north where there weren't people killing each other. He had his flight to Delhi in the morning, and I had mine, to a gritty village in the south where men were dying in the night.

16.

Plasmodium Falciparum

Hotel Grand gave me an early wake up and I preferred to get flying as soon as possible. And, since sunrise at that time of year was 05:45, I had asked the crew the night before to be ready for a six o'clock departure. They didn't want to wake up any earlier than they had to, however, and such an early morning request was met with indignant slouching and grunting.

"But Cap'n, saa," whined Babeesh, one of the engineering technicians. "Pe'haps dat too early? Raipur quite hazy in dee morn'n."

"No, man. Those guys in Konta are counting on us to take off early," I said. "You're so handsome anyway, you can skip an hour or two of beauty sleep."

Not quite understanding my little shot at humor, he stared at me with a wrinkled brow and, with BK's agreement, suggested that the much better option would be sleeping in and waiting until the sun cleared off the fog. I was outnumbered but held the veto vote. In the end, the fog was a valid argument, though, so before retiring for the evening, we reached a compromise in the hotel hallway, agreeing on a 07:00 takeoff. Still dissatisfied, their contemptuous stares and glares followed me into my room.

The seven o'clock departure meant I had to have my plan faxed to my friends at AAI by five, before they became busy with other operators. I had the alarm set for four, the first coffee down my throat by four-fifteen, and the flight plan filled out by four forty-five. Taking the elevator down to the lobby, the darling clerk at the front desk wasn't nearly as happy to see me as I was of her, and she became even less enthralled when my mouth lost all control of the early morning flirtations coming out of it.

She was the first young woman I had talked to since Delhi, but in no way did she share my enthusiasm for conversation. Showing me where the fax machine was, she then tried to hide at the other end of the desk, but I was feeling the effects of too much sugar and coffee and continued rambling on and on, until she was rescued by her phone ringing.

The morning went smoothly, although, like Chatterjee's, my phone was overworked. Before takeoff from Raipur Heliport, Rabinesh called multiple times with a change in the mission program: we were adding a landing in the village of Chintalnar. Then I checked in with Raipur ATC by telephone. They said visibility was a mile and were concerned about our flight. My crew hadn't been far off from the truth the evening before: the skies were indeed quite hazy. I told ATC not to worry, that we wouldn't have any problem at 500 feet and that we were getting ready to start.

"Okay, Captain," the controller said. "Radio the tower as soon as you're airborne. Five hundred feet AGL, initially."

"Thank you, sir. I'll call you when airborne."

After taking off and reaching 500 feet over the city, the tower asked for my opinion about the visibility. I agreed that it was no more than a mile, and then he asked for the FIC and ADC clearances that I'd been up so early for. After I gave him those, he continued, "No known traffic in the area. Your cruising altitude request?"

"Stay at 500 feet, call you for climb."

It was murky enough that if we climbed any higher, losing sight of the ground was a possibility. ATC cleared us direct to Dantewada, our first landing, and as we flew further from Raipur, the visibility improved, allowing us to climb higher.

Settling into cruise, the helicopter purred along nicely and the aircraft instruments agreed. I listened to radio traffic between Raipur Tower and a distant, inbound Air India flight, glad we were airborne and out of their control zone before they could give us any senseless and time-wasting routing instructions. Glancing at the cabin behind me, I felt satisfaction at having all four seats available for passengers and medevacs.

BK was in the left seat, chin on chest and dozing from the early morning start. Close to forty and mustachioed, about average height and a muscular 190 pounds, he had a wife and two kids in Mumbai and was one of the more mature lads on the crew. He had been with the company for over a decade and was looked up to and respected by the other engineers. Though he was quite competent and professional, he always had a relaxed, easy smile or a joke.

Since the flight further south to Konta covered a lot of miles, a full fuel tank out of Raipur wasn't going to be enough and while we refueled from barrels in Dantewada, Rabinesh greeted us with sweet coffee and biscuits. He had plastic chairs set up in the shade, but at first I was reluctant to sit—relaxing didn't come naturally when there was work to be done. He insisted, though, and knowing that BK had it under control, I relented and walked across the big concrete helipad to join him, Rabinesh's grin getting wider and brighter.

Always grinning and bursting with energy, Rabinesh was one whose glass was always half-full. If not quite half, he'd cut glass until it was. More beef than pudding, he stretched to six feet tall and kept his mustache trimmed fastidiously, like BK. In fact, they could have been brothers, though BK was a turban-less Sikh and Rabinesh a Muslim. He was married to a schoolteacher and once remarked that his in-laws didn't approve of their daughter's choice and thought that she was marrying down. Nonetheless, Rabinesh and his wife had a son and daughter and, at times, both could be seen ripping around the helipad, getting spoiled with treats from the troopers.

He was the man in charge of helipad operations in Dantewada and, although never officially acknowledged as such, was my main contact with IPS and for any of the government helicopter requests. If anyone in Chhattisgarh, whether it was the IPS districts, state government honchos or the CRPF, desired our helicopter transport, the request would go through him and then he'd coordinate the flight with me.

He said there were two wounded men to airlift out of Konta, but that the landing in Chintalnar was now more critical as a malaria-stricken trooper there was approaching death. Rabinesh assured me that they knew I was coming and that proper security would be given.

"Rabinesh," I said, "I wanted to make that flight yesterday, but we were up against the wall with sunset and darkness."

"Yeah, I know you did, buddy. But you made the wise choice, the weather here wasn't good late in the day."

That was contrary to what he had told me over the phone.

"It was better that you didn't come," he said. "Besides, after the initial attack, there wasn't anyone left alive who needed to be airlifted immediately."

Seven troopers, including a higher-ranking officer, had been killed by the Maoist-Naxalites, and another three were wounded in the ambush. They had traveled on a farm tractor and trailer from Konta base camp to Bheji, twelve miles away, to deliver rations. After delivering the rations, they were returning to Konta when their tractor was hit by an IED. The guerrillas then opened up with rifle fire on anyone still moving.

With the troopers dead or wounded, the Maoists seized all their rifles and ammunition and left behind Maoist-Naxalite propaganda. Of the three wounded, two were critical. The third did not need further medical attention in Jagdalpur, where we were taking the other injured. Rabinesh was now more concerned with the malaria patient in Chintalnar.

"You need to pick that guy up," he said. "He's in a real bad way and can hardly stand, just skin and bones. The camp commander said he's as yellow as an egg yolk."

Thirty minutes later, the helicopter was refueled and ready, coffee cups and chairs were taken away and, with the cattle cleared from the takeoff path, we started up and took off in what was becoming another white hot day.

The GPS coordinates were true on this, my first flight to Chintalnar, and the yellowish smoke signal indicated all was clear for landing. We spiraled and circled our way down, BK and I both doing contortions, peering out the windows for anything or anyone out of sorts.

By the time the dust settled on the dirt helipad, the malaria patient became quite apparent; being supported by a man on each side, he looked to weigh no more than ninety pounds. He had a rag tied from the top of his head to underneath his jaw and wore an oversize jacket, though the temps were over a hundred, but his yellow, jaundiced face was the most striking. His eyes were mostly closed as his mates half-dragged, half-carried him to the helicopter, and I thought, *We may be too late for this fellow*. BK helped get him aboard and propped up against the seat and window. Then he turned around to confront a couple of trooper-goons who thought they could just hitch a ride as well.

We were repeatedly turning away guys like this. Rabinesh always made it clear not to take any more than the number of guys he specified. It appeared he was worried that certain elements of the jungle troopers might go AWOL. These two were told that we had casualties in Konta to extract and that there was no room for able-bodied men. BK turned them away and cleared off the helipad. All the while, they were looking angry and hostile, ready to start trouble. We departed and were barely off the ground when the security personnel guarding our perimeter began traipsing back and were already filing into the buildings, making me wonder how secure we really were.

Konta was another thirty-five miles to the south over rough terrain; counting the climb and descent, there would be twenty to twenty-five minutes of flight time. All this area was considered dangerous, and the villagers, who lived without even the basic services of running water or electricity, were heavily influenced by the Maoists. We could expect no help from anyone down there in the event of an emergency.

Though smaller than Dantewada, Konta and the landing area within was still considered safe and, after the IED blast of the previous day, there was a substantial troop presence. I shortened the sequence of our descent and dropped in near a string of waiting trucks and tractors. Of the two wounded, one could walk but had bloody bandages covering half his face and left side of his body. His left arm hung in a bloody sling off his shoulder. The other trooper had to be carried on a stretcher, but upon reaching the helicopter, we discovered there wasn't enough room for it. He had to be lifted painfully off the stretcher and laid on the floor, face-up at the other patients' feet, his moans and cries heard clearly over my screaming engine. The one stricken with malaria did not or, more likely, could not move during the entire process.

Two troopers again sauntered up next to the helicopter with their bags and gear, wanting a ride. First they looked expectantly at me and then BK, who dismissed them immediately with a wave of his hand. We would be back to Konta in the afternoon; those guys could try to beg a ride then. With the amount of misery already in the back seats, there was no need to make it worse with overcrowding.

We set course to Jagdalpur forty-five minutes away. For several miles, we followed the Sabari River north until we reached Sukma, where our track diverged and the river waters disappeared in the haze off to the east in Odisha. It was such beautiful country, with wild rivers and stony hills—beauty tempered by people lurking in the trees, wanting to kill.

Upon landing at Jagdalpur, two ambulances were waiting for us, unnervingly, they started reversing toward the helicopter before I could hover to my parking spot and set down. Some of our technicians and security personnel were able to stop them and allow me to get on the ground before helping the wounded out of the back, from which, there was a strong smell of blood and general direness; the supine chap had abdominal wounds and moaned steadily.

Before returning to Konta, we refueled and took time for lunch. Beebu the cook and one of his house-lady helpers brought a dozen stainless-steel tiffin containers to the airport containing the usual tongue-tingling spicy dishes. In front of the old airport shack, we stretched out on the soft grass in the shade of royal palms planted during British colonial times, hungrily devouring our meal. When a bit of biryani fell on the ground and was ignored by ants, BK cracked jokes about Beebu's cooking skills.

"Aha, Beebu, take a look at dat!" he laughed, pointing at the retreating insects. "You see? Even dee ants are afraid a' yo' cooking!"

On our return, the security presence around the helipad had grown and now included two armored troop carriers, each sporting a .50 caliber machine gun. At a mile out, I dropped the collective lever and floated down to the treetops surrounding the helipad. Turning a half-circle to point my nose into the light breeze, kicking up clouds of dust and weeds, I came to rest on the white H they'd marked with lime. The dust was still much in the air when several Tata Mahindras slid to a stop next to the helicopter. Our passengers for the afternoon were not IPS but camouflage-wearing paramilitaries of the CRPF, one of whom had been killed in the attack. The two groups worked together in the fight against the Maoist-Naxalites, and we routinely flew troopers from each, although they usually, but not always, kept separate camps.

After the two troopers from earlier and two spit-and-polished officers boarded, we took off for Dantewada, their destination for meetings regarding the attack. We had enough fuel for the entire route back to Jagdalpur and, after delivering the officers in Dantewada, BK gave the helicopter a quick look for leaking oil or bullet holes, then he climbed back in, and we sailed back to Jagdalpur.

Landing at the airport, the crew went to work giving the Astar a scrub down. Not minding the extra work, I was keen on helping out also, but my slick-haired driver, wearing a black muscle shirt that showed off broom-handle arms, was urging me to climb in the car and go. The scrawny bugger was more persistent than I cared to hear at the end of a long day. I needed to stretch, walk around and reacquaint myself with Earth, and his little four-door sedan looked as appealing as a sun-soaked, vinyl-lined coffin.

"Would you like a beeya, saa?" he asked, flipping the car keys in the air and catching them. "I can take you past the beeya shop."

He knew which buttons to press. A cold, frosty one sounded good. Looking at the crew surrounding the aircraft with buckets and brushes, there didn't seem to be room for me anyway.

"Yes, yes, I would."

I gathered my flight kit, thanked the dozen or so engineers and technicians for the great job and crawled into the car. Out to the beer shop we ventured, but after a half-hour of traffic near-misses, I was close to admitting defeat. Traffic, even in this small town, was the usual cacophonous mayhem, and at one point we were bottle-necked and pinned between a surge of traffic on the driver's side and, on my side, the ass of a loitering cow, which was taking up one lane of traffic. Heaven forbid anyone should disturb the damn cow and clear her off the road.

This was precisely the same moment the fat beast's bladder reached critical mass, and she hoisted her tail into the air like a flag at morning reveille. Practically tearing my rotator cuff rolling up the car window, I was just able to seal out all of the fiendishly aimed golden flow.

My near afternoon hot shower was a great source of amusement for the driver, Mr. Broom-Handle Arms. He giggled, snorted and continued honking the horn, and as the yellow waterfall rolled down my window, tears were rolling down his cheeks. Nearly doused by gallons of steamy excreta, I did not share the jocularity of the moment, but felt victimized from the assault and close to needing professional help.

17.

Red Menace

The Red Menace; that's one of the tags given the rebels by the newspapers that I got my masala-stained fingers on. Other short and not-so-sweet versions included *Maoists*, *Naxalites* and the plain and monosyllabic *Reds*. Their attacks and carnage were increasing throughout the countryside, which had developed its own label, *The Red Corridor*—the region in East India that was experiencing the most Maoist-Naxalite insurgency.

The area had one of the highest illiteracy and poverty rates in the nation and included parts of Chhattisgarh, Andhra Pradesh, Bihar, Jharkhand, Odisha, and West Bengal. Close to 500 paramilitaries, civilians and Maoist-Naxalites had been killed there during my first several months in the country; all sides shared in the burden of death, although civilians appeared to have the worst of it.

The deaths were troubling enough, but it seemed the Maoist-Naxalites waged war against progress too. Schools were burned in certain villages, cellular phone towers and power lines damaged or destroyed, roads and bridges—which provided the most basic form of communication and contact between people—were blocked. They also dismantled or damaged railroad tracks in an effort to cause derailments. Without good infrastructure, education suffered and the cycle continued; Maoists recruited heavily from the people who were most disadvantaged.

As time went on, our operation settled into a rhythm. Most mornings, our first takeoff was at eight. I kept up pressure for an earlier start but was met with resistance from both my crew and the IPS. I argued that the earlier the start, the cooler the temperatures and that we could be done sooner or have time for an additional mission. Plus, we could possibly get in and out of those places before the bad guys woke up and had their nefarious plans organized for the day. On several occasions, when I was able to convince the crew of a seven o'clock takeoff, we found that the IPS would not be quite ready, though we had confirmed the time with them the night before. Everyone grew comfortable with an eight o'clock start, so we stuck with that.

Now and then, a new village or landing zone was added to our growing list of destinations, and on one evening a mission to such a place materialized, demanding my attention late into the night, planning flights and verifying locations. Rabinesh sent a text message with the new coordinates but, as I entered his numbers into my GPS, he would send another text with different coordinates to the same place. By the time he sent his third amendment, my cussing had become articulate and quite foul. Even a small error would have huge consequences; one digit off, and I would be searching for the landing zone miles away from the intended destination, and we were to have the Home Minister of Chhattisgarh aboard this flight. Over the hostile jungle was no place for discrepancies, and it was after midnight before all the questions were, somewhat, settled.

When he thought he had the final coordinates sent, I called him. "Now, you're sure these are the true coordinates, Rabinesh?"

"Yes, yes, those are correct, my friend!"

"There seems to be confusion from your local source, bhaiya *(the Hindi word for brother)*. Let me read them back to you just to be sure."

"No, no, Mista Mike. You have 'em... They're correct!"

He was tired and wanted to get home.

"You can trust me on that," he said. "If I'm wrong, I'll have my wife make you sweets," he chuckled, and then laughed, a little too loudly to inspire confidence.

My sleep offered little rest.

The mission was to take the home minister from Raipur to Farasgaon village where, a couple of days prior, Maoist-

Naxalites riding motorcycles had attacked and gunned down a high-ranking IPS officer while he was at the village market with his family. The victim's funeral was being held, and the government wished to show sympathy and solidarity with the IPS, who had been getting hit quite consistently in the recent months.

We arrived in the morning at Raipur with plenty time to spare, had our usual wait and drama when the VIPs arrived, but everything went smoothly, and on out to the new patch at Farasgaon we flew. There seemed to be nothing but rice paddies or trees in every direction; the smaller mud hut villages were not seen until I was right on top of them over the thick jungle. Rabinesh's coordinates proved true, though, and we were lined up with the landing zone when a signal canister was lit off and the sulfurous smoke rose above the treetops.

Babeesh pointed excitedly and yelled over the intercom, "Da smoke, saa... d'ere's da smoke!"

Every couple of days, BK had begun relinquishing his flying crew chief duties to his junior man, Babeesh. Babeesh was the guy willingly at the butt of most jokes amongst the crew; with wild hair and wild eyes, he was five and a half feet tall, about a hundred-thirty pounds and thirty years old. He liked the bottle and the betel nut leaf and had to be prodded into doing work from time to time, but he always did a fine job with me out in the bush, watching for bad guy junglies and keeping order at the helipads.

We kept the spirals and circling to a minimum, once again figuring that security was never going to be as good as it was then, and hovered down into our dust cloud next to a volleyball net at the IPS compound. Pausing for a few moments, we let the dust settle before setting loose the septuagenarian home minister and his assistants into the small village of Farasgaon.

There looked to be electricity and running water in a few of the rundown stucco shacks, but most of the dwellings were basic one-room structures surrounded by sandy soil, the only vegetation being twenty- to thirty-foot dust-covered trees. Water came from a hand-pumped community well.

While the VIPs were escorted away alongside their throng of followers, Babeesh and I were given steel folding chairs on the veranda of the one-story IPS building next to the helicopter. Hundreds of locals more interested in the helicopter than the politicians stood lined up along the security cordon, dividing their time between pointing and gawking at the aircraft and pointing and gawking at the pilot.

When nervously asked by two female police assistants if I would like chai tea, I requested coffee instead, thinking that coffee was as common as dirt anywhere on the planet. Not wanting to appear hard to please, I ended up doing just that. They nodded in the affirmative, glanced at each other uncertainly and came back balancing a tea tray five minutes later. They had still brought chai tea. I gulped it down with a slightly scrunched face, reaffirming that the taste was much akin to boiled paper and sugar.

An hour and a half passed, and we reboarded the VIPs, flying them the fifteen minutes to IPS district headquarters in Naranpur. Naranpur village had a population of ten thousand and, like the other districts we routinely operated in—Jagdalpur, Bijapur, Dantewada, Kanker, Kondagaon, and Sukma—it had a vast and scattered rural population of about 150 thousand.

We used Naranpur's parade ground for our landing zone, and someone had the foresight to send the water truck to sprinkle down the brownish-orange dirt before we arrived. The two-acre square was protected by a double row of fences topped with concertina wire to the south. Barracks buildings and troop tents formed two sides, and on the north was the three-story main building. Perhaps a hundred troops lined the perimeter, with the majority congregated around a half-dozen armored troop carriers spaced evenly along the wire. Using a smoke signal was redundant with the amount of security provided, but they lit two canisters anyway, and the resulting thick smoke engulfed the entire building. Wafting through the open windows into rooms and hallways, it sent people scurrying outside for fresh air.

A group of high-ranking IPS and CRPF officers and representatives of the local political parties were at the landing zone, and they stood in line welcoming the visiting delegation. Officers and superintendents gave salutes and handshakes while the politicians and supporters adorned our passengers with flowers, garlands, lavish praise and smiles. The most vocal of them pumped his fist in the air and offered up a Hindi version of the acclamation, "HIP, HIP, HOORAY!" or, "THREE CHEERS FOR THE HONORABLE HOME MINISTER!" to which the other followers shouted their response.

The hoard was divided into a fleet of a dozen waiting SUVs and sedans, but two chaps were forgotten and left behind when the cars began driving away without them. They peered hopefully into each one as it passed, not wanting to lose this game of vehicular musical chairs. In a cloud of dust, the drivers revved their engines and raced past our helicopter toward the exit, only to bottleneck at the guard gate in a flurry of red brake lights, kicking up more dust and enveloping the guard shack in a mini-sandstorm. Surprisingly, no one was on the horn.

While the politicians were having lunch and meetings elsewhere in the village, we were offered food and a chance to relax in air-conditioned comfort in the headquarters building. Before we could do that, we had to address our fuel supply. They had fuel drums waiting for us and after Babeesh checked them for contamination, we filled the tank for our return to Raipur.

It was two hours later in the afternoon when the meetings and meals had concluded and, surrounded by the same entourage that had greeted him earlier, the home minister arrived back at the parade ground, climbed in our helicopter and we flew back to Raipur. Then, although we could have made it to Jagdalpur from Raipur with no additional fuel, I shut down and had Babeesh top off the tank one more time at the heliport. I was glad I did—it would be needed.

There were always extra engineering technicians appearing mysteriously in the ranks, and while this ragtag contingent finished the refueling, I fiddled with the FIC/ADC. But then ten minutes before takeoff, I received an urgent call from Rabinesh requesting an emergency medevac. Maoist-Naxalites had attacked a convoy of IPS vehicles near Bijapur, destroying all six of them. Four troopers were killed and two had life-threatening injuries. They needed to be flown to Jagdalpur for better medical care.

My original flight plan called for a route between Raipur and Jagdalpur, but to get AAI to change my routing to include a landing at tiny Bijapur—a considerable dogleg seventy miles out of the way—changed everything. It would take an hour, at least, for the sloth-like paper pushers to give me their new clearances. I knew the area south of Raipur's control zone, including Jagdalpur and Bijapur, was pretty much mine. There was no one else flying in the area; if there was, I would have been told so by my contacts.

Getting airborne off the Raipur Heliport, I called ATC and, replying to their queries, said, "Yes, affirmative, my destination is Jagdalpur," not bothering to tell them about my emergency medevac in Bijapur along the way.

They asked for my FIC/ADC clearances, and I gave them what I had. They cleared me, saying, "No known traffic in the area."

I knew the only aircraft that would be flying at my altitude in the entire state of Chhattisgarh would be the Chief Minister's Agusta 109, and that was back in the hangar collecting pigeon poo. Punching Bijapur in on the GPS, I set a direct course, flying close to the few dirt roads where practical.

There was rain in the area, and it would only become worse as we flew further south into the rugged hill country. Sunset was also a concern, as Jagdalpur would be another one-hour flight from Bijapur, more if I had to deviate around any weather. We were going to cut it a little tight. I requested that the patients be ready for us upon landing, telling Rabinesh that I didn't intend to shut down, but I knew a request like that fell on deaf ears. They only wanted to hear that the helicopter was en route.

The flight time to Bijapur was an hour and twenty minutes and, when we reached there, the skies were a sea of splotchy medium-to-dark grays, and there was lightning from the darker smudges. Evidently they were out of smoke canisters at the helipad because we circled for three minutes with nary a sign of one. We did see a heavy security presence, though, and it was a similar setup to Naranpur's IPS headquarters: a large parade ground protected by tall walls and concertina wire. The area surrounding it was rice paddies and police barracks, so I figured we were safe. I dropped the lever and floated down to the helipad.

There was no sign of the patients, however, and I had Babeesh talk to the head security chap to determine their whereabouts while idling, although not a lot of info was garnered. The weather was worsening, and daytime was clicking by too fast, but needing to conserve fuel, I shut down.

After an anxious, pacing forty minutes, they were brought out to the helicopter; just teenagers it appeared, maybe fifteen or sixteen years old. They didn't look old enough to be in uniform. Both were unconscious and had bloody chest wounds, among other injuries. Babeesh fetched an olive drab plastic tarp from the IPS to keep their blood off the seats, laying it on top of the bright orange flowers and garlands our earlier VIP passengers had discarded. The sweet smell of the blossoms was replaced with that of gore. Carefully as possible, the chaps were laid in the back, one across the floor, the other across the seats. One walking wounded trooper was able to sit upright in one of the seats with the chap's head on his lap.

I was stressing about the weather and darkness to be sure, but at least I didn't have oozing chest wounds.

We took off and pointed our way over the wicked hills to Jagdalpur, dodging rain and low clouds along the route. When we reached our airport, a squall had already engulfed one end of the runway, the advancing downpour devouring yard after yard of tarmac, and I was just able to land midfield at our parking area in the gusty winds that preceded it. If I had arrived five minutes later, the airport would have been socked in, forcing me to land at an alternate or circle until the weather cleared, which was improbable in the darkening evening.

While I cut the throttle and shut down, big raindrops started splattering on the windscreen and the tempo quickly increased to a deafening roar inside the cabin. Our patients endured a drenching downpour while being stretchered to the waiting ambulance, but it's doubtful they felt it.

18.

Culture Clubbed

A Sunday morning. Sometime during the night, the power had been cut, but I and the small squadron of marauding mosquitoes didn't mind. One had its blood sucker sunk in up to its eyeballs on my temple, and when it was sleepily brushed away, a fine gush of blood oozed down my cheek and onto the pillow. In fact, my entire pillowcase was beginning to resemble the drop-cloth of a careless, ochre-obsessed painter.

I laid there in the non-air conditioned quiet and rising warmth, watching the little bastards fly from one side of my mosquito netting to the other, trying to escape the barrier that should have kept them out. They were so overladen with blood that they could not hover out of ground effect and were summarily smashed into my bed sheet, which was acquiring an ochre-colored camouflage pattern itself beneath a pile of mosquito carcasses. The cleaning ladies the day before had changed my bed linens, but in so doing had compromised the net integrity of my nocturnal mosquito fortress. Repair work awaited, and a week of sleeping on blood stains.

A Catholic church was not far from the guesthouse, and I was contemplating attending services for the first time in many years; it would be in Hindi, but I had been to enough Mass in my early years to follow along. I only had to spiff up my cherubic look before going. Unsurprisingly, though, while scrubbing the last bit of jungle loam off my boots, an emergency call came from Rabinesh, and church had to be forgotten. Initially, there was an officer requesting a medevac due to illness. But twenty minutes later, after we had preliminary preparations started and most of the crew woke up, the flight was canceled, the officer opting for ground transport instead. It appeared we would have a day off after all.

I had a loitering, lazy breakfast of egg roti and coffee. The former was roti with egg slapped and fried on each side in something resembling thin French toast, and the latter was now coming in a real four-fingered coffee cup that I had bought at the market, not the little quarter-cup sized, sissy tea sipper that had been the usual demitasse.

After breakfast and a shower, and weary of my increasingly long-haired-gone-native look, I set out on the mile or so walk to the barbershop. Along the way, I passed the now-finished church services, sharing the road—no sidewalks here—with honking cars, people of all shapes and colors, and countless stray but friendly dogs. The cattle I inevitably encountered were just as tame and friendly, and I fantasized about how easy it would be to rustle one, thus, to satisfy my red meat cravings. Firing up the barbecue cooker discreetly under the many watchful Hindu eyes would be the hard part.

After putting it off for a long while, this was to be my first haircut in India. My mullet days were fondly remembered but ungrudgingly far behind me, and I did not cut it as a hippy. A good clipping was in order, and I didn't know what to expect, but I was hoping to avoid the more serious of skin contagions from the community coiffeur.

What I received was the best scissors haircut a person could hope for. No electric clipper in this shop, and the barber's chair sat so close to the busy main road, I could've high-fived each passing motorist over the open sewer in between. The barber was a little rough, cuffing and nudging my head this way and that to get the best angle, more like he was carving a Thanksgiving turkey than styling someone's hair. And he was unnervingly distracted by both the Bollywood movie blaring on the old TV above the doorway and his old acquaintances on the street, shouting at them over the traffic noise as they walked by. With eyes and attention elsewhere, he kept snip-snipping those scissors around my ears, making my palms sweaty where I white-knuckle-gripped the armrest.

Holding up a cracked mirror behind my head, allowing a reflective review of the back-skull styling he performed, the barber inquired multiple times, "Okay yes? You like, saa? It is good, saa?"

Running my hands over my close-cropped, stubbly landscaped cranium, I said, "Yeah man, feels good!"

After I convinced him that I was indeed satisfied with his shearing, he inquired about a head massage. I had watched the previous patron accept this offer and then have his head callously clubbed from top to bottom and pummeled side to side in what I guessed passed for tenderness locally. I declined.

Final tally for services, twenty Indian rupees. Less than fifty US cents; my head was so smooth and aerodynamic I felt quick, like Forrest Gump after losing his leg braces.

Back at the guesthouse, lunch was the familiar chicken curry. For some reason, one that I was never able to discern, the chicken—bones and all—was always chopped into tiny pieces, causing me to spend most of the meal with fingers in my mouth, picking out bone fragments. It's as if the bird was tenderized highway style: with a car tire.

Later, dinner was a spicy fish curry, a freshwater species caught out of the Indravati River that flowed through Jagdalpur. With all the chilies in meals like these, I guzzled water like a hungover and cotton-mouthed drunk just off a three-day bender. Between the spices and liquids consumed, sleep could be sporadic during the night, and the next morning, the curry was no kinder on its way out than on its way in.

Not a week went by that someone didn't ask me, "Do you like India, Captain?"

Never skipping a beat, I'd always reply, "Yep! India's a great place!"

Still, I wasn't quite ready to apply for citizenship.

Indeed, living in big-city Mumbai would be an adjustment for a Westerner, but neck deep and isolated in the Indian jungle could be suffocating and soul crushing at times. The open sewers and filth, sociopathic drivers, the belligerence and pushiness, and always the constant gawking and glares from the locals. My own housemates could not keep their eyes off of me, especially during meal time. I can understand certain curiousness at first, but after weeks of sharing the roti and sabjee, I'd still have four or five pairs of eyes staring me over at the dinner table. If I stared back, their silent, empty and hollow gaze just lingered.

I was a monkey at the zoo. There were times in the jungle when the culture shock was overwhelming, and the learning curve was especially steep at the beginning. My colleague, Zach, the pilot who made India possible for me, was on assignment in another part of the country. But our paths crossed occasionally, giving us both a chance to converse, share a common thought process and, most importantly, blow off steam.

The Maoist-Naxalites kept up their killing. I received a call late one night from Rabinesh that there had been an attack on an IPS convoy near a place called Madapoti village. This was significant as it was considerably closer to the state capital of Raipur than any of the previous attacks. Out of a convoy of four vehicles and forty-one personnel, there had been nearly a dozen killed with more wounded. Rabinesh said the ambush had started, per the usual modus operandi, with IEDs being triggered, destroying three vehicles, then the rebels had opened fire with rifles, inflicting further casualties.

We launched from Jagdalpur early in the morning and headed north with full fuel, expecting to take the casualties on to Raipur. The landing area at Madapoti was another dusty, sunbaked clearing with near brown-out conditions. Heavily guarded and secure, though. We loaded the first three wounded, bandaged and bleeding, and one attendant who had his hands full with IV bottles and medical kit. Seating became tight with them all aboard, and they had to half-sit and half-slouch on the back seats, only adding to their misery and pain. The smell of blood and body fluids, along with their screams and moans, filled the helicopter.

The couple hundred troops gathered nearby, readying themselves for patrol into the jungle to find the group of assailants, were covered in clouds of dust as we departed the landing zone and headed for Raipur Heliport. With the short distance in between, there was no need to refuel on the first sortie, and after landing and watching as the casualties were wrestled from the back seats and into the waiting ambulances, I advanced the throttle to FLIGHT and headed back out for a second load.

I thought Raipur ATC would have been more accommodating when it came to life-saving emergencies, but it seemed their mission that day was to impede the flight wherever they could. Aircraft need adequate separation, *bonne idée*, but flying a direct route between the heliport and Madapoti, our helicopter would've been miles away and thousands of feet below any traffic in the area at the time. Their usual, annoying instructions to deviate course or hold and orbit for departing or landing traffic were only time- and fuel-consuming on normal days, but on days like this they were life threatening. Between phone calls and my radio calls, they were well aware of the emergency situation. I requested direct course to Madapoti from the heliport at 500 feet, a route that would have taken me no closer than six miles to the airport, but was refused. They insisted I route over the airport, losing a precious twenty minutes in the process. Common sense was in short supply when it came to helicopter traffic and AAI.

Once reaching Madapoti for the second time, we loaded four more wounded. Two were able to walk and assist the other two, who were more badly injured. The onsite commanders readily accepted our offer of further flights after we refueled in Raipur. Although two troopers had succumbed to their wounds, there were many others lying about and scattered on stretchers in the shade of nearby dusty trees who were in dire need of medical attention, and waiting to be transported.

Heading back to Raipur Heliport, ATC was again making life miserable. One problem was that blasted FIC/ADC clearance. They wanted a new clearance for every leg, which, in the interest of saving lives, I simply did not have the time to obtain.

Upon our second landing at the heliport, news of the ambush had reached the Raipur citizenry. Mobs of curious onlookers had surrounded the perimeter, and more havoc was created by three TV news channels who were giving live coverage. I was worried about my tailrotor and the potential for an overexcited journalist to lose his head before I could shut down. I reminded BK of the threat, though the warning was unnecessary. He was quick with his usual, efficient crowd control while I secured the engine. The wounded were mob-loaded into the ambulances, with dozens of troopers encircling each stretcher in an effort to carry their comrades, and then adding their shouts to the chaos when they could not get close enough. Once loaded, with engines screaming and sirens wailing, the wounded were sped demonically through the civilian-packed street, swerving around pedestrians as they went.

Refueling a total of three times in Raipur, we flew several more medevacs out of Madapoti before heading for home, and I was used up by the end of the day. Arguing on the phone for expedited clearances from AAI, then ATC when I could not get them; also having to reach someone in Madapoti, Jagdalpur and Raipur for weather reports; filing and faxing new flight plans—only to find the fax machine was down—and so forth. My idea to have a dedicated operations team to assist me had been broached to the company, but nothing had yet been decided.

Back in Jagdalpur, I just wanted to relax in a quiet place, watch the distant lightning, drink a cold beer and reflect on my exhaled cigarette smoke as it disappeared into the darkening night. The crew thought a night of Bollywood music, spicy food and whiskey was a far more fitting way to spend the evening. And they were right.

19.

Paradise City

As with people, helicopters need a checkup occasionally, and one for our Astar, the hundred hour inspection, had the helicopter grounded for a couple of days. I was always hopeful that these inspections would never take much longer. If it was only a routine inspection, and all the checks turned out alright, it would be kept short, but if they found an item that required replacing and the part was not in our small stock of inventory, it could be a long wait for it to be shipped to Jagdalpur.

I partly used this lull in action to catch up on emails and tidy up my living space, but mostly I slid into a rut of indolence and profound slackerdom. Seizing every chance, I did remain adept at antagonizing the cook and housecleaning ladies around the guesthouse, though.

We lived in Sun City. The name conjures up an image of palm-tree-adorned bungalows on a beach in paradise, but in reality it was just a few rows of cookie-cutter stucco houses adorned with spindly banana trees grappling for existence in a sunbaked Indian village. I vowed to, at some future point, start a banana plantation on our own postage-stamp-sized lawn in front of the guesthouse.

It was a ten-acre walled and gated property development built on land that, in a previous life, had been rice paddies. A walled and gated community would have seemed secure except that, in places, the eight-foot brick walls had sections missing where anyone could walk or ride their bicycle or motorcycle through. The few gaps were not large enough for a car, but for unknown reasons, someone was knocking out the bricks one by one on a certain wider section and making progress in that regard. Perhaps they had their own brick wall to construct elsewhere and could not be bothered with acquiring bricks the usual way.

There were a few uniformed guard-type persons scattered around, and one chap always near the gate at the real entrance, but it was never closed and the guard didn't project the slightest feeling of security. He just glared at the cars while they passed through, if he was awake.

It was the Indian version of a small-town, middle-class neighborhood of about fifty homes, with more construction ongoing. There were at least two doctors, or health practitioners, scattered around, a businessman across the street, and a school administrator a couple of doors down from us. The administrator's sons had good English skills and were always out on the street riding bikes or kicking a soccer ball around. The older of the two was twelve years old and fancied wearing a #80 Green Bay Packers jersey.

After the third day in a row seeing him wear this NFL sanctioned gear, I figured he must share my cheesehead allegiance and queried if he liked Donald Driver or James Lofton better. He looked at me as if I had sprouted feathers and asked, "Who?"

"You know, two of the greatest wide receivers to play for the Packers?"

Blank, vacant stare.

"They played football for the Green Bay Packers... They're whose jersey you're wearing," I explained.

That did not ring a bell with the young lad, and I assumed any neighborhood fantasy-football leagues were out of the question. We went back to kicking the soccer ball back and forth, until an errant launch off the tip of my foot sent the ball deep into the sewer.

The guesthouse was only a half-mile north of the airport ramp where the helicopter was parked. By egressing through one of those broken-down wall sections, I could walk to the airport in about twenty minutes through the backstreets, slums and cow poop, but I preferred being chauffeured in the company car. The horn-blaring, death-on-wheels traffic with its accompanying dust clouds meant that the walk was neither enjoyable nor relaxing.

Along the streets and around our house were open sewers filled with sludge and tepid water. The sewers in town, like the one in front of the barber shop, were three feet wide, and cement or wood bridges allowed you to access whatever business was on the other side without having to perform a long jump. The sewer around our guesthouse was about a foot wide and had a small cement bridge to drive over into the car park. If the wind was wrong, the sewer smell was carried into the house. All the standing water and sunshine made ideal conditions for mosquitoes, and sneaky snakes too. More than once, the cooks had to chase yellowish-colored snakes out of the kitchen and back into the sewer. I always made sure the door to my room was shut and the bottom crack plugged with a rug.

Directly north and across the street from the house were two empty and trash-strewn lots. With its few grassy spots, this was a favorite spot for the stray neighborhood cattle to graze. Rubbish was everywhere, and the empty lots became the local dump, being that garbage collection services had not caught on there or anywhere in India, from what I had seen.

The cattle enjoyed it, though. Paper of any kind was an appetizer to them, and cardboard a delicacy. The cattle would have slobber fights amongst themselves, huffing out big globs of snot at each other while butting noses and heads in an attempt to gobble down the last of a ditched gift box. Just kitty-corner from our house was the officially undesignated, but locally designated spot for cardboard and paper. Most of the neighborhood cleaning ladies would dump their trash there, and small herds of cattle would pick through it all day long.

The most peaceful spot to be found and where I spent my sundowns was the airport itself. It was well guarded by the IPS and surrounded by a high wall topped with concertina wire. Late in the afternoon, when most of the sun's heat had drained away from the sky, I would go there for a jog along the runway. I'd do two laps. And, if feeling energetic and spunky, carry on further. Afterward, I would enjoy a long cool-down walk, relishing the peace and quiet of the deserted airstrip. My airstrip. Faraway were the car horns and the obnoxiously loud and shrill air horns of the Tata commercial trucks coming from town. Distance subdued the noise, but still some truck-driving heroes had horns loud enough to wake the dead.

Usually, a relaxing and cool light breeze would be coming from one end of the runway or other, but never a dusty, squint-inducing gust. Other than during the occasional thunderstorms, the winds were never stronger than ten knots throughout that region, which made headwinds quite predictable during flight and fuel planning.

Bordering either side of the runway were tall grass and short brush. The scrub trees were tall enough to provide nesting for birds, and their singing was therapeutic. Among them were the Asian Koels, talking back and forth with their loud, crazy-sounding whistles and calls. In the future, when traveling around Asia and I would hear their call, my mind's eye would see a sun setting along an empty and peaceful, mile-long runway lined by gently waving bushgrass and leafy saplings.

Other creatures in residence included a burgeoning group of stray dogs. Upon seeing me, a few would begin their obligatory barking boldly from a distance, but as I ran closer they would melt back into the brush or go back to chasing the snake they had been after.

Snakes were well represented too. While I was jogging along one evening, a five-footer slithered across the runway yards in front of me; I hurried to catch up and examine it more closely, but it was in the weeds by the time I reached its point of crossing. I turned my head while running by, watching the spot where it disappeared. Then, with snakes on my mind, I looked forward again and glimpsed what I thought was a snake attacking my ankles. I freaked and jumped and skipped, almost breaking my neck trying to elude snakebite from a crooked and snakey-looking stick that the dogs had dragged out.

It was a great place to clear my head and, when the time zones worked out, I would call family or friends back home and continue my long walk of the runway up until sunset. Just at sunset, not a minute before, mosquitoes would come out of their daytime hiding and, in hungry swarms, descend upon me. They never bothered the crew, who came to the airport after waking from their siesta to check the helicopter. Or, more likely, to engage in a heated game of cricket in the parking area next to the runway.

They were all passionate about cricket and endeavored to teach me the game, occasionally offering me the bat. I was a slow work in progress in that regard. Choking up on the grip like Robin Yount, I would swing for the bleachers, launching the tennis ball they were using far into the head-high grass. Regretting their decision to let me swing, they'd put their hands on their hips, looking at me like I was a three-year-old and explain how to hold the bat in a proper cricketer's stance. I got the hang of it, though later rather than sooner.

20.

Security Insecurity

I always requested that the next day's mission details be given to me at a reasonable hour the night before to allow time for proper planning and coordination. A reasonable hour to me would have been five or six in the evening, but that type of rationality was a pipe dream; usually it was after eight and closer to ten before the IPS would send a text or give me a phone call outlining what they wanted flown and where they wanted it flown to. After receiving the first message, it would not be surprising if later, fifteen minutes into flight planning, I'd receive a second call or message to make amendments to the plans.

At dinner time one evening, Rabinesh sent me a text. I glanced at my phone while scooping rice into my mouth but thought of putting him off until after dinner. That wasn't soon enough, though, as he starting calling immediately. I excused myself from the table and went to my desk.

"Good evenin', Mista Mike!" Rabinesh always kept his side of the conversation to short drum rolls. "How are you this fine evening, buddy?"

"Great, but having dinner, my friend," I answered. "Hey man, would it be alright to call you back?"

"It's okay, it's okay, this'll only take a minute!"

Phone calls with Rabinesh never lasted less than a minute. He had a few questions concerning fuel and other items, items that could have waited until after dinner, but after ten minutes we had the details sorted out and bid each other goodnight. The next day was to be a busy one and, after finishing dinner, I started work on the flight planning; then, at about ten-thirty, while I was reading a book and dozing off behind my mosquito netting, he called me just one more time for revisions and changes. Buggeration.

In the morning after breakfast, Babeesh and I climbed in the heli and took off for Dantewada. With the possibility of a few rain showers later in the afternoon, the day was becoming hot, humid and hazy, with temperatures climbing to their normal 100 to 115. I made sure the vents were open and cracked my little side window a tad to suck in more ventilation. Breakfast sat in my gut like the iron ore being mined from the nearby hillsides, but after the recent maintenance, the helicopter felt strong and smooth as we headed west, clipping along at 120 knots.

Greeting me at the helipad, Rabinesh asked if I could fly to Gollapalli first instead of Kistaram as the plan had called for.

Gripping my hand, he yelled over the engine noise, "Good mornin', buddy! Hey, I'm waiting for one more trooper to make muster for Kistaram, he's late and I'm gonna kick his butt!" He made a kicking motion with his camouflage-trousered leg. "Can you go to Gollapalli first?"

Gollapalli and Kistaram were relatively close to each other. "Yeah," I shouted back. "No problem, let's go!"

We made the first flight to Gollapalli, overflying Kistaram along the way and, when peering down, everything looked normal: a few cows, goats and villagers milling about, getting baked by the sun. Dropping our passengers in Gollapalli and taking aboard four troopers rotating out, I took off and climbed northeast, paralleling the tall ridgeline that separates Gollapalli from Kistaram, and headed back to Dantewada for fuel and the second load of passengers for the day.

Rabinesh had the red plastic chairs out again, so after shutting down I joined him for biscuits and coffee. It seemed the one trooper he was waiting for still hadn't showed up, wouldn't answer his phone and his family did not know where he was. The decision to launch for Kistaram was made anyway. We would take the three who were ready and, after picking up two troopers from Kistaram, the plan was to head over to Bheji and pick up two more.

Rabinesh was telling me about the discipline problems the IPS had with those guys they recruited out of the jungle villages.

More than a few of them just stuck around long enough for the paycheck and then disappeared until the money ran out. Rabinesh, himself university schooled and academy trained, knew that on one hand it was advantageous to have guys recruited straight out of the area, who were familiar with the terrain. On the other hand, he explained that many of the recruits lacked maturity, education and any ambition to do better for themselves, and sometimes their loyalty was in question. I didn't give it much thought. I had been in India long enough to know that when it came to ambition, there was never an overabundance. A trooper's absence did not surprise me.

Refueling complete, we loaded the passengers, started up, took off and climbed to four thousand feet, pointing south. Babeesh, sucking on his betel nut, was lost in thought and seemed nervous, saying less than usual during our flight and occasionally glancing at our passengers.

When we arrived overhead Kistaram, the smoke was already deployed, and we immediately started our downward tight spiral and approach. During the descent, I noticed what looked to be villagers out and about and didn't see anything out of the ordinary, except for one thing.

Anywhere in the world, a helicopter attracts attention. Even in major cities, where a helicopter can be expected, most people cannot help but watch these noisy flying machines, especially as they come in to land. In the backwoods of India, seeing a helicopter is like witnessing rare magic. Everyone stops to stare, and the story of the sighting is perhaps passed on to sons and grandsons.

Therefore, when I saw about a half-dozen villagers do nothing—not look up, not glance in our direction, not even move—I thought, *Hmm... that's a little odd*.

I saw our normal guards around the perimeter, too. All of *those* guys were watching the helicopter, many of them holding their rifle barrels forward by one hand, with the buttstock over their shoulder in a relaxed and nonchalant posture. I had complained repeatedly and unsuccessfully to the IPS and CRPF to get troopers to change those bad habits, to be more alert and to watch the bushes and trees, where the threats would most likely come from instead of staring ceaselessly at the helicopter. Since no one else did anything about it, I wrote a memo addressing the lapses, had it translated into Hindi and distributed to the camps we landed at in the hope of clarifying what was expected of security at the helipad.

There were no indications of impending violence or danger, and things seemed routine as we landed on the grass next to the wire. We spent the usual thirty to forty seconds on the ground, perhaps a bit longer, while we offloaded one group and Babeesh haggled with the other group, convincing them we could only take two passengers. Just as Babeesh had the other stragglers sorted out, one tall chap came running up with his duffel bag and rifle. It appeared that he and these other lads had had enough of the country cooking and fine scenery offered in the tropical paradise of Kistaram and were ready to vacate. While his comrades all glared and stared at me with hostile eyes as they slouched back to the camp gate, this tall chap was all smiles and waves.

This was the first time any of these guys had showed any emotion other than hostility, especially after being told to back off, and he was making me feel bad. Babeesh nudged him one final time away from the helicopter and then, seeing that Smiley wasn't walking back to the camp gate, gave the aircraft a quick look-over, jumped in and slammed the door shut.

I felt a little sorry for Smiley as I raised the collective lever and came to a hover, blasting him with downwash and dirt, sorry my helicopter wasn't any bigger for the old boy. At the helipads, it was always, for the majority of times, an undisciplined free-for-all; any normal-thinking person would assume the camp commander would determine which of his troops was flying, but that was not the case. For safety, we did not want to dally on the helipad. And it wasn't our job to pull out a list of names and determine *who* was going, just that *someone* was going, and one of the tricks that my crew chiefs used when confronting too many passengers for the limited seating available was telling them we would be making a return flight to pick them up. This was usually less than truthful, but we told them anything to get them cleared away from our departing helicopter, and I know that's what Babeesh told Smiley. So with hopeful eyes, determined to stand first in queue next to the helipad until our supposed return, he gave us one more happy wave, and then we were gone.

Departing the jungle camps was no time to coddle the engine. I always pulled maximum power, keeping one eye on the gauges and one eye on the flight path to obtain best angle of climb. The further away from Earth and the faster we got there, the safer we were. With a reasonably light load like the one we had departing Kistaram that day, the powerful Astar could gain altitude quickly, and that may have been the difference between life and death.

Suddenly, Babeesh lurched forward in his seat and thrust a filthy pointy finger against the window toward the ground. The words coming from his mouth were unintelligible and almost immediately drowned out by what sounded like the beginning of a hailstorm, though we were flying through cloudless sky. Three or four pops of sound rapidly escalated into a cacophonous staccato where I could not discern single hits anymore, only a continuous pelting. Like lighting the fuse to a string of a thousand firecrackers, it started off with two or three singles, then each *crack* became swallowed by the next until all I heard was a steady barrage.

"Those fuckers are shooting at us," I said, "We're being shot at." Not that anyone aboard needed this illuminating clarification.

"Saa! Go up, go up, go up!" Babeesh shouted, big saucer eyes and betel nut juice dribbling down his chin.

The two troopers in back were shouting too, and even though they were shouting in Hindi, it was quite clear they wished for me to go up as well. Of that, I was in full agreement. Quickly glancing around, I didn't see anyone shooting from my side, so with a steep, banking turn to the right, we angled away to the south, and the helicopter slowly—too slowly—climbed away from our would-be assailants.

During this melee—which seemed to last for two minutes, but was only about ten seconds—I was expecting to see bullet holes erupting out of the floor or through the chin bubble at any instant. We were climbing through one thousand feet MSL, which was around 700 feet AGL and still within range of most rifles. With all that shooting, how could they miss?

Perhaps they didn't. At one point during the attack, I had felt a slight tap on the foot pedals, so slight that it might have been my imagination. After the shooting had stopped, but still climbing with all available power, I kept checking and rechecking the gauges for anything out of the ordinary. Nothing looked to be, although I was curious about that tap on my feet. I briefly considered continuing the short distance to Bheji and landing there to check it out. But, once reaching safe altitude, I reduced power and, with no negative signs from the gauges or unusual vibrations, dialed in Dantewada on the GPS and steered our ship that way. Bheji could have been overrun by bad guys at the same time, and I figured there was no sense jumping from the frying pan into the fire by landing there.

I certainly wasn't landing back at Kistaram for a look-see, bad things were assuredly happening there, and landing anywhere else in the jungle was hazardous. The closest, safest landing area was forty-minutes away, in Dantewada. That would give us all plenty of time to settle down and realize we were away from peril, if the helicopter held together that long; I imagined the exterior must have been riddled like Swiss cheese. Still amazed that no bullets had penetrated the cabin, I looked all around but did not see any evidence of the attack. Wiggling my toes inside my boots, I took inventory and was rewarded with responsive motor skills in all lower extremities.

21.

Smiley and the Reaper

"Everyone alright?" I asked, looking around at Babeesh and the two passengers, "Is anyone hit?"

They were all drenched in sweat that had nothing to do with the heat, but there were no signs of injury, and no one was shrieking in pain.

"S-Saa, w-we waa fired upon, saa!" Babeesh spluttered. He had managed to wipe the betel nut juice off his chin and must've swallowed the rest.

"Do you see any damage on your side?" I asked. "I don't see anything... How 'bout behind me?"

"I'll check it out." He was wearing a nervous smile, thankful to be alive, as were the rest of us.

He took off his headset and shoulder harness to maneuver around his seat, checking the floor behind me and the rest of the cabin interior for holes or damage. Our two passengers were standing up off their seats staring at them, apparently afraid they'd take a bullet in the keister if they sat back down. I continued watching the gauges for any signs of trouble, but we'd been lucky so far.

Babeesh settled the passengers down and after finding no damage, I asked him, "What did you see at Kistaram? I saw nothing from my side."

"Three mans with AK47s waa firing at us, saa."

As we were making our turn a hundred yards from the IPS camp, three insurgents on his side of the helicopter had come running out of the tree line into the rice paddies. They stopped, took aim and started firing. It was then I recalled those odd "villagers" that remained motionless while we flew over them. It wasn't that they had been disinterested in us—quite the contrary—they were setting up an ambush. The attackers were well within the IPS's allegedly secure, one-and-a-half-kilometer sanitized perimeter zone.

Babeesh said their rifles looked like AK47s with banana magazines, but he couldn't know for sure from our distance and speed. The Maoist-Naxalites had been killing and pillaging the government's rifles for years, and they had others in their arsenal, including the Indian made INSAS assault rifle, which used the 5.56 mm cartridge, while the AKs used the heavier 7.62 mm. From what I understood, the Maoists used a hodgepodge of weapons, everything from bows and arrows to recoilless rifles. Whatever they used to attack us, I was just glad that their aim was poor.

I kept monitoring the gauges with particular interest to the fuel quantity; it didn't seem to be diminishing any more than normal, which would have been the case if a round had gone through the fuel tank. There were no vibrations or noises that indicated any problems. No noises other than Babeesh, anyway; he was yammering away to the passengers in back, and they were shouting back and forth over the sound of the aircraft.

He put his headset back on and, over the intercom, reminded me about the missing fourth trooper who was supposed to be on the flight from Dantewada. The two lads in the back seats knew him and that his allegiance to the cause had been called into question in the past. There may have been a more sinister reason why he wasn't on the flight, as in, he knew beforehand that an attack on Kistaram was coming and went AWOL to avoid it.

Babeesh said he had been considering the missing trooper and just such a violent outcome since taking off from Dantewada earlier, hence his brooding and ruminating. I glanced at Babeesh. For all his backwoods betel nut ways, he was a clever chap.

"That thought didn't cross my mind," I said. "You should've spoken up, buddy, we could've avoided this mess."

"Saa, yes saa," he said, but in his culture, subordinates didn't usually speak unless spoken to.

Wishing for a tailwind that I knew would not come, I wanted badly to have Dantewada fill my windscreen and get the bird on the ground. By the time we did start our descent, the talk and chatter had subsided again. Everyone was thinking about our narrow escape. Hovering just above the pad, I had Babeesh shout through the window to Rabinesh, telling him to inspect the landing skids for any damage. Rabinesh's usual grin transformed into a puzzled look, then he bent down to check our skid tubes and, standing back up straight, gave us a confused thumbs up. I gently set down on the oversize concrete helipad, slowly letting the landing skids take the aircraft's weight, hoping they had not been blown apart during the attack, and idled down.

The passengers could not get out of the helicopter fast enough; as soon as Babeesh had the door open, they bolted down the dirt path for home. I let the engine cool down while he went on a quick check for damage. From all that firing, I was expecting grim news. Walking around the backside of the helicopter to my open door, Babeesh held up one finger and hollered, "Tailboom!"

After shutting down and climbing out, I was amazed that there were no fluids leaking, no bullet holes, not even a paint scratch, nothing on my side of the helicopter that indicated we had just been through an assault. But as I walked back to the tailboom, my pulse quickened a couple of gears. Three feet forward of the end of the tailboom, a hole was blasted top dead center of the tailrotor driveshaft fairing, and it was big enough to stick my fist through. We only found one small bullet hole on the bottom of the tailboom, but by the time the projectile exited the top, it had expanded and accumulated larger pieces of metal to blow out the gaping hole. We unscrewed that damaged section of fairing to examine the driveshaft itself and what we found had us speechless, nearly.

The tailrotor driveshaft is as vital to flying a helicopter as the engine. It's a tubular length of steel that connects the engine gearbox to the tailrotor gearbox, which in turn drives the tailrotor. Without the tailrotor, there is no yaw control, and the helicopter would only spin end to end due to the torque effect from the main rotor. Depending upon the airspeed, if a sudden loss of power to the tailrotor occurs, one of the emergency procedures the pilot is trained to use is entering autorotation and landing. The problem in a high power setting and low airspeed configuration—like takeoffs—is that a sudden loss of yaw control can quickly have the pilot disoriented and beyond a recoverable point.

Though the pilot may be able to lower the collective lever all the way down—removing the torque effect from the airframe—and achieve autorotation, the aircraft's high power setting and torque beforehand, combined with the sudden loss of tailrotor thrust, may have the helicopter spinning end to end and pitching about uncontrollably. The chances of regaining control would not be good.

Dead center in my driveshaft was another jagged hole, and this one was big enough to put my finger through. But by the bullet's hitting the *exact* center of the driveshaft, it saved our lives. A quarter inch to the left or right would have weakened the driveshaft enough to allow itself to shear into two pieces. Impacting in that precise spot left sufficient steel on both sides of the bullet hole to provide strength in the shaft to keep it rotating in one piece. That little thump I felt in the foot pedals during the attack was not my imagination at all, but the bullet that nearly brought us down.

We scoured the rest of the helicopter and were quite amazed to find only one other bullet hole. Looking up at one of the composite main rotor blades, about mid-span and three inches from the trailing edge, there appeared to be just a little paint chip missing, but inspecting the top of the blade, we saw an eruption of material where a bullet had passed through. Astar rotor blades are remarkably robust and, unless a bullet hit the leading edge of the blade, they could take a few bullet hits. I would not be the pilot to stand in line for the test flight to determine how many, though.

The entry and exit points of both bullet holes indicated a near-vertical trajectory, meaning the gunmen had been directly below us. With all that aircraft surface as a target, we had only been hit on a blade spinning close to 400 RPM and in the only place on the tailrotor driveshaft that would not shear. It's cliché, but something like that might make a person religious.

The news spread quickly, and by that time Rabinesh and quite a number of troopers were crowding around the helicopter. Rabinesh said he was receiving little radio communication from Kistaram, but now knew that a battle was raging there. The Dantewada IPS district brass and superintendent were driven down to the helipad to investigate, and thereafter began an afternoon of debriefings and explanations to the IPS, CRPF and my company.

The helicopter was not airworthy and would have to spend time grounded in Dantewada. Rabinesh quickly had his troopers erecting a sandbag defensive screen on the jungle-exposed side of the helipad to stop any potshots from the Maoist-Naxalites. It would be a couple of weeks before the replacement parts would reach Jagdalpur, and then we'd bring them to Dantewada for installation. BK and other members of our team had driven the hour-and-a-half road journey from Jagdalpur and were securing the helicopter as best they could for the long grounding.

As the sun was heading down, and after most of the excited buzz had left the helipad area, Rabinesh and I chatted quietly while the engineers finished covering the windscreen. I asked him what news, if any, he was getting from Kistaram and how the camp was holding up. He said that after we flew away and escaped, an unknown number, but probably hundreds, of Maoist-Naxalites attacked the camp. The battle had lasted for five hours and that many of his troopers were hurt or killed. Two of the killed had their bodies set on fire. He knew the men well, and I could tell that one in particular was a tough loss.

"The one chap was going on leave today," Rabinesh said, shaking his head with a little quiver in his voice. "His wife is having a baby soon."

Remembering Smiley back at Kistaram helipad and how he came running up to the helicopter optimistically hoping for a ride to Dantewada, I described him to Rabinesh: his tall height compared to the others, his happy demeanor, the friendly smile and wave.

Rabinesh smiled himself and gave a short chuckle. Then, his smile fading and staring over my shoulder into the distance, he said, "Yeh, Cap'n, that was him. He was always a happy man, *always smiling.*"

22.

Beereaucracy

The night's ride back to Jagdalpur was long, dark and had its own element of danger; it was not unheard of for the Maoist-Naxalites to come out of the trees at night and set up roadblocks to harass off-duty IPS or CRPF, or shakedown travelers before allowing them to pass along the road. We left Dantewada while the sun's last rays burned the green hillsides into the color of scorched gold, and not long after that, the jungle darkness became as thick and black as overused engine oil.

Our plan, if stopped, was to say that we were tourists sightseeing in Dantewada. There was an ancient Hindu temple located there that did attract distant diehard devotees, we just had to hope that the helicopter tools and parts would not be noticed. My mates were excellent smooth talkers, but I didn't know if they would be able to explain that evidence.

I found myself on a dark and dangerous road once again, fearing the loss of body organs or worse: especially if the bad guys were able to deduce that I was their enemy, the government's contracted helicopter flyer.

There were a few tense moments when the road dipped into a shallow valley and our headlights shone on two suspicious-looking desperados who held up a hand each. After a quick consultation with my companions in Hindi on whether to stop or not, the driver gunned the engine, honked the horn and aimed his headlights straight for one dude's belly button. The suspected highwaymen hesitated, but then dove out of our path, shouting in a way that I would not describe as neighborly. We craned our necks for the next five miles, watching behind us and hoping not to be pursued.

During the drive, Babeesh was the center of amusement and ribbing as his colleagues blamed him for being our bullet-dodging source of bad luck.

"Babeesh," I said, "we need you to enlist with the police and go through rifle training before we go to Kistaram again. Then we'll take off your door and clear you to go hot, Rambo style."

"Good idea, saa," BK said, "but we start him with a slingshot before the real gun, eh?"

We were relieved to see the lights of Jagdalpur come into view, the familiar sights and shops, everyone going on about their business as usual with no threat from the jungle. By the time we rolled to a stop in front of the guesthouse, we were stiff, sweaty and thirsty; the day's happenings had my throat extra dry, and I craved a beer. Changing into more comfortable clothes, we walked to the nearest beer shop. But upon reaching my usual source of suds, we were told that all liquor sales were halted due to elections taking place.

Making my usual pitiful attempt at humor, I said, "Babeesh that sounds like ignorant *beer*eaucracy, doesn't it?"

"Saa?"

"You know, *BEER*eaucracy. Get it?"

He gave me a quizzical, sideways glance, but his disregard and wrinkled brow stifled any further attempts at comedy.

Discouraged and thirsty, we headed down the road to a place rumored to supply the brew black-market style; we were never to find it, but the rain gods, seeing my parched predicament, offered to help in the form of a tropical deluge. Pelted with drops the size of billiard balls, Babeesh suggested we climb into a bicycle rickshaw we had found, where five or six of the drivers were huddled together. At first they were reluctant to pedal anyone during the downpour, and I didn't blame them; there was a cover to keep the passengers dry, but no protection for the driver. Babeesh was finally able to strike a deal with one skinny, semi-ambitious chap, enticing him with a large wad of rupees out of my wallet. We climbed in back and out of the rain.

Babeesh and I combined weighed no more than 300 pounds, both of us having the narrow waists of diet-conscious bikini models; still, when we sat in that tiny seat, our butts were pinched together like warped sardines in a tin can. Sizing up our driver, I harbored doubt that we would even roll. He looked to be no more than a hundred pounds, including his soaking wet turban, and when he started pedaling, it was with grunts and great lurches on the pedals. I wondered how he did that all day long, especially with the weight of an entire family aboard. But a fair amount of pain must've been diminished by the strange smelling, hand-rolled cigarette he was sharing with his comrades before our damp intrusion. Twenty minutes of his leg-straining exertions later, we were moist, but safely returned to the dry and liquor-less guesthouse.

The next morning broke bright, clear and sunny. The always cheery Beebu fixed me a cup of sweet coffee without asking, and I took a stroll outside, past the open sewers and scavenging stray dogs, out to where the neighborhood cattle were gathering for a morning graze in the vacant, trashy lots. Their morning munching was a calm and relaxing way to ease into the new day; they were ignoring the sparse shoots of grass attempting to grow and instead tore off and gobbled down great slabs from a discarded flat-screen TV cardboard box.

Events of the previous day clouded my mind: the image of ripped steel and a nearly destroyed tailrotor driveshaft—the image of a tall, happy chap, smiling and waving as our downwash blew dust all around him, some of the detritus catching in his shaggy hair.

I was grounded in Jagdalpur, and it would be many days before the slow, indecisive wheels of my company were to gain traction and have the helicopter airworthy again. Sitting around with so much flying to do was driving me up the wall. I continued my late afternoon runs at the airport, and that was the highlight of my days. Like a penitentiary prisoner being released into a fresh air exercise area, I enjoyed the sweat in the late-day sunshine.

I attempted to work with Beebu and his helpers to tame down the spicy food for my Midwestern-tempered palate, and one evening after coming back from my therapy session at the airport, they eagerly served up what they described as a special meal for me. They claimed they had reduced the amount of chilies and had convinced the chicken butcher to leave bigger pieces of chicken for the masala.

"Saa, try dis, saa," said Beebu, "You like? Less spice, saa. You like?"

They queried me with anxious eyes and waited for my response. I was hopeful for an improvement too and even drooled a little with anticipation. But it tasted and tortured just the same as before, my gums tingling like every tooth might fall out.

"Yeah," I answered, while my tongue slowly succumbed to green-chili paralysis. "You guys did great!"

That made them both proud and happy, and as they went back to the kitchen congratulating each other, I tried to douse the volcano in my mouth. My guts weren't proud or happy, though. Starting at midnight, I was on the toilet every ten minutes. By morning and throughout the next day, there was trouble at both ends of me. When not in the bathroom, I was in the fetal position on my bed, awaiting the angel of death.

Everyone else had eaten the same dish, but I was the only one who was half dead and could not walk five feet from the nearest toilet. By the second day, I was able to start eating again, but had no appetite for masala. I hid from Beebu and had Babeesh smuggle in a half-liter of vanilla ice cream from the shop to soothe my suicidal guts.

A few days later, I received word to come to Delhi. The powers in the office tower wanted to discuss the shooting incident and our company's future activities face to face. They seemed not keen to continue our flights with the IPS, citing the security breach and lack of protection, especially the kilometer-and-a-half perimeter that the troopers were supposed to ensure. To say the least, I was worried about that as well and told them I would happily fly somewhere safer.

A part of me didn't want to abandon the operation, though. The flying was steady and continuous, but yet I was not overworked; the aircraft one of my favorite types to fly, and my crew had settled into a comfortable rhythm with the operation.

Nevertheless, I found myself on hell's highway, retracing the route from Jagdalpur to Raipur. It was, predictably, a much better drive during daylight hours than at nighttime, but it was still dreadfully long, and still narrow and hazardous. At least my driver could see the hazards before he hit them, if his eyes were open. The heat and monotonous distance had made him sleepy; the car's air conditioner needed recharging and wasn't cooling properly, so the already danger-strewn highway became even more perilous with him nodding off at the steering wheel. I offered to supplement his blood sugar with tea and snacks, but he refused, saying he did not want to waste time by stopping.

It would have been an interesting drive for a photojournalist, with a wide range of bizarre sights to see. In a watering hole stood a herd of cattle up to their backs in the water, and not ten feet away a group of men were having a bath, and not ten feet from them another group were doing their laundry in this frightful soup. We passed one village where a group of men were using an elephant to move logs; I immediately felt compassion for the old beast and wished to run down the road and ask them to stop. There were many stories just on one old stretch of crumbly road, and I allowed myself a brief fantasy where my photography would grace the covers of *National Geographic Magazine*.

Reaching Raipur Airport unscathed and in plenty of time for my flight, I told my sleepy, half-lidded driver, "Thanks bhaiya, good job." Then, passing him a few extra rupees before being screened by security outside the entrance, I said, "Now get a decent meal and some sleep."

An hour later, my bored-to-bradycardia heart sank at finding out the scheduled eight p.m. departure was delayed until eleven. I waited and slowly decayed in the cramped and non-air conditioned departures area, and it was well past midnight before I landed in Delhi.

I had messaged Sami from Raipur about the delay but didn't get a reply. The delay had apparently given the company driver ample time to become further stoned, and he was slurring his words when we were able to reach each other on the phone; he was upset that I was late and hadn't picked up his call.

"Listen, the flight was delayed," I told this Indian version of Cheech or Chong. "I sent Mr. Sami a message, and of course I couldn't pick up your call, I was in an airliner."

"Saa, you should ha' picked up my call," he said, trying to focus his eyes.

I was quite cranky from the tense jungle drive, the dulling wait and then delay. Strangling this half-wit with his own turban was becoming a not-so-remote possibility.

With the driver pissed up and unsteady but happy to be moving, my own mood was swinging low as we went back out to the company guesthouse at the monkey-ranch. There were more than a few white-knuckled close calls to keep my fear for life and limb in practice along the way. A storm had blown through, and trees were lying broken across various sections of the road. For that time of night, traffic was terribly jammed. His little van was a stick shift and combined with his ineptitude and lack of sobriety, it was a miserable ride.

When the traffic did move, he would rev the engine up, dump the clutch and send us rocketing forward twenty feet, then stomp harshly on the brakes, sending me lurching into the seat belt. The cycle repeated itself as the stop-and-go traffic persisted. One good thing about the traffic jam was that he wasn't able to accumulate enough speed to kill us, but at times I had to keep him talking and alert, otherwise his chin would fall to his chest and the minivan would be nearly up on the sidewalk, running over the cattle resting there.

Reaching what would be my home for the next couple of days, I washed my face and hit the sack a little after three in the morning. I was beat-tired and grumpy from the daylong journey and profoundly disgusted with India, as most situations seemed more trouble than need be: food poisoning, frenetic travel, idiot drivers and the foul conditions of the guesthouse.

That night, I'd about had it with the ancient South Asia land of a thousand gods. On a short phone chat with my buddy, Zach, who was also in Delhi, he readily agreed that just when you thought it could not get worse, India found a way to knock you into the gutter again, and then again. And, while you were lying sprawled out and face down, it would kick you in the kidneys and steal your money.

23.

Bhubaneswar

Sleeping later than usual the next morning, I awoke craving my usual dosage of coffee. Cracking my room door and poking my head out, I peered down the steps to the main floor below and said into the darkness, "Hello? Anybody there?"

It only remained quiet as my voice echoed off the bare walls. The houseboy didn't answer either; nothing or nobody stirred within the house. Only the faint din of Delhi outside the tightly locked up windows and doors could be heard, humming along at its normal tumultuous tempo. I had been left to fend for myself. Frightening.

Slowly walking down the cement steps, I looked all around for signs of life, but none showed themselves except for the ants gathering at the remains of someone's gooey gray breakfast left on the dining table. Ignoring those fine morsels, I continued on to the kitchen. Then, remembering the angry looks I'd received from the local rats the last time I disturbed their brunch, just before entering I gave the door a good five-second *knockity-knock* for their benefit and ample warning. Hearing a bit of scurrying from within, I waited until all was quiet. Then I opened the door and was relieved when nothing attacked my ankles and the kitchen was rat-free.

Out of sight, out of mind.

Entering this disaster zone, I maneuvered around rainbow-colored puddles of mysteriously textured, inedible mush, both on the floor and on the counter—even the walls—searching for the coffee fixings and requisite cup. Frustrated with poor search results, I began to consider boiling water in a pan and drinking from that, if I could just find one, and if I could find the damn coffee.

Concern began to mount. I was running out of shelves and storage space to check. Reaching up for the handle on one of the last cupboard doors, I was already thinking about what I would have to do, where I would have to go to find the delightful roasted beans. That's why when opening it, I was hardly prepared for the eight-inch furry rat that launched himself out, whizzed past my ear and arced over my shoulder to a graceful, four-point landing on the floor below.

About a week into my stay at Delhi, I was graciously moved to a hotel near the airport. My company had various managers visiting from its satellite offices, and they preferred to all stay together at the guesthouse. To make room for the intrepid travelers, I was volunteered to relocate, and it was a welcome reprieve from the detention-center style existence at the company quarters.

The food took a turn for the better too, and on the top floor was a gym to eliminate any chance of chubbiness due to the increased caloric intake. The hotel wasn't a five star by any measure—unless the company guesthouse was the yardstick—but it was less than twenty years old and in good condition. My fourth-floor room overlooked the busy main road on the perimeter of Delhi's Indira Gandhi International Airport, and through the haze and dust I could watch airliners landing, the sound of their thrust reversers rattling the windows. The bustling road was also a trove of unique and bizarre sights.

One morning, while surfing the internet news by my room window, I noticed a young man having difficulty in the middle of the road. It appeared he was either on drugs or having mental problems. I happened to glance down while he lay spread-eagle over the first of three lanes on the road, occasionally rolling back and forth. The horde of pedestrians walking by barely noticed him, and the traffic kept streaming on through, the buses, trucks and cars swerving to avoid him.

At one point he ripped off his tattered shirt, folded it neatly, laid it next to him, and then suddenly somersaulted from one side of the road to the other. I cringed when he was almost wiped out by a horn-honking bus. Pulling off his shoes he threw them toward its windows while it passed around him, nearly scoring a direct hit through an open one; the passengers inside watched, expressionless and indifferent, like it was an everyday occurrence.

One citizen tried to help by offering him a couple of bananas. He ate one ravenously, then peeled the other open and smashed it on his head, rubbing it into his already-filthy hair. A few minutes later, another passerby offered him a bottle of water. Standing up to drink it, the cool liquid going down his throat must have triggered the bladder to release overflow; a dark stain blossomed on the front of his trousers and a rivulet formed around his bare feet and ran down the sloped pavement to mix with the other roadside nastiness. Pitching the half-finished bottle at someone's Mahindra, he gazed up at the sky and stretched out his arms like Willem Dafoe in *Platoon*. Eventually, a traffic cop came along on a bicycle, not to offer assistance, but to chase him down the road with a stick.

The company was developing an alternate plan to flying in Chhattisgarh. Although not as enthusiastic as I had been with flying there—near-death tempers the zeal—I still felt it could be done as long as the IPS and CRPF convinced us they would reliably secure the landing zones. In the end, it was up to the bosses, and the final planning and meetings, unsurprisingly, did not include me. It was decided that once our Astar was repaired, I would fly it to the company's small base in Bhubaneswar where it would be put to use for other charter operations. It would also be used for the occasional company flight to their iron ore mines and steel mills; that sector being the main focus of the company, their aviation division only a sideline.

Upon hearing the city of Bhubaneswar, I thought of Anika and her prediction that we would meet again. She had turned out to be quite correct, and I called her with the news.

"See, Michael," she said when I was able to get her on the line, "I told you we would meet again! And once you're here, you *will* take me to dinner!"

"Once I'm there," I said, "*You* will take me to dinner, since I have no wheels, but I'm happy to get the check."

"No wheels... no... What did you say?"

"A car, I don't have a car, dear Anika."

"Well, of course you don't," she said impatiently, and then sweetly crooned, "Although I do, and cannot wait to pick up my dashing pilot!"

She had me promise to call prior to departing Jagdalpur so she could prepare herself.

The days clicked slowly by, but eventually I received word to fly to Raipur. The parts required for the Astar were on a truck somewhere in the middle of India and would be arriving in the jungle soon. Flying first to Mumbai and then spending the night, I met up with Chandru, our chief engineer, who would be supervising the repair work in Dantewada and Jagdalpur. The next day, we flew Air India to Raipur with his tools and engineering weaponry. Chandru was able to hire a car and driver at the airport for the long slog through the countryside and, with all his gear, the little Tata was cramped and squatting on its tires.

We stopped once, about halfway through the journey, on the south side of Kanker for tea and masala at a dusty, bustling open-air wayside eatery. It was filled with truck drivers and road warriors like us making the jungle journey to or from Raipur. The sun was again showing off its strength, the temperature reaching beyond 110 degrees. That, combined with a spicy dish and hot tea, did not sound like a good mix, but I scarfed it down anyway to my almost immediate regret. Although the car was a deathtrap, climbing back in at least provided air conditioning for me and my violated stomach.

Reaching Jagdalpur, the base technicians helped Chandru with his gear, and I helped myself to a beer that Beebu had chilling in the grimy refrigerator. It was a reunion of sorts between Chandru and the others, and it felt like home to me, being able to put my feet up and relax with a smoke and a cold beer in familiar surroundings with familiar faces once again.

The crew was relieved to hear that we would be shifting operations, albeit for a while, to Bhubaneswar, and they were eager to get started on the repair job. But the truck carrying the parts was having difficulties out on the road. Besides getting lost multiple times, the old Tata ten-wheeler sprung a radiator leak and had to contend with flat tire issues. The exact date of arrival was in question.

Rabinesh, at Dantewada, was glad to see us reclaim our aircraft when the parts did eventually arrive; it had caused him security headaches as the bad guys wanted to blow it up in the worst way. It would have been quite a victory for them to send a helicopter up in flames. He had to increase his guard patrols, especially at night, and the bunker of sandbags had grown substantially since we were last there. It now towered above the helicopter by about three feet.

I complimented him on the fine sandbag construction work. He laughed and said, "Anything for my favorite pilot, anything!"

"Do you guys do pools?" I asked.

"Already done!" He pointed to a muddy pond just off the end of the helipad that held half a dozen water buffalo, sharing a good soak in the slurry.

He was aware that we were ceasing operations temporarily, but I told him there was a good chance we would be back soon, just that my company wanted the situation to cool down a tad. He said that lately the higher-ranking officers were more in favor of having the troopers use roads instead of relying on the helicopter—not that they had a choice—although it was more dangerous, they would use this time to make a show of force to the Maoist-Naxalites. By traveling in larger patrols, they felt they could provide safe travel to the troopers and resupply convoys and, in so doing, show the villagers that they too could travel as they wished.

It took the crew half a day to replace the tailrotor driveshaft and after installing the battery, which had been on a trickle charger back at base, I started up for a ground run. All the systems performed satisfactorily and upon shutting down, the engineers rechecked all the fittings and cowlings, then gave me a thumbs-up for the flight to Jagdalpur.

I shook Rabinesh's hand. "So long, my friend. We'll try to get back soon. Be safe!"

Grinning, he said, "No worries, Mista Mike, I'll be here. You fly safe!"

Starting up, we flew back to our home airport where the work was only beginning for the crew. The next few days required the bullet-damaged tailboom to get patched, and the hole in the main rotor blade needed to be addressed as well. First, they tried switching out the rotor blade with one from their other Astar, but after multiple tries they could not get it to balance with the other blades. The three rotor blades come from the factory matched to a specific aircraft, so attempting to swap one from another aircraft was generally a waste of time. Shifting tactics, they looked at the bullet hole in the original blade and decided just to patch it with composite material.

With repair work complete and my possessions packed, we launched east for Bhubaneswar. It was a two-hour flight over beautiful hill country. Even though the area was still considered to be under Maoist-Naxalite influence, they were supposedly not as strong through this region. That fact made the country even more pleasant. There were a few rain showers and squalls to avoid through the hills, but we had an early enough start that in the morning, the weather was still settled.

BK and Chandru were aboard, along with two other technicians, all of whom were unable to stop chattering away happily. The crew was glad to be leaving the jungle behind. But the fact was, this was a temporary move; we would be back in Jagdalpur at some point.

Bhubaneswar was larger than Raipur, at well over one million people and, like Raipur, was situated near the Mahanadi River. The capital of the state of Odisha, it had a human history dating back thousands of years and, as with many Indian cities, was home to hundreds of temples. Its airport had a one-runway airstrip providing a half-dozen scheduled flights in the morning, another half-dozen later in the day, and a few scattered throughout. It was not a busy airspace.

Upon landing at our hangar, there were more than a few people on hand to welcome us, but when the handshakes and "Namastes" tapered off, I dug out my cell phone and dialed up Anika. Answering on the first ring, she promised to be at the hangar within fifteen minutes. How she knew where the hangar was or how she intended to gain access to our isolated parking area I left up to her. Evidently, she knew the right people because our hangar seemed to be positioned in a forgotten corner of the airport.

It was outside the walled and fenced perimeter of the airfield and even to taxi the aircraft to the hangar from the runway, we had a half mile of ground to cover. This included passing three guard shacks along the way that were bordering the airport ramp. Likewise, to access our driveway by car from the nearest city road, a ten-acre, thistle-infested field had to be crossed. We shared this isolated, weed-strewn part of the airport with two other companies and their separate hangars, but it appeared an impractical location for any aviation charter business. It looked more like a Wild West trading post overrun with tumbleweed.

When her little Suzuki Swift came bouncing along our dusty dirt driveway, it looked to be swallowed up by the oxcart-sized dips that lined the track, and due to her tinted windows, I didn't even realize it was Anika. The first clue that it was her appeared below the opened car door after she had stopped; glittery sandals, red toenail polish, slim feet and ankles that were draped by lime-green material from a golden-bordered saree. I was tongue tied and awestruck as she stepped out and turned toward me and my ogling crew, pushing her mane of raven-black hair over a shoulder. Her dark, heavily mascaraed eyes and tan face were lit up by a smile that was white as snow. The saree she wore offered small peeks of well-defined waist, her curves accentuated and exotically draped by the Indian dress. I was in the presence of nearly unimaginable beauty once again.

Holding out both her hands, she said in her delicately accented English, "Hello, Michael. With great happiness, I welcome you to Bhubaneswar!"

She squeezed my hand within both of hers like she was making a snowball. I replied with some blabbering response, giddy as a schoolboy, then went about introducing her to the crew. We gave her a short tour of our hangar and helicopter; and I noticed she wasn't shy or bashful in the least and was respected by the other Indians, speaking with certain eliteness.

The crew started to unwind with Bollywood music and booze. The meet and greet session over, I grabbed my bags, threw them in the back of her car and, with a wave to my gossiping mates, climbed into the passenger side and shut the door. She backed out of the parking space and then deftly gear-jammed through the first two gears, bouncing and bumping down the driveway out to the main road, out to a dinner she promised I would not forget.

24.

Lock and Load

The company guesthouse, Bhubaneswar version, sat on the perpetually jammed and busy two-lane main road that ran all the way to Puri and the Bay of Bengal. While it was only two lanes, the traffic used it like it was four or six lanes at times, and the horn blowing, especially from the commercial trucks, was relentless and deafening. To anyone who has not been to India, this constant source of bedlam would be difficult to imagine. It comes off to a Westerner as mindless, rude and unnecessary. I was the lucky one who took up residence on the back side of the building, overlooking a quieter alleyway and hundreds of grimy two-story residences.

Our building had four floors. The first two floors held company offices that administered the regional iron ore mining and steel plant activities, the third floor was guest rooms and a kitchen, and the fourth was unfinished and vacant, unless you count spiders and pigeons as occupants. The easily accessed flat rooftop had a decent view of the centuries-old temple grounds across the chaotic road and the sky-darkening flocks of pigeons that made them their roost.

This being the tallest building around, I could look east from the roof and just see the white Dhauli Hills Peace Pagoda a few miles away on the banks of the Daya River. Looking around to other parts of the city, I saw numerous temple spires jutting into the sky, but they were outnumbered tenfold by the ubiquitous mobile phone towers. I did calisthenics and laundry up on the roof by day and, toward the evening, it was a good spot to unwind with a beer and a smoke. I claimed it as my own territory, but shared.

After a cool rain late one evening, I felt it was a precious gift from above that the loud, John Deere tractor-sounding air conditioner in my quarters would not be required for my evening

Lock and Load

sleep. The temperature remained cool even after the rain had stopped, and I was content to set the ceiling fan on low, read a while and peacefully drift off to sleep. I'd learned, however, that my definition of peaceful was vastly different than the average Indian's definition.

No surprise then, that sometime after midnight I began to hear a whistle blowing at regular intervals. It was like a policeman's whistle. In the beginning, it was barely audible through semi-consciousness and earplugs, but soon it became louder and louder outside my third story window. Half-awake, at first I thought it was a juvenile delinquent messing around looking for attention. The sound faded as he moved on, and I snuggled deeper into my pillow, hoping to fall back asleep.

No such luck. Just as I was dozing off again, there came the whistleblower once more, and I was fully awakened. I jumped up and scampered to my window, barely in time to see the offending whistler go around the corner of our building. But I could still hear the bastard; so if he came around again I planned on being ready for him. Running a few gallons of water into a bucket, I set it next to the window. Locked and loaded, I was poised for an ambush.

I eased open the window, ignoring the squadron of mosquitoes that were undoubtedly sneaking in. My noisy target was headed my way again, coming closer and closer, blowing his whistle each time until his lungs were empty. Then, as he came within range, I triggered my attack and sent cold water over the ledge, nailing the sucker mid-whistle. The whistling stopped with a sort of gurgling sound, and the startled soloist ran off a few yards. He turned, looked up and shouted something in Hindi that, if I'd understood it, probably would have found quite offensive, judging by his tone. Mission accomplished, though, and feeling quite proud of my aim, I returned to bed and wasn't disturbed the rest of the night.

The next morning at breakfast time, I saw Vihaan, one of the company's airplane pilots who, with his wife, also shared the third floor. I bragged about the ambush and my defense of peace and quiet at our great castle. His eyes became big and, half-whispering in Indian-accented conspiratorial tones, he said, "That was you? Mike that was a security guard you nearly drowned last night! I heard them talking this morning!"

"Why the hell was he blowing his whistle in the middle of the night?" I asked.

"Well, to scare away any troublemakers. Security guards sometimes blow their whistles all night to keep criminals away."

"What criminals? Are you kidding me? What about people trying to sleep?"

He glanced at his wife, smiled and said, "We don't seem to have trouble sleeping through the loud noises or disturbances that bother other people."

"Give me the pills you're using," I demanded.

We were laughing, but I swore him and his wife to secrecy. I didn't need any trouble from the security guard or his twelve-gauge shotgun.

Vihaan flew the company's small, Italian-built twin-engine six-seater airplane and, like me, wasn't kept as busy as he wished. He had a few charter flights with minor politicians and around an equal number of company non-revenue flights. I had a few flights as well, but mainly with our company executives, and it was nothing like the daily operations tempo back in Jagdalpur. Many days I would be at the Bhubaneswar hangar trying unsuccessfully to be useful and, when the pace was exceedingly slow, I'd read a book or go pester the engineers until it was time to leave.

Mahesh was the operations manager for Bhubaneswar, and he was in love with me. That is perhaps a stretch, as he had a wife and kids, but the guy could not stop staring at me. In a land where I was stared at everywhere I went, this guy took the eyeball idiocy to new levels. If I walked into the office and he was talking to a colleague, his voice would trail off mid-sentence and his eyes would follow my every movement; meanwhile, his colleague who was in the middle of taking instructions and notes was sitting there, pen poised, ready to continue copying, wondering about Mahesh's mental health.

If he walked out into the hangar, and I was at the far end of it, his eyes would search me out, lock and hold gaze while talking or discussing company information with the other lads. Then, turning back to the office, he would look around and gaze at me five seconds more before continuing in through the door. He showed no self-consciousness about this. If I stared back, he would only continue giving me the puppy dog eyes, falling deeper and deeper in love. Although I'd had my share of it wherever I went in India, his case of the gawks was creeping me out.

It probably wasn't, but our dimly lit and pigeon infested company hangar looked as old as the World War Two vintage airstrip that Bhubaneswar airport was built on. There was sufficient space for perhaps three small aircraft inside, and it was large enough to accommodate the company's Mi17, but at the time it held just my Astar helicopter and Vihaan's P68. There were stacks of old and timed-out main rotor blades from the massive Mi17, one of its thirty-five-foot-long blades encompassed the entire rotor diameter of the Astar. Seeing the oversized helicopter parts caused me to think about my old friend Chatterjee and wonder how he was getting along in Shimla.

Due to the ridiculousness of our hangar's position in the airport and strict security measures of the government, we were not allowed to board any passengers at our hangar. First, we had to start-up, reposition to the ramp adjacent to the main terminal and shut down. Then the pilots and crew had to go into the airport, through the security line like any regular passengers and back out again to the aircraft before flying away to the destination. On the way through the airport, pilots would meet and collect the passengers, and then we could all compare the color of our socks while going through security together.

The ATC in the tower, for whatever reason, would have me park as far away from the terminal doors as they could, making it so that everyone had a hot sweat going on even before climbing into the locked-up oven of the helicopter cabin.

The lack of consideration for general aviation by the AAI was confounding.

Certain evenings, Vihaan, along with his wife, and Anika and I would dare death by crossing the murderous traffic in front of our guesthouse and walk to the old Hindu temple grounds on the other side. The actual grounds were somehow kept in good shape—the thick green grass was trimmed and pleasant for strolling—but the sandstone temple spires themselves were deteriorating. After countless years of rain, wind and pigeon poop, that's hard to avoid I would guess.

There were five taller spires, about forty to fifty feet tall, and twelve shorter ones half as tall. The larger spires could hold a few people for prayers or chants in its base, but the smaller structures were too tiny for people. Peering into them I could see candles and usually a picture of a Hindu god adorned with offerings and incense. Vishnu and Shiva were probably the most popular deities, according to my Indian mates, but there were many others.

The sites for a Hindu temple, Anika explained to me, were always near water and gardens where lotus and other flowers bloom, where swans, ducks and birds could be heard, where animals could rest without fear of injury or harm. That sounded like compassionate good sense. The incessant traffic with its ear-assaulting horns sort of broke the peace though. Other than cattle or dogs, the occasional hawk could be seen from time to time, chasing one of the hundreds of pigeons, but presumably the swans and ducks had moved on to more tranquil digs.

The little concrete-lined pond near the tallest spires did hold some type of tough, sludge-breathing fish, however, and in the early mornings it held many assorted bathers too. In fact, all day long people would stop by to break out the soap and give themselves a nice luster. How much of a luster was another matter; the water would change from a mysterious dark green to dark brown depending upon the way light shone on it.

25.

Scandalous Diversion

It was an early five o'clock wake-up, and downstairs I went to the front door where Anika was waiting to drive us to the tennis courts. After several days of trying, she had convinced me that what I really needed in the morning were tennis lessons, not to sit around drinking sweet coffee, lazily watching the sunrise. It seemed a good idea at the moment, but the last time I'd picked up a racket was back in high school and even then, I was no tennis ace.

For me, it wasn't so much the quality of play. Just being able to smash the ball on return with no heed of the boundary line was good exercise and fun. Anika did not appreciate my reckless volleys, however, and suggested that I spend more time with the resident tennis coach. He helped as best he could but kept our sporadic lessons short. At times, while he was teaching me to volley, baseball reflexes from my youth kicked in, and I would smash a line drive back toward his noggin—not on purpose of course, but hey, it felt good to really get a hold of one!

Backing away, he would tell me to practice volleying against the wall. Meanwhile, Anika and her sister were battling back and forth in a heated match, with one of her sister's kids on either side of the net providing a doubles partner. Sometimes they would let me join in and play, but they would argue over who would have to take me for a teammate.

They certainly let me join them for breakfast afterwards, though, and it was wordlessly assumed that I, the dashing and cosmopolitan pilot, would pay. I was alright with that, the food was good and so was the company. We would go to a nearby hotel, the Mayfair Lagoon, for breakfast, and the place was magnificent. It had to be five-star rated and was one of the cleanest places I had seen in India. A mind-blowing contrast to the grime and filth just at the end of its driveway, it had well-kept gardens, pools, ponds, peach-faced lovebirds, cockatiels and other birds, plus ducks patrolling the lagoon. The days we were able to get together for tennis were early wake-ups, but they were a groovy diversion from the monotony of my slow flight schedule.

On one of those tennis outings, Anika found out that her teaching schedule had been canceled for the day. After breakfast, she convinced me to skip hangar duty, which wasn't hard, and go sightseeing. She had been talking about the Dhauli Hills Peace Pagoda on the Daya River before and thought that we should go check it out. A phone call to my old buddy Mahesh verified that I had no flights coming up, so I agreed to the jaunt.

Dhauli Hills was four miles outside of Bhubaneswar on the road to the Bay of Bengal. It was the site of a massive ancient battle between the local people of the time, the Kalinga, and a ruler named Ashoka. Ashoka was a butt-kicking Indian emperor who ruled the entire Indian subcontinent during the second century BC—a region that stretched from the Hindu Kush Mountains in the west to Bengal and the Ganges delta in the east. Around 260 BC, Ashoka waged war against the Kalinga and conquered them. At first, news of the victory made him proud because none of his ancestors had been able to defeat them. But then, after touring the battlefield and witnessing the mass deaths from the war, he was shocked into peacefulness and embraced Buddhism.

On top of the hill, a dazzling white peace pagoda had been built by Japanese Buddhists in the 1970s. In the early afternoon, Anika and I sat in the shade of a few trees near the entrance, overlooking the plains leading to the banks of the Daya River. We were munching on potato chips and washing them down with Thumbs Up cola while trying to imagine what the scene would have been like all those years ago; thousands of people dead or dying, the river red with blood. I wondered what type of weapons they used, what they used for transportation and what drove a ruler like that, who reigned over a large amount of land already, to continue attacking and killing in the lust for conquest.

We had strolled around the ten-acre shrine in the late morning heat and, after relaxing a while, she handed me her car keys and said, "Come on, let's go cool off." Then, with a mischievous grin, "Do you think you can handle a Suzuki Swift, *Captain*?"

"I think I can avoid breaking anything," I replied. "Will the captain be told where he's going, or will he need to read minds?"

"Ah, don't you worry... I am your navigator!" Balancing her pop bottle on top of the overflowing trash bin, she jogged toward the car and shouted, "Let's go, pokey!"

She showed me a rutted trail that led downhill to the river. It caused the car's suspension to squeak and groan, nearly forcing me to eat my words regarding not breaking her car. At the foot of the hill, there were concrete steps on the river bank that led down to the water. Walking to the bottom, we sat on the ledge and dangled our feet in the cool, gentle current.

Anika was wearing turquoise pajama bottoms and an Indian ladies' white kurta top complete with a scarf, or dupatta, that she would sometimes drape over her head. It wasn't quite as sexy as a saree—it was more pragmatic for everyday wear and hid a lot of her voluptuousness—but she was still drop-dead gorgeous. We chatted about everything and nothing. I was trying unsuccessfully to find a good skipping rock, and she was doodling in the dust with a twig.

Throwing the twig into the river, she giggled and said, "Come on, I have an idea... something we might like in the car."

Stashed underneath her car seats were two large, well-traveled bottles of beer. The labels had been rubbed away from rolling back and forth for so long, and the glass was scuffed up. The outside air temperature was nearing an India-typical hundred degrees, and the contents of the bottles might have been near their boiling point.

"What are we gonna do with those, Anika?" I asked. "Make noodles?"

Still giggling like a teenager, she held them up like trophies and said, "Let's drink them!"

"Drinking in the early afternoon? Scandalous!"

She laughed louder and dug around in her glove box for something to open them with. "Oh, don't be such a teetotaler, Michael!"

"That's something I've never been accused of, my dear. Listen, I have a better idea, let's buy cold beer, or at least find ice for these pitiful bottles, go back to your apartment and relax in air-conditioned comfort."

She wasn't quite convinced that *that* was a good idea, and she insisted on having the hot beer. Leaning on her car in the shade of a eucalyptus tree, we popped open a bottle and then made funny faces and groaned every time we took a sip of the warm, foamy brew.

Not every day was a holiday though, the company had enough flights to keep me mildly busy and except for a rare occasion, they all involved mineral mining or steel and aluminum plants. India was going through an industrial metamorphosis, and there were large projects scattered across the countryside. One mission involved transporting Bhushan Steel executives from Bhubaneswar to one of its newer projects near a place called Angul, up in the rolling hills fifty miles away.

Again, just when you thought an unpleasant situation could not possibly get worse, India always had a way of proving you wrong. I quickly found out that filing a flight plan in Jagdalpur was a walk in the park compared to the goat rodeo general aviation pilots had to prepare for at a tower-controlled airport like Bhubaneswar. The same cockamamie procedure of FIC/ADC clearances had to be obtained, but gladly, after a few flights and then a bit of negotiating with our Bhubaneswar operations boys and my number one fan, Mahesh, a system was developed where they agreed to assist me.

Still, the pain in my behind started about two hours before any particular takeoff time. In countries where I had worked before, the system was so comparatively simple that it left me ruefully reminiscing. The Indian system appeared determined to hinder a pilot in every way to keep them from flying; many times, my exasperated voice could be heard saying to anyone that might listen, "Why the hell do I have to do that?"

No one *was* listening, of course. Eventually, my bullheadedness faded, and I resolved to live with the nonsensical grind.

With my flight plan faxed to AAI and awaiting their clearance, the next step was a drive to the airport meteorology office, which was in a separate building located just outside the airport in the shadow of the air traffic control tower. There, a man who looked to have one foot in the grave would, at his time and leisure, provide me the requisite pre-departure weather briefing. His job was to give me a detailed verbal account of the forecasted weather, complete with gigantic hand-drawn and penciled-in weather charts. No animated Doppler weather radar here. In fact, I didn't notice any equipment that might have postdated 1955.

Indicating my anticipated cruising altitude of four thousand feet, he spared me the Winds Aloft and such charts meant more for those airplane and jet jockeys; and while I respected his knowledge and experience of many years studying the weather, there was just little value in my visits to his office. VFR helicopter pilots, with our relatively short flight distances—I'm hopeful not to sound pretentious here—can usually look out the window and determine if it's a go or no-go weather situation. However, the meteorology office was a necessary step at an Indian tower-controlled airport.

After the meteorology officer signed off my flight plan, it was back out to the company car and a short drive to a guarded security checkpoint, after which, I walked to the air traffic control tower. Once in the tower, I traipsed up flights of stairs to the control room, stopping halfway to receive another signature from the dark and mysterious communications office. A simple, "Namaste, sir," to the officer within seemed to be the only requisite needed for his authorization.

When I arrived in the top structure itself, depending upon the controllers' workload, I waited and then discussed my flight plan with them. They checked that all boxes had been filled correctly, signatures in the appropriate places and verified my FIC/ADC clearances, if I had them. If not, I would give a cross-my-heart, hope-to-die promise to call after I *did* get them. That being followed by the controller's stern gaze and reluctant final signature for approval of my flight plan.

Back down the stairs and back through the security checkpoint—on the way out the guard again scrutinizing my identification—and back to the waiting company car. After another fifteen minute bouncing off-road-rally-ride around the airport and through the ten-acre thistle field, where groups of men, women and children would be squatting in the weeds for their morning business, we arrived at our hangar. Then, while dealing with the niggling little changes that were bound to come, I waited for the FIC/ADC and preflighted the aircraft.

The aforementioned process having just been accomplished and all systems go for the Bhushan Steel program, I jumped in the helicopter and radioed the tower two miles away for permission to start. Ignoring me the first couple of calls—out of some unwritten air traffic controller code—they then granted me permission, instructing me to "Observe all safe practices at every moment" and to radio back when ready to taxi.

Due to our position not quite over in the next township, it took twenty minutes to start up and taxi to our parking space on the ramp and shut down. Only then could we order up the refueling truck. If he wasn't too busy refueling another aircraft the delay would be short, but if it was a long delay, I would have to contact first AAI for an FIC/ADC departure revision and then call my new friends in the tower to inform them of the revision. It would have been a cold day in hell if I was connected to any of those places on the first, second or even third attempt to reach them.

Refueling complete, I headed into the small departure lounge, tracked down my passengers and cranked up my normally hard-to-find extrovert side. Together, we went through security and then out through the terminal doors. At times, if the executives were deemed sufficiently important, a shuttle car would be arranged from the terminal to our waiting chariot of the sky. If not, or there wasn't enough room for me in the vehicle, I would do my impression of Gandhi walking across steamy India.

That day, there was no car. Reaching the helicopter, passengers and pilot were in full sweat mode and, after receiving their hopeful query about a climate controlled cabin, I did not delight them by answering, "No, I'm sorry. Our helicopter doesn't have air conditioning installed."

BK was helpful, offering cold bottles of water from our cooler, but their disappointment was evident. I recklessly gave them false hope by saying that, once up in the air and flying, the vents would provide cooler air, but unless we could climb substantially higher, all the vents really did was force the hot air to circulate like the inside of a furnace.

With everyone strapped in, I called ATC for permission to start and takeoff without further delay, or heat stroke. We were lucky to receive immediate start authorization but, upon lighting off, running through the after-start checks and lifting to a hover, I received a taxi and hold instruction to wait for landing traffic.

There was only one aircraft incoming, and it was still miles away, so I requested a taxiway departure on course to our destination. This is a common procedure at quiet airports in other parts of the world, simple enough to understand and execute, and what helicopters were built for. We would have been no factor to the inbound jet, but Indian ATC treated helicopters like they were jumbo jets that needed a mile of runway to takeoff. They refused my request.

I set down and idled the engine to wait for Air India to land. The passengers were close to asphyxiation. I can handle a little heat and sweat, but the high-flying executives in the seats behind me were having second thoughts about hiring a non-air conditioned helicopter. Knowing that pinning the blame on someone else worked for politicians, I tried to explain that ATC was the culprit and that they were making us wait for a landing airliner many minutes away. BK stayed busy, handing out more water and absorbent paper towels.

When we were finally able to line up on the runway and be cleared for takeoff, the fifty miles to our destination were covered in twenty-five minutes, less time than the whole rigmarole at the airport. No doubt the passengers were happy when the steel plant came into sight. The executives had said it would be hard to miss, and at over five thousand acres of ongoing construction and excavation, it was not. Massive building frameworks of blue steel and large green conveyor belt assemblies stretched for miles. There were hundreds of Tata ten-wheeler trucks crisscrossing back and forth across the complex, hauling construction materials, equipment and excavated dirt. They kicked up a towering cloud of dust that could be seen from miles away.

After landing, my baked and broiled passengers nearly ran to the waiting Mahindra SUVs. They were most anxious to avail themselves of the modern comforts of air conditioning. Over the commotion of the idling helicopter, they shouted their intention to return to Bhubaneswar in mid-afternoon. I hoped they would be well rehydrated by then.

26.

Two-Wheeling

I had available to me a road-weary Honda motorcycle that, depending on who wanted to put gas in it, was alternately kept at the hangar or the guesthouse. As with many Asian countries, motorcycles were popular, and India had millions of them. Two-wheelers, as they were more commonly referred to, were versatile and hauled everything from goats to grain. They were also highly maneuverable through heavy traffic, easy to park, great on gas and cheap to acquire.

Tata Motors was trying to elbow into that market by selling a tiny car called the Nano, and the price of a new car at the time was just a bit higher than that for a motorcycle. A bare-bones, slight upgrade from a two-wheeler, this alternate mode of transport kept passengers dry, but that was where the benefits ended. Three to five people could regularly be seen riding a two-wheeler with no apparent discomfort, and the car initially wasn't a hit. Even at that low price. Indians loved their two-wheelers.

At first the thought of riding a two-wheeler in that deranged traffic was intimidating. I had ridden dirt bikes quite often as a youngster and adolescent, managing nearly to kill myself more times than Mom ever found out, but driving in Bhubaneswar looked exceptionally dangerous. Still, I was tempted one day when walking to the guesthouse and the company's two wheeler was sitting in front with the keys in it, just beckoning me to ride. On impulse, I jumped on, kicked it over and, with the security guards pointing and smirking, I eased into traffic and sputtered away down the road.

Surprising myself by still being alive after a mile, I kept going. The engine was a 250cc four-stroke, so no land speed records were in danger of being broken; in fact, top speed was not much above fifty miles per hour, and the throttle was cranked when I reached the Daya River Bridge, where traffic thinned out. I had left the greasy, worn-out and possibly mange-infected community-shared helmet back at the house, so with wind through my hair and bugs in my teeth, I motored down the highway.

Cruising for a while and halfway to Puri Beach and the Bay of Bengal, I reached the town of Pipili. I had been here once before with Vihaan and his wife when they were buying wedding gifts for relatives. The town was known for its handicrafts and had displayed on both sides of the main road brilliantly decorated clothes, blankets and other goods. Bright reds and whites were the popular colors, but all colors of the spectrum were in view. It was a bright contrast to the drab green trees, brown patches of dirt and grubby shanties that were the usual scene on either side of the pavement. From one end of the town to the other, I slowed and put-putted through waves of color.

With the sun up high and figuring it wasn't much further to Puri Beach, I kept my little two-wheeler pointed in that direction. Stopping once alongside the road for a Fanta Orange, I inquired from the gawking locals the distance to Puri. I received much pointing and gesturing in the direction I was heading, but the distance remained a mystery. No matter, I knew it was not far, and before long I came to the city by the sea. Not knowing how to negotiate through town to the beach, I had to stop at several police checkpoints before catching the smell of ocean. Then the wide blue expanse of the Bay of Bengal opened up before me.

Stopping at the curb on the beachfront road, where several other two-wheelers were parked, I stepped off, took the key and walked down the steps. Pulling off my socks and shoes and rolling up the cuff of my cargo pants, I hit the lonely beach; it was mid-afternoon on a weekday, and there were not that many people about. I didn't see one swimsuit and certainly no bikinis among the thin crowd. A few women were splashing around in their sarees and kurtas, but most of the beachcombers and all of the men present preferred to stay dry up on land, content simply to watch the ocean.

The tawny sand was clean by India standards, and the ocean was active, having frisky four-to-five-foot waves. In case I never made it back to Puri, I wanted to at least walk in the surf and be able to say I'd been in the Bay of Bengal. The waves looked too menacing for a casual swim—the potential for riptides was high and, without a swimsuit or place to shower off, it would not have been a good idea. Far up the beach, too far for my ambition in the wilting heat, I spotted a few beached fishing boats, but that was all. It was mostly deserted although I assumed at evening, away from the hot sun, people would come to enjoy it in droves.

I had read that a killer cyclone hit Puri in 1999, killing over ten thousand people, millions of livestock and causing billions of dollars' worth of damage; it was the strongest tropical cyclone ever recorded in the North Indian Ocean up to that time. The International Red Cross was prepared to send substantial monetary help from its Disaster Relief Fund to India, but in what could be categorized as government incompetence or, at the least, government disconnect, the Indian government refused the money, saying the cyclone was not a national disaster. Many people died of starvation and disease after the storm.

Satisfied with my impulsive solo beach foray, I headed back to the two-wheeler and, after a few wrong turns, drove out of Puri. Returning back the way I had come, through Pipili and its roadside colors, I neared the Daya River and noticed a paved trail on top of the dike paralleling the large stream that other two-wheeler traffic were using. Curious, I braked at the end of the bridge and drove off the road and down the steep embankment to see where it led.

The trail was just wide enough for two converging motorcycles to meet and not slice into each other. Still, when meeting the shocked and wide-eyed local riders, I slowed way down, stopping at times. My knee felt achingly vulnerable sticking out into their oncoming front wheels, and I inched off the narrow path as far as possible without tumbling down the twenty-foot dike to the river.

Passing little mud-hut villages along the way, I drove until abeam Dhauli Hills. Stopping under one of the many trees that lined the trail, I dismounted to take in the sights and snap a few photos. Directly across were the concrete steps where Anika and I had cooled our feet days before, and towering over it was the brilliant white pagoda. The riverbed was a half-mile wide there, though most of it was exposed sand at the time. It was a little late in the day for proper drying, but I saw a group of women doing laundry in the silty water. Showing good sense, they were upstream from a large herd of buffalo cooling off from the afternoon sun, the water up to their black, furry shoulders.

While the other two-wheeler traffic kept buzzing along the trail, a man around forty-years old, with glasses thick as Coke bottles and riding his own Honda, pulled up and stopped, glaring at me like I had stolen his last bajji snacks. With a brief wave, I said, "Namaste!"

He didn't return my greeting. His magnified eyes just stared back at me, and then suspiciously looked back the way he had come and the way he had been going.

I wondered if this was the riverbank where I would lose my liver or some other mandatory body organ.

I tried to return attention to my photography, but any sense of comfort had disappeared. It was hard to ignore his gawking up there on the path while I was a few feet below crouched in the gravel. Minutes went by with me trying to appear casual and him attempting to clear his sinuses and throat with loud snorting and hacking. The sound echoed off the water as he spat something out that sounded like an egg being dropped on concrete.

Finally, I heard him start his engine and watched as he drove away, glancing over his shoulder at me one final time before shifting into second gear and accelerating. My warm and fuzzy tranquil riverbank reverie busted, and assuming he went off to see who of his mates needed a fresh kidney, I climbed back up to my Honda and hastily began kicking it over to start. It did not.

Setting my camera in the crook of a nearby tree, I fiddled with the key switch, checked the gas tank and choke, but still no start. Getting desperate, I reached for the spark plug wire and it fell away with just a brush of my hand. Somehow the loose wire had provided sufficient spark to the plug over the many miles I had rode it, but there on the isolated river bank, with my future in suspected jeopardy, it would go no further. I slipped it back over the spark plug, pressing it on until I heard and felt it snap satisfyingly into place. I feared the engine was then flooded, but after four kicks it popped off, idled roughly a few seconds, and then I was shifting through the gears back to the main road, relief in my wake.

I was racing along, glad to be mobile and becoming absorbed with the many other sights along the river, when Gawker Guy came roaring up behind me, blowing his horn and shouting. Startled, and all but launching myself off the dike into the river, I glanced back to see him waving something in the air, and it did not look to be a weapon. I braked, and he pulled up beside me. Staring at me with no expression through the thick binocular-like glasses perched on his nose, he handed over my camera that I had left in the crook of the tree.

On my eventual return to Bhubaneswar, I rode directly to the hangar. Earlier, Mahesh had informed me that there would be a celebration in store. A DGCA officer had given the company hangar and operations offices an annual inspection and spot check, and according to Mahesh, we passed with flying colors. The man was pleased with what he saw in our dark and damp hangar and gave us a clean bill of health.

"Perhaps," I suggested, "the officer might've needed his vision checked?"

My comrades and colleagues, never short on excuses to throw a party, thought that getting a satisfactory review during a spot check warranted just such frivolity, and no time was wasted in breaking out the whiskey. Enough whiskey, it was emphatically decided, did not exist at the hangar, so two of the lower-ranking chaps were dispatched on the two-wheeler I recently returned to fetch more. It was a two-man job, one man to hold the bottles of booze and give road directions, and the other chap to drive and give directions on holding the booze.

However, torture and death were considered appropriate retribution when they found that I had returned the two-wheeler with an empty fuel tank. Babeesh and the others glared and grumbled under their breath, probably determining where best to dispose of my body. One sneering dude was holding a shovel.

Reprieve was only awarded after BK gave a more accurate reading of the tank's quantity. He determined that, indeed, there was sufficient fuel for the short drive to the gas station, and my empty-gas-tank-of-a-life was spared.

That cataclysmic problem solved, loud and distorted Bollywood music was cranked up and immediately sung along to. The first glass of whiskey into Babeesh launched him onto the hangar floor, dancing with himself to the hoots and cheers of his colleagues. It wasn't long before others joined him in the all-male dance-a-thon.

Wild kicks, arm swings and fist pumping accompanied by streams of screams, screeches and squealing was the most popular way to boogie. Even though great skill and mastery of complex dance moves was most unnecessary, I was content to relax and sip whiskey. Regardless of my friends' chiding, the dancing was too aggressive and gender biased for me. Someone was going to get hurt.

27.

Cold Milk

In our distant corner of the airport, another expat helicopter pilot, Rodrigo from the Philippines, flew a Robinson R44 for a mining company out of the neighboring hangar. There were several mining companies in Bhubaneswar, but ours were the only two that had helicopters and an aviation department. He was at the end of a two-year contract with his company but had just signed an extension worth more money. On a rainy afternoon, he invited me over to celebrate and "hangar-fly." Beer was mentioned.

He also had the study material for my upcoming DGCA Air Law exam, which I needed to borrow if I was to have any chance of passing. The questions were notoriously tough, and more than a few expat pilots had to re-test after failing it the first time. I wanted to get in, get out, be done and never have to go back.

As a former Astar pilot himself, Rodrigo was amazed when I showed him the photos of the bullet damage done to my tail-rotor driveshaft back in Kistaram. Like many others, he was astonished that it hadn't snapped into two pieces. He slapped me on the back and said, "*You* are a lucky man!"

"I know it," I said. "Every time I glance at those pictures, I think how close to broiled worm food I was."

"Do you carry a horse shoe in your flight kit?" he asked. "You should have it gold plated."

Several days later, with my company's typical indifferent attitude toward scheduling and preparedness, they informed me two hours before the flight that I would be heading to Delhi for the exam. I knew the day was coming at some point, but again, at least a half-day's notice would have been nice. While rushing to the airport, I called Anika and told her the news. We had evening dinner plans at one of the expensive restaurants she preferred. Unperturbed, she told me just to call when I returned and hung up.

One positive aspect of the Delhi trip was that I would save money. Although I didn't mind going to the new Pizza Hut in Bhubaneswar, Anika enjoyed a higher degree of maintenance and required slightly more sophisticated trappings. She was always insistent on something romantic, and it was usually a restaurant at one of the classier hotels with candlelight, wine and a hefty tab. I enjoyed the romance and wine, the drain on my wallet not so much.

Being a tad high maintenance myself, I was disappointed when the head office tightened their purse strings and did not offer to put me in the airport hotel; it was back to the skeevy company guesthouse for the duration while in Delhi. I thought it a good omen, though, when the driver who picked me up from the airport in the evening wasn't inebriated, but traffic was its usual stop and go. By the time he dropped me off at the front door I was feeling surly and ready for a little inebriation myself. Dumping my gear on the bed, I reminded the houseboy about breakfast in the morning and walked to Bennigan's Bar. Later, with one beer in my belly, another on the way and an order of chicken wings on the table in front of me, my mood had improved tenfold.

It was a couple of days before the exam, giving me time to study the test material. Rodrigo told me that some of the questions were common sense and based on similar regulations to the rest of the world, but there were others that were India-specific. He said about half did not make sense at all unless you'd specifically read the question in the study material. Either way, I felt confident and looked forward to getting it over with. During the days, I studied and listened alternately to the pigeons cooing, the monkeys squealing, dogs barking and the laundry woman's tied-up kid wailing. But happy hour would find me at Bennigan's, drinking cold beer and eating hot wings, being ignored by pretty office-working women who had finished for the day.

When the day of the exam arrived, Sami and I drove to the DGCA headquarters at nine in the morning, but it wasn't until after one o'clock that I was able to sit down and start answering questions. My stomach was grumbling from lack of lunch. A samosa graciously given me by Sami did little to help and made my mouth taste crappy. As Rodrigo had said, about half the exam read like FAA questions, but there were many that were oddly phrased and hard to decipher. I finished and, feeling a lot less confident than before, grumpily went looking for something to eat. There was a decrepit old snack machine on the first floor that I wanted to raid. Sami stayed to receive my test results.

Finding me outside with my nose inside a bag of potato chips, he said, "Good news, Captaaiin, you passed!"

"That's a relief," I said, brushing crumbs off my cheek. "A few of the questions were hard to figure out."

"Oh yeah? Well you should've left those blank, Mike. The exam proctor was to fill in the correct answer for you anyway."

"...What? Are you kidding me?"

Sami just grinned like a mule eating briars.

The India Ministry of Tourism had an advertising slogan at the time, *Incredible India*. Experiencing the country's many vagaries, at least once a day I felt like shouting, "Incredible India!"

A flight to Bhubaneswar could not be arranged quickly enough for that day, so the day after, I packed my bags for a late afternoon takeoff. But, before leaving for the airport, I was concerned about dinner and—heaven forbid—the chance that I would miss it; asking the houseboy to fry up a quick omelet in the rat condo kitchen, I then washed it down with a quarter-liter of milk.

Another habit I found odd about the Indian diet was that they always drank their milk hot. Not warm, but tongue-scalding hot. Not knowing any better, I thought that was absurd and always insisted that my milk be cool, the colder the better, and had already drank it that way many times.

On the way to the airport, again stop and go through the rush hour traffic, I started feeling a little unease in my stomach. Eating hurriedly and then having the bumpy, uncomfortable car ride was the likely instigation, I thought. Perhaps I would feel better once my feet were on the ground at the airport.

Once there, however, the intestinal unease did not go away. While I checked into the flight, my stomach started making noises that were not normal, and I felt bloated. Since my flight required extra time to ride the shuttle bus to the airplane, we were called to board early, and while waiting in line at my gate number, something was growing quite discontent behind my belly button. I felt flushed and clammy, more sweaty than usual. I needed to spend quality time at the nearest toilet, but missing my flight was not an option.

Going through the cattle chute to board the cracker box of a bus and out to the waiting 737, I reflexively placed a hand over my stomach in a pregnant woman's protective pose. I didn't want anything or anyone to bump it, even slightly. With the other space-robbing passengers' body odor filling my nostrils along the way, I was ready to pry open the doors and jump in front of the next oncoming bus.

Arriving at the aircraft, the heat from the tarmac made me light headed, and I just wanted to board quickly, takeoff and lock myself in the bathroom. By the time all passengers were seated, my gut was distended and still growing. Removing my belt helped a little, but buckling up the seat belt took concentration. I didn't want even the slightest pressure on the deleterious alien spawn apparently growing within my belly.

I knew something was wrong but figured that, if I could just survive the two-hour flight to Bhubaneswar, all would be okay. After taking off and climbing, I was way too early in unbuckling my seat belt and stumbling to the lavatory. Perhaps I looked like death warmed over, for at first the air hostesses appeared ready to sit me back down, but upon seeing my ashen but determined face and purposeful locomotion down the aisle, they closed their mouths and stifled orders of, "Get back to your seat!"

They glanced at each other, seemingly ready to help, and their stern authoritarian scowls melted to those of motherly concern. I think one reached for a defibrillator. *Maybe they'd divert the plane*, I thought. Regardless, nothing or nobody was stopping me from availing the lavatory.

Transcendent relief was had there. Physically I was still seated on that cramped airline one-holer, but the momentary easing put me in another dimension, a near-meditative state, or possibly vegetative. The pain returned with vision-blurring vengeance, however, when taking my seat once again. I felt likely to explode. Dizzy and clutching the armrests with splayed fingers whenever a spasm or cramp gripped me, time slowed to a crawl.

The captain's call for descent was like angels singing when it came, but it was followed by a lengthy weather hold, and we circled the airport for another twenty-five grueling minutes. We finally landed and taxied to the ramp, but the ordeal was far from over.

In most parts of the world, politeness is observed when disembarking a plane by letting the passengers seated in front of you off first in a relatively calm and orderly manner. Not so in India. Even when the airplane is still rolling to parking, against the futile objections of air hostesses, passengers are in the overhead bins gathering their bags, and a few are inching toward the exit. And when the aircraft comes to a complete halt, it's a free-for-all. Passengers jam the aisle, pushing their way to the door.

Negotiating my way out from the seat about halfway through this stampede, I joined the herd and gripping the railing tightly, inched down the airstairs—no skybridge in Bhubaneswar—into the evening breeze. Walking from the plane to the terminal without any accidents was a challenge.

It was one of my worst cases of food poisoning ever, one which will be remembered to the end. Lying there bedridden, seemingly helpless, I even had my pallbearers picked out. And they would've had an easy lift as my body was nearly shriveled to nothing. Once more, I was either on the toilet or on my bed and could not eat normally for days, and then just an ice-cream-only diet.

Further investigation revealed from my mates that the milk I had drunk was raw and unpasteurized and that it was more than likely buffalo or goat milk. Divulging that I prefer my milk cold, they looked at me as if I needed fitting for a straightjacket.

Vihaan shook his head quite disappointedly and said, "You must never drink cold, untreated milk. People die from such foolishness!"

Okay, boil that milk.

28.

Red Planet

The chairman was the biggest of my big bosses. He had founded the company in the early 1990s and built it into a large, successful family-run business with his wife and two daughters. A war veteran, he flew jet fighters against Pakistan back during one of the Indo-Pakistani wars but, choosing to discharge out of the military, had pursued his fortune in business and construction. He was a Yale graduate and had been a classmate of Senator, then Secretary of State, John Kerry, a fact that he felt should be mentioned occasionally.

His main office was in Mumbai, but from time to time he would visit his interests in Odisha. He had come to Bhubaneswar with the intent to fly to one of his iron ore mines. The mine was near Barbil, 120 miles northwest up in the hills, and flying direct, our flight path would take us across Charbatia Air Force Base—if they'd let us fly through. Early-morning attempts to receive permission to cross were unsuccessful. Besides the normal FIC/ADC, an additional authorization was required before entering their airspace. It turned out to be only a minor problem for the unusually enthusiastic Mahesh, who was on the job and able to sort it out with only a brief delay.

I met the chairman at the airport VIP lounge, where he shook my hand, smiled and said, "Ahh, Captain Mike, it is nice to finally meet you. I have heard many good things."

What good things he would have heard, I had no idea. The only noteworthy act I had done in India up to that point was nearly getting blown out of the sky and converting his million-dollar helicopter into a smoldering heap. He was laid back and relaxed while we walked through the airport lounge and then the security checkpoint; chatting nonstop, he inquired about me, my family and background. A gentleman, he listened to what I said and, although it was just small talk, nodded intently as if my tedious life was a captivating story.

Our operations department had come through with a win and provided a shuttle car for us from the terminal to our distant helicopter. BK had completed the refueling and was looking busy and engaged for the big man as we pulled up, wiping down the already clean tailboom and hustling to carry the luggage with his all-business facial expression.

"For what reason did you park so far away, Captain?" the chairman laughed. "You're on the other side of the city!"

"Well, sir, that's where ATC parks me."

"Mike, Mike," he said, shaking his head, "Indians like to deal. You have to negotiate with them, and they expect it. They inherently want to debate."

"I'm beginning to realize that," I said, "but I didn't want to cause too much of a fuss and be escorted off the ramp by gunpoint."

As we approached our helicopter, the temperature was warming up, but it was still morning, so the Indian blast furnace had a few hours before it reached maximum smelting temperature. His two male assistants climbed in back. Then, saying he had not been in the front end of a helicopter for a long time, he climbed into the copilot's seat and watched my start-up procedures with great interest, knifing in a question when he could. Once fired up and with the idle stabilized, I gave a thumbs-up to the stern-looking BK and, after dismissing the fire-watch, he climbed aboard and we were able to get down to business.

The flight to Barbil took a little more than an hour, and it was a comfortable flight; due to the time of day the sun was behind us, and at four thousand feet the temperature was tame, cool even. The chairman chatted pleasantly on the intercom, usually over the top of a radio transmission from ATC, but not in a bothersome way. He told me, among many other things, a war story about his mission to bomb a dam somewhere in Pakistan.

He said he had been low level amongst hills to avoid radar, but then, flying over a rise in the terrain, had come head to head with point blank anti-aircraft fire. He saw the puffs of smoke from the guns and didn't know how the enemy had missed him at such close range. I asked if he found his target.

"Bombed the shit out of it," he said, in what was the first and last time I heard him use rough language.

Barbil was easy to spot. A red dust cloud rose up over the town and the nearby iron ore mine, and it could be seen from many miles away. Our Astar was equipped with a sand filter, and I engaged it to avoid damaging our engine while we flew over both the gaping maw of the strip mine and the hundreds of Tata ten-wheel trucks hauling the ore. Not much that we saw resembled organization or orderliness. The once-green hills were being blasted apart and hauled away, truck by truck. What trees and flora remained were covered with fine red dust. It was one of the most aesthetically deficient scenes I had come across.

Landing at the small airstrip at the foot of the mine, there was a brightly colored mob of people to welcome us. Flowers and cheers were given and an oversize wreath of blossoms was hung around the chairman's neck. It looked to weigh about twenty pounds and was quite similar to what was given to the equine winner of the Kentucky Derby. The local citizens adored the man and, after a short speech, they whisked him away in a waiting SUV.

BK and I took our time tidying up the ship and making sure all covers were in place and on tight. With the amount of fine dust in the air, stirred up from iron ore trucks, it was imperative the covers were properly secured. It wouldn't take long for the abrasive grit to infiltrate somewhere it shouldn't be, say if an exhaust cover or pitot tube cover blew off. BK, ever the wise and grizzled veteran, had the first aid box out and was offering me a surgical mask to keep the dust out of my lungs. I gave him a wink and put it on.

Driving through the sad, red streets of Barbil from the airstrip to the guesthouse revealed numerous tire and truck repairs taking place along the crumbling road. Most all of the work was done outside in the weather because there were not sufficient garage structures to handle all the broken down rigs. Axles, radiators, tires and dismantled trucks were crammed into every open space. Men taking a break, covered in black grease and smoking cigarettes, sat on old truck parts and stared blankly at us as we drove past. The mechanics or drivers not on break were crawling around in the mud and dirt alongside the road, making adjustments or inspecting underneath their rigs. A few were wrestling with a stuck lug nut, trying to break it free with a five-foot length of pipe slipped over the wrench, the smaller man of the bunch jumping up and down on it in an exercise of roadside tire repair acrobatics. In one scene, the guts of an engine were laid out on a tarp while men surrounded it and stared, hands on hips, saying in the universal body language, "Now what?"

The chairman had remarked that we would all be staying at the same company guesthouse in town, and that it was a new building and comfortable, with all the modern amenities. Hearing that, I assumed the guesthouse would be in fairly mint condition, perhaps even a swimming pool. After all, he was a wealthy man in charge of a large company. I figured his taste in accommodations would lean toward the clean and bright edge of the spectrum. Pulling into the driveway, the main office building was quite modern and pleasing to the eye. Though it was remote and out in the sticks, the architects had made an attempt to add artistry to the building's lines with marble and glass. It was a diamond in the rough compared to its bleak surroundings and drab neighboring buildings.

The guesthouse was to the side and behind. Like the office building, it had four floors, but in appalling contrast were the heaps of trash and busted concrete surrounding it. Stray dogs were running amok and barking as we pulled up and climbed out of the car. The trash was shoulder height and stretched the entire width of the entrance stairs; it was difficult even to find an opening in the rubbish to access them. I looked at the bleak, paan-stained walls, and my hopes of decent digs disappeared.

Walking up the stairs to our third-floor guestrooms, we saw that the stairway and corridors were coated several times over with dried red spittle and trash; from chest height and down to the floor, the walls were covered all along with someone's nasty paan-juice expectorate. A new building it may have been, but its insolent inhabitants preferred a more apocalyptic motif. Incredible India.

Inside, our rooms were not so bad—spacious and comfortable, in fact. More importantly, clean. The windows and doors fit well, and I *assumed* there'd be no problems with mosquitoes. The bed felt of the right firmness and appeared new. I looked forward to the night, when I could enjoy a peaceful sleep away from the usual noise and hustle-and-bustle at our guesthouse in Bhubaneswar.

Two smiling lady cooks materialized and introducing themselves, then endeavored to practice dormant English skills; with much giggling and a short game of charades, we were able to agree on my brunch, some of which included iron-flavored local fruit. Then, with the day's heat in a race to the top of the thermometer, I grabbed my camera and ventured onto the dusty red streets. When perusing those photos later, a red hue caused by the iron ore dust clinging all around made it appear like I had been sent on a charter flight to Mars.

29.

Spiderman

The next day, the chairman had a meeting in Keonjhar, a small village about twenty minutes of flight time from Barbil. A mercifully short flight, for I'd had little sleep.

I hadn't been ambushed by mosquitos but, rather, by chiggers or some other type of evil vermin. They had kept me awake all night long. The evening before, the chairman had rounded up a few business big hitters from Barbil and invited BK and me along for an enjoyable evening in his flat, with whiskey at cocktail hour and wine with dinner. Figuring I needed my beauty sleep, I had excused myself at eleven, went up one floor to my room and hit the sack. But just as I was contentedly dozing off, the power failed and the air conditioner stopped.

Moments later, while lying there with no blanket or sheet covering me, the dirty little parasites found me and began their torment. So much for beauty sleep. The power stayed off the rest of the night, and it was an eternity before the eastern sky began to turn gray in my early morning torture chamber.

At Keonjhar, the chairman left us at its tiny little airstrip while he went to see to business in the nearby village. We were given a tasty lunch, possibly the best Indian food I'd had, and washed it down with sweet coffee from a generous security guard's thermos. Strolling after lunch, I examined the small runway and guessed that it was built by the iron and steel companies to help serve their interests in the region. There were numerous World War Two-era airstrips in India, but they each encompassed a lot more land with longer, wider runways. This airstrip did not appear large enough to handle any warbirds.

Beaten by the sun and heat, I retreated to the little concrete shack that made do as the jungle pilot lounge. Its windows were open to the steamy outdoor temperature, but the guards had plenty of electric fans to keep BK and me alive and merely on the verge of heat stroke. I even caught up on some sleep as an old, semi-clean cot in the corner met my tired stamp of approval for sleepy time. I woke up later just a little sore, but a lot cranky.

With his business concluded, the chairman arrived back at the helicopter in mid-afternoon. It was not the worst part of the day to fly, but during monsoon season we were guaranteed to see rain showers. At least the cloud cover gave a little protection from the sun. Still, with the chairman sitting next to me once again on the way back, it was more than warm. When he used his handkerchief to dab the sweat off his face for about the fourth time, I mentioned our need for air conditioning and, with a droplet of sweat dangling off the tip of his nose, he agreed.

Keonjhar was between Barbil and Bhubaneswar, and the flight back to base was short; deviating course two or three times for rain squalls, we then made our approach to the runway and taxied to our assigned parking area. Shutting down in front of the airport terminal and popping open the doors, steam from a recently passed rain shower rose off the tarmac and filled the cabin like I had landed at the hot springs in Yellowstone.

Part of the entourage awaiting us included a leggy and stunningly attractive young lady that I had not seen before. The chairman introduced her as Sabeena, his chatty and beaming new personal assistant. She wore a white short-sleeved blouse tailored snuggly around her plentiful chest, and from her slim waist down began a tight black skirt that was cut well above her knees and made her bare legs even longer. The high stilettos she wore had her almost eye level to me, and I thought she belonged in the Miss Universe pageant.

The chairman kept a home in Bhubaneswar and suggested we all get together at his house for drinks later. I did not object. While his group walked to the waiting SUV, I could not help myself, and kept stealing glances at the retreating figure of Sabeena. BK's eyes were big, and he cared nothing for *stealing* glances; his eyes were locked on her backside until she was in the car.

In stunted English, he said, "Mmmm, Cap'n, dat girl... ver' beaut'ful, hmm?"

"BK," I said, "Break out that first-aid kit again, I need medical attention."

Later, at the chairman's sprawling estate, several of us sat in the great room, getting acquainted and drinking wine before dinner. The gathering included Vihaan and his wife, four honchos from the company, the chairman, Sabeena and me. The chairman took down a framed picture from a shelf and asked me if I recognized anyone. I could see it was a photo from his Yale days and sure enough, there was a younger version of John Kerry alongside a dapper and youthful Indian man, our chairman.

Vihaan and his wife did not drink, but the chairman insisted that they do so, asking several times. Each time, Vihaan would politely decline, saying the fruit juice they had was fine. With a bizarre sense of logic, the chairman said, "It's been my experience that the best pilots are the ones that aren't afraid to drink. I remember a time..."

Then he launched into war stories that invariably involved alcohol. I drank more than my share, though Chuck Yeager or Chuck Aaron I was not, and figured the quantity of nip had no correlation whatsoever to flying abilities. But if a study were to be done, I could be swayed to volunteer.

Sabeena was single, about thirty and had recently resigned from her position as an air hostess at Kingfisher Airlines. She was an outgoing woman with a gorgeous, engaging smile and, for the evening, she had changed into a Western-style V-necked pink top and designer blue jeans, a style of dress quite popular in Mumbai for sure, but seen only occasionally in Bhubaneswar and never in the backwater of Jagdalpur. With her beauty, it was like I was blind and suddenly could see.

She was staying at one of the vacant rooms at our guesthouse for the evening and flying out on Air India with the chairman in the morning. When we returned there from the chairman's house, Vihaan drove with his wife next to him, and I sat in heaven, sharing the backseat with Sabeena. Her perfume was a hypnotic musk and, combined with the wine, it compelled me to say all sorts of silliness during the drive.

Arriving at the guesthouse, Vihaan and his wife claimed tiredness and had gone to their room, calling it a night. Sabeena and I decided we needed a nightcap. We found a cold bottle of beer in the refrigerator and, grabbing a couple of glasses, we giggled our way up to the roof. We were already half in the bag from wine at dinner and forgot the bottle opener in the kitchen. We were laughing a little uncontrollably, trying to improvise a way to get the beer open. Finding the correct angle on a piece of metal in a window frame, I knocked off the cap to vigorous cheering and applause.

The guesthouse rooftop, by day, could not have been less romantic. Huge swaths of paint missing, unfinished concrete work, the noisy street below and line after line of hanging laundry made for a dismal, if not depressing, scene. But after dark when the noisy traffic died down, it could have been the Eiffel Tower, if one was distracted properly.

The beer gone and the hour creeping toward midnight, I walked Sabeena to her door and bid her good night, wishing her "Safe travels on the morrow."

Then, feeling a little buzzed, I determined the best thing for that was a smoke before bedtime. Searching my room for cigarettes turned up nothing, though, so grabbing a handful of rupees, I went downstairs to the front door for a quick dash to the shop. It was late, so late that the security guard had the iron gate in the wall surrounding the building closed and locked. I tried to explain to the guard that I needed to go to the shop for a pack of Gold Flake ciggies.

He seemed to think that walking the streets at that late hour was a foolish idea and didn't want to open the gate. Banda, the cook, happened to be awake and roaming around the building for some mysterious reason; he understood little English but more than the guard and, noticing my pleas for freedom, ventured over to see if he could help. After a little back and forth between him and the guard, he informed me that the gate wasn't to be opened. "Poe'licy by da company, saa," he said.

It smelled like BS to me. Looking at the guard, I reckoned he may have been the chap I water-bombed all those nights ago. *Okay, guard dude*, I thought. *Revenge, is it?*

Feeling like a prisoner, I climbed the stairs back to my room, but once reaching the third floor noticed the open windows in the small lounge area directly across from the kitchen. Glancing out and below, I could see Banda and the security guard. They looked to be enjoying the moment, talking and laughing, pointing at the gate and wall. I was directly above them and noticed that, the way the building was constructed, someone like me might have been able to shimmy down the multi-angled concrete facade floor by floor. Then, to reach outside the gate, swing from my arms just a bit and hurl myself off the first floor overhang to the patch of concrete at street level.

Without further thought of repercussions or death, and feeling escape was possible, I slipped out the window and quietly did my Spiderman impression down the front of the building. Although there were street lights dimly burning, I remained in the shadows due to the various building ledges and columns. My climbing surface was dry, and I had no problem climbing down to the point where I would have to execute my swing-and-jump trick.

Reaching the first floor eave, I gripped my hand hold and eased my body out into space. Hanging from my arms, I glanced at Banda and the guard. They had not noticed me and were preoccupied, jabbering away about the slick move they had just put over on the pilot. I focused on my landing zone, swung once and back. Then, seeing that I had plenty of momentum on the second swing, launched into a short six-foot plummet while releasing my breath in a screaming, blood curdling, demented Tarzan howl. Hitting the ground and crawling, half hidden behind a concrete column that supported the front gate, I continued my shrieking until my lungs were emptied.

Banda started shrieking himself and his eyes were saucer-shaped. The security guard, who had his back to me and was facing inwards toward Banda, pushed the little cook halfway through the narrow doorway into the building. Getting their legs tangled, they tripped and went down. The guard ended up on top of Banda in a howling, shouting flurry of ankles and elbows.

I peeked around the corner of the gate and shouted, "Blow your whistle now, fucker!"

The guard, up on all fours and looking back at me with fire in his eyes, returned my insult with plenty of his own in Hindi. Banda was lying in the doorway still shouting and moaning along with genuine crying. His faded gray trousers showed a wet spot in the crotch, and I felt sorry for him—later. Right then, both of them scrabbling around in the doorway was the funniest damned thing I had seen in a while, and could not stop laughing.

I turned and jogged off a ways, not wanting to be within blast range of the guard's twelve-gauge shotgun, and laughed to myself while walking to the shop. I giggled so hard that tears came to my eyes. The streets were deserted, luckily. If someone would have seen me in that condition, they would have thrown me in the looney bin. It was hard to compose myself, even when reaching the shop; giggling like a fool, I spluttered out my order for a pack of smokes while the shopkeeper eyed me warily, surely thinking this strange white man was off his medications. I was still beyond control when walking outside and lighting up, chuckling through my first cigarette.

A realization eventually hit me that I had to return to the guesthouse, though, where an excitable man held a weapon, and where most of my daily meals were served.

Ahh, but it was worth it!

30.

Bossus Interruptus

A lazy Saturday morning and Anika persuaded me that it would be an endeavor of great consequence for us to head to the local zoo. Twelve miles out of Bhubaneswar, the Nandankanan Zoo and Botanical Gardens maintained seventeen hundred animals on a thousand-acre spread, and according to a news article, the zoo's death rate was one of the lowest in India. A positive, I guess, but mentioning death rates and zoos in the same sentence was probably not the best way to promote it. Perhaps announcing birth rates would have been a better idea. I hoped the caged critters were dying from old age and not neglect, but given the general indifference of the populace toward animals other than cattle, I was not optimistic in that regard.

It was full-on monsoon season, but the morning was bright and sunny. There were only a few cumulus clouds floating about and giving little protection from the sun, which seemed intent on melting all solid matter in the vicinity. If the sun wouldn't melt us, then the humidity would surely force every bit of moisture from our pores. As Anika parked and we stepped out, a trickle of sweat was already forming on my brow. She was dressed Indian style, with yellow pajama bottoms and a light-green kurta top with matching dupatta. The latter she placed over her black hair for protection from the sun's rays. I had on my well-worn, million-mile olive drab cargo pants and a faded, short-sleeve light plaid button down. I would have favored cargo shorts, but only wore those around the house. Bare legs were rare—I saw them only once or twice when backpacking Europeans had come through, never from an Indian in the Bhubaneswar public.

At the entrance gate, there was an elderly, gray-haired beggar woman that looked in quite poor condition. She was on her knees and bowing to the ground, with her hands held together around the collection cup in front of her. Most visitors walked past, but Anika bent down to her, saying gentle words and dropped in fifty rupees. I wondered if the government would see to her welfare, but Anika said there were not many services like that and the elderly woman and folks like her had to fend for themselves.

It was a sprawling place, and there was a lot of ground to cover in one day while enduring the tropical heat, but there were many unique animals to see, and the place was especially abundant with tigers. Also inside the zoo grounds was a 150-acre lake filled with lotus flowers. Renting a little paddle boat, we cruised around and through the giant floating green pads for almost half an hour; Anika, playing the diva, claimed heat exhaustion and tiredness ten minutes into the voyage, which left me as the sole source of propulsion. She was not too tired or shy about barking out orders, though, and more than once was in danger of being sent into the green water and keel-hauled. Occasionally a slow breeze would catch us, giving a little push, and that cool breeze was a gentle reminder of heaven.

After returning the boat, we relaxed in the shade overlooking the water on an old wooden bench that was missing one front leg. It had to be balanced just right or we would teeter over onto our knees. But it was the only shady spot available, so wobbling a tad, we guzzled bottled water and watched grimy, threadbare kids fishing with long cane poles. Every now and then, they would pull in a little four-or-five-inch sliver of a fish and, shouting their triumph, would raise it into the air like they were at the Bassmaster Classic.

Cooling off a bit in the shade, Anika and I were only halfway through seeing the animals, but we were scorched and decided to come back and finish another day. My clothes were already soaked with sweat, but Anika looked fresh as a spring flower—though at times she whined like the winter wind.

"How about a swim?" I asked and pretended like I would throw her in the lake. Her eyes flashing with brilliance, she half giggled, half screamed, and ran off a few steps.

Then she turned, squirted the bottle of water into my face and chest and shouted, "You know you should shower first before swimming!"

The other zoo visitors stared while we chased each other with water bottles; they didn't know what to think of this foreigner and Indian girl. By the looks on their faces, they did not approve. That type of behavior in India, if it did occur, usually would only take place between people of the same gender. Indeed, if you happened to notice two people walking and holding hands, they were most assuredly of the same sex. Flirting, the way we had been, was rare. Perhaps in larger cities it happened more, but not there. Anika was a free spirit. She didn't care what people thought, being more self-possessed and unfettered about such perplexities compared to her compatriots.

Getting each other soaked and out of breath, we tossed our empty water bottles in the trash bin and hatched a plan. We'd had enough sunshine for one day and planned to hit the video store, rent a couple James Bond movies, then go back to her apartment and cool off.

Giving me a sideways glance, she said, "I have a bottle of wine chilling in my refrigerator, Captain..."

"Fantastic! That was a great year for wine!" I said.

"But, I didn't tell you the vintage."

"Still, it's perfect."

"You're a strange man," she said. "If you behave, I might share it with you."

"I'll behave, you always bring out the best of me."

"Oh, is this your best?"

A few hours later, relaxed and in a near-meditative state, I could see Daniel Craig's lips moving, but he wasn't saying anything. What came out of the TV speakers was an excited, high-pitched Hindi voice that began after Bond's mouth was already moving and still rattled on after his mouth was closed.

The disembodied Indian language was not a problem, though, as the pirated DVD provided English subtitles.

We were relaxing on Anika's couch in the cool, air-conditioned breeze. After leaving the zoo, we stopped at Café Coffee Day for lunch, then walked to the video shop to peruse the dusty new videos on display. The shopkeeper was eager to offer us the latest two Bond films with the blue-eyed Daniel Craig as Bond.

Pointing and grinning at my blue eyes, the shopkeeper said, "You, saa? You are James Bond, yes?"

"Ahh, no," I chuckled, pointing at an adjacent DVD cover. "More like this guy, Johnny English."

"Oh yeah!" Anika chimed in. "That is more your style for sure!"

My clothes had been drying nicely in her chilled apartment air, and the wine was indeed *fantastic*. Anika was considering dinner later on at one of her favorite restaurants, and I was considering my wallet, the short supply of funds within, and how to persuade her to consider more inexpensive eatery alternatives without putting a damper on the evening.

Negotiations were going smoothly between us until I got a call from Delhi and Mr. Bad Timing, Sami. He told me to drop anything I was doing to start planning and making preparations for a flight to Jagdalpur and four further landing zones the next morning.

"Captaaiin!" he shouted. "We're still setting it up on this end, and there's more information to come."

"Hey, that's great news," I lied, and hoped that it didn't come out sarcastically. "Do you have the coordinates for..."

"I'll get back to you, bro!"

Click!

The line was cut, and Sami was gone in a cloud of dashed evening expectations.

Reluctantly, I broke the news to Anika that I needed to get back to the guesthouse for my flight planning materials and GPS. Looking at her from the front of the TV where I had placed my phone, she was draped over the couch like a supermodel at a photo shoot. Lying on her side with her long legs bent at the knees, she had one hand holding up her head and the other resting on her curved bottom. Her long black hair was hanging over the arm of the couch and the V-neck material on her top was drooping slightly, revealing the tops of exquisite, caramel-colored breasts. Her dark, heavily mascaraed eyes smiled back and she quietly asked, "Do you have to leave right now?"

As it turned out, I did not have to hurry straightaway.

Sami had me wait until ten p.m. before I received the final details: fly from Bhubaneswar to Jagdalpur, then from Jagdalpur to a village named Gadchiroli, which was west of Chhattisgarh in the state of Maharashtra. This was out of our normal area of operations and in unfamiliar country, where we had never flown before. And still a dangerous region. Gadchiroli was the sight of an ambush that had killed sixteen IPS, five of them women, a few weeks prior, and intelligence showed that Maoist-Naxalites may have been moving more personnel into the area.

Several IPS top honchos were having a meeting there and desired an aerial overlook of the combat zone, while even hoping to see the enemy from our roving observatory in the sky. Knowing Sami, he probably said and promised whatever the customer needed to hear in order for them to approve the flight. I'm sure he overstated our ability to spot any movement and set their expectations high for the reconnaissance in terms of what they could see from our helicopter.

Good luck with that, I thought. *Not a snowball's chance in Bombay will we see anyone through that jungle canopy from four thousand feet.*

I had the earliest possible takeoff time from Bhubaneswar determined, but many of the other timings and fuel requirements were unclear. I talked to BK and told him to make sure my fuel tank was full by departure time. What fuel I required from Jagdalpur would have to be determined upon reaching there. I had rough, unconfirmed coordinates for Gadchiroli, and once those were verified for certain in the morning, I could figure my fuel calculations and add accordingly.

Weather was a concern, and I was awake past midnight checking and rechecking diversion routes and safe diversion helipads. Later, sleep was elusive. New landing zones, unfamiliar territory, fuel worries and the monsoon weather were all weighing on my mind until morning, when my already-awake self slapped off the five o'clock alarm. I was heading back to Maoist-Naxalite territory, and those fuckers wanted to kill me.

31.

Joyriding Rainman

The body odor funk in our hangar was particularly revolting in the overcast and misty monsoon morning. I wasn't sure who the smelly bandito was, and it may have been multiple banditos—B.O. banditos. The odoriferous assault made me want to get off the ground and into the breeze posthaste, but Mahesh was still working out a delay obtaining FIC/ADC for our flight to Jagdalpur, and I was trying to receive a reliable weather report from our IPS contact there. The guy was being way too apathetic with his weather prognosis.

"Yes... Cap'n," he mumbled. "Da skies are clear 'f weatha'... You kin fly."

Then he realized that I realized that he was full of shit and, thinking it was better to be noncommittal, he said, "D'ere are clouds and d'ere is sunshine... rain has stopped... for now."

With that I knew the guy was still in bed, probably even had his eyes closed. I hung up and decided to launch anyway, telling Mahesh and the rest not to disappear from the hangar. If the weather showed the slightest tendency of blocking me in, I would return.

I always started my preflights by switching on the battery and checking fuel quantity. To my early-morning surprise, I saw that the fuel was only at seventy-five percent, not full like I had requested. In that model of Astar, the fuel gauge was read in percentage, and I had planned to arrive at my destination with about twenty percent remaining in the tank. That's normally plenty of reserve fuel. If it was a short flight with good weather, I might plan for less, but if it was a longer flight with uncertain weather, I would plan for more reserve. Monsoon season in the hills of India patently qualified for uncertain weather, and I wanted all that could be sloshed into the tank for the unforeseen diversions. To save time, BK had said he would have my fuel topped off from the extra fuel barrels we kept at the hangar.

"What gives BK?" I asked. "I need more fuel."

"Yes saa, fuel pump defective, saa," he smiled innocently. "More fuel needed at airport ramp."

"BK, buddy, you're killing me. That's gonna put us an hour behind schedule." Sleeplessness was making me cranky, "You should've called me as soon as you discovered the problem, bhaiya."

I did the calculations. On a clear summer day, we could have made it there by a hair with the fuel we had aboard, but in monsoon season, with its assurance of fickle weather, we were a no-go without more fuel. There went an hour, or more if the fuel truck was engaged. I hadn't cranked the starter yet and already had to call for a delay.

Repositioning to the ramp just to refuel sounds easy enough, and it would be at most airports in most countries. With Indian regulations, and especially with our hangar position, it was a discombobulation. The real drag started after the twenty-minute repositioning exercise and refueling request.

Showing no sense of logic, AAI policy required the pilot and engineer/crew chief to go through the passenger security check inside the airport, even when we had no passengers. To walk inside, we had to show the security guard at the terminal doors our already screened and vetted official DGCA *Airport Security Pass*. Once through the doors, we would find the end of the line that passengers were waiting in to go through the security screening. Through that, we again would have to show our airport pass to the same security guard at the same doors and then head back out to our aircraft, *which we had just arrived in*. We were only getting fuel. Why the hell go inside the terminal when we had no passengers waiting there?

Easily an hour was shot to refuel. All that time, the phone stuck to my head like some rectangular growth. FIC/ADC, the tower, and of course, the boss, calling every ten minutes to check our progress and hurry us along.

By the time we were cleared, the weather had deteriorated, and I had to request Special Visual Flight Rules (SVFR) in order to depart. There were spotty patches of rain in the area, and the visibility was low, but just good enough to carry on with our journey to Jagdalpur. The arid hills, mountains and valleys that we had flown over a few months prior were now cloaked in luscious green vegetation from weeks of rain. With the low cloud cover, maintaining a comfortable altitude above the hilly ground proved difficult. At times, I had to reverse course and try the next valley over before getting on track again. Deviating like that was the only way to get through, and only by taking maximum fuel were we able to continue. It made me consider the hilly territory between Jagdalpur and Gadchiroli: that terrain had few roads and fewer villages, mostly hills, jungles and bad guys. It was to be a long, wet day above the jungles of East India.

Breaking out of the hills and low ceilings, we emerged over the plains that stretched east of Jagdalpur, and with the relatively flat land, the visibility improved. It was still overcast, with numerous rain squalls on the horizon, but the terrain elevation had dropped, giving us more elbow room. We overflew our old home airport at 500 feet and could see that we were expected: a small army of technicians had fuel barrels lined up for us. Circling and landing, I set down right next to them to avoid having to move the unwieldy and heavy barrels again.

Immediately upon landing, my phone was ringing. What I needed was to have a coffee, but I answered several calls from the IPS and Sami, plus Mahesh, who was wondering if we had arrived alright. The officers in Gadchiroli were wondering about our ETA and, explaining my soggy plan to them, I then verified their helipad coordinates, telling them their further reconnaissance waypoints I would obtain once on the ground there.

Sami reiterated for the umpteenth time how important this mission was, how important it was for business. He and the officers in Gadchiroli did not seem to consider the bad weather, but I reminded them of it, saying there was a strong chance I would have to abort due to the rain and clouds. Their lack of concern for my weather report was predictable.

According to them, it was good holiday weather in Gadchiroli and barely a cloud in the sky.

Having the important requirement of coffee met and with my fuel tank once again filled to the top of the filler neck thanks to a borrowed hand pump, we were ready to launch into the misting sky. I received the FIC/ADC from Mahesh, thanked the crew and, less than half an hour after landing, was airborne once again. The ease of operating out of that remote old airstrip compared to Bhubaneswar airport felt liberating.

BK was not feeling liberated, however. His body language and grunting told me he would have rather stayed dry in Bhubaneswar. He was worried about losing visibility and flying into the side of a hill. Looking at the sky, he gave a faint, nervous smile and said, "Hmm, Cap'n... this weatha'... it not so good, eh? We cancel, saa, have more coffee and aloo paratha, eh? Eh?"

"BK," I said, "We'll give it a shot. If it looks like it'll get worse, I'm gonna turn us around, don't worry, my friend."

He would have been happy to call off the flight, and I gave it thought too. If we flew and the weather closed in behind us, we might have to set down at one of those diversion helipads I had studied the night before. Having to spend the night in a mud hut with cows for company concerned me more than flying into a rain cloud. I would have us on the ground before running out of visibility to fly. That was the practical beauty of helicopters.

In good weather, Gadchiroli would have been a little over an hour's flight from Jagdalpur. During the monsoon, though, deviating around squalls would add to fuel consumption. Knowing they wanted to give reconnaissance to the surrounding terrain, a tankful of fuel from Jagdalpur was not going to be sufficient. The IPS had informed us that fuel barrels had arrived at the camp, but having none of my trusted crew on site, I had to rely on the troopers' ability to maintain the fuel drums and safeguard them. I wondered about the age of the fuel and whether it was contaminated. Did they have sufficient quantity? Would our borrowed fuel pump function correctly?

The weather en route was overcast and gloomy with mist, but it did not become worse. There were frequent squalls popping up which led to deviations around zero visibility and hills, but we landed in Gadchiroli an hour and a half after departing. The sky over the camp was just as overcast and misty as the rest of the area; predictably, the skies were not as good for flying as was promised by the bozo I had talked to on the phone.

We field tested the fuel barrels before firing up again. My fuel tank was slightly over half full, so if their fuel was contaminated, we could fly on to a more hospitable and safe helipad with what I had remaining. All of the fuel barrels tested showed no moisture or contaminants, but knowing that five officers desired to fly the reconnaissance flight, we held off refueling until after, thereby keeping the weight low for takeoff out of Gadchiroli's small helipad. The Astar had great performance and would have handled the extra fuel weight, but it's better to fly light if possible, and this saved us from refueling more than one time while in the bush.

After the requisite meet and greet with the officers, lubricated with the caffeine of sweet coffee and the carbohydrates of biscuits, we boarded for the magical mystery tour. With five passengers flying, BK stayed on the ground and paced through the rain puddles. I knew we would not see much through the jungle canopy, especially with the foul weather, and I told BK to expect us no more than a half-hour later. They had four points that they wanted to see, and I entered those in my GPS. I gave them a short briefing about the helicopter and warned them one final time that we weren't going to see much. Then, with a slap on the back to BK, I climbed aboard and hit the starter button.

Mist and rain covered the windscreen, but as I slowly raised the collective lever and increased pitch, downwash from the main rotor intensified and blew most of it off; then as we gained forward airspeed, the water droplets feathered off even more, revealing the white murkiness of an unfathomable horizon. Gadchiroli and the surrounding area was at around 700 feet of elevation and, being near the banks of Pranhita River, it was relatively flat compared to the hilly country encountered on the way from Jagdalpur. Once we reached twenty-five hundred feet AGL and were just below the ceiling, all I had to worry about was staying out of the clouds and flying circles around the officers' designated points.

Approaching each of their points, I would turn my head and shout out its name, then slow to sixty knots and orbit once around clockwise, then make a slow, banking turn to the left, completing an orbit counter-clockwise and, thereby, giving everyone a good view out their side of the aircraft. As good a view as they would find that day, anyway. The ground was obscured with low clouds, misty haze and fog. The Maoist-Naxalites, if they were moving, would be unseen. After two orbits around each point I would give my passengers a look, hold a thumb up and ask, "Okay?"

My questioning look would be returned with vague disinterest and blank stares, like they were waiting for me to perform tricks. They seemed to focus their attention on the side of my head or the cool little gauges on the instrument panel instead of the terrain outside. Orbiting the last waypoint and with no further input from my passengers, I pulled all power available, put the aircraft in a shallow dive for maximum speed, and pointed the nose back to Gadchiroli. Screaming along just under VNE back to the helipad, I wondered, *Am I playing around in the rain today for a goddamned thirty-minute joy ride?*

I landed and let the engine idle and cool, then shut it down. A sodden-looking BK opened the doors for the officers, and every one said thank you on their way out. They all turned to wave at the edge of the muddy helipad and stood conqueringly, posing for their staff, who were snapping photos of them in front of the machine after their perilous mission. BK then directed the beat-up old Tata truck containing the fuel barrels to stay away from the drooping rotor blades while it reversed.

We needed to get airborne as fast as possible and back to Jagdalpur; we did not want to get stuck in Gadchiroli. Regardless of the offer of a pleasant overnight there, the camp resembled a soggy *M*A*S*H* episode—without the consolation of a distillery in the officers' tent.

During refueling, the mist picked up, and we had to delay, fearing moisture mixing into the fuel. We were only able to resume again when one ambitious trooper found a halfway clean tarp and, with the assistance of four other chaps, held it over the fuel drums and fuel spout while we recommenced refueling underneath. It was a bit of a muddy struggle, but we filled the tank. Politely declining the adamant late lunch offerings, we shook hands all around and said goodbye. Our stomachs were grumbling, but my concern was the weather worsening. I made a call to our Jagdalpur weatherman, but he only knew one reply.

"Yes, Cap'n." At least he sounded more awake since morning. "Da skies are clear 'f weatha', you can fly... d'ere are clouds and d'ere is sunshine, rain has stopped... for now."

What a joker.

The skies were nasty on the way back but void of any thunderstorm activity: just a lot of rain, obscuration and scud running. With the company putting me up at the Hotel Devansh after landing, I relaxed under misty skies on the roof after having a five o'clock lunch. My hectic day and lack of sleep the night before caught up with me and I was staring at the street scene below like a zombie. I downed the first two whiskeys quickly and felt the tension fade. I was sipping a third and neglecting a lit cigarette when Sami called with a report from the IPS. He was elated with the mission, saying they appreciated the flight and were impressed with what they were able to see.

I half-chuckled and said, "What they were able to see? Sami, all they saw were a few minutes of up-close monsoon. It was borderline foolish to fly that mission today."

"No, no, no, Captaaiin! It's all okay. They valued the flight time and wished to thank you for a job well done. They want to fly again tomorrow. Isn't that great news!"

32.

Tirathgarh Falls

It started at the edge of my consciousness as one or two soft beeps while the morning light slowly oozed over the horizon and filtered through Hotel Devansh's dusty curtains. I buried my head deeper into the pillow and tried wedging the ear plugs deeper into my skull in a futile attempt to block out the first intrusive horn honks of the day. My auditory sense was aroused, though, and involuntarily began to search out other sounds, like dogs fighting or the panipuri peddler pushing his cart along the street, shouting and selling his treats.

Surrendering to the dawn, I cracked open an eyelid only to view the water damaged, discolored ceiling. Lacking proper repair materials, but showing creativity, the hotel maintenance staff pasted over the stain with letter size copy paper, a ream of the repair material sitting in the corner. The rest of the room was well kept and modern looking, with wood-paneled walls and polished granite floors. Reluctantly waking up further, I called downstairs for coffee, then rolled out and shuffled over to my fourth-floor window overlooking the street.

The sky was dark and ominous, bleeding out gray drops of itself onto the Indian countryside below. Opposite from the Devansh, a gathering mob of working women had assembled and were forging forward into another day at a construction site, their simple sarees stitched with all colors. This rainbow of women, with metal buckets on their heads, made a bright contrast to the immense pile of dark, aggregate stone that they were moving, bucket by bucket, from the roadside to a concrete mixer. In that impoverished region of India, construction equipment was rare, and the solution was a workforce of hard-working women.

Spending a few days in Jagdalpur and with poor weather making flight operations difficult, I thought we should use the down time to visit a local attraction. Tirathgarh Falls in Kanger Valley National Park was a forty-five minute, reasonably secure drive from Jagdalpur and, after a sluggardly morning of coffee, breakfast and sprawling about, I walked out to Sun City to see who of my mates was up for sightseeing. When reaching the guesthouse, I found my colleagues in full-on relax mode, and it wasn't until after an early lunch of mysterious vegetables that the few who volunteered were ready to go.

During the winding drive, we came close to wiping out a flock of gray geese when coming around a corner too fast. The fowl-farmer panicked, diving into the ditch and leaving quite frightened honkers in the middle of the road as our driver locked up his brakes on the wet asphalt. A loud verbal exchange between the two erupted, both of them claiming right of way, and just when it seemed headed toward violence, they threw up their arms and the argument faded. A head count was done of the fowl, and then they were marched off the road. With our driver spitting his paan out the window and grumbling, we carried on.

Once reaching the falls, we visited the ancient Hindu temple that was on the site, and it appeared to attract as many visitors as the falls. You could not swing a stick in India without hitting a temple, it seemed. Trees sprouted everywhere, except for the car park, which sat on top of the flat plateau that formed the falls. Along the path from the parking lot were a dozen shabby, corrugated tin huts sheltering snack shops and trinket vendors. Walking with poise was impossible due to the recent rains and the thick mud it created. At every step, I had to clinch my toes or risk losing my flip-flops in the sticky muck. The warm red mud oozed between my toes like a fresh cow-pie on Grandpa's farm.

Guarding the long, steep stairway to the base of the falls were dozens, if not hundreds, of those twitchy and thieving rhesus monkeys. A family of four Indians whom we were following made the mistake of carrying a bag of potato chips within sight of the fearless little buggers. In an instant, a four-year-old's snack was snatched out of her hands by the hairy culprits, causing frightened squealing from the kid and a taunting victory chant from the animals, which scampered up into the trees, clutching the looted chips. Seeing what a crime-ridden neighborhood we were venturing into and wanting to avoid becoming victims ourselves, we armed ourselves with the heaviest sticks we found to bolster our defenses.

Reaching the bottom, I looked up at the rushing, cascading falls and declared them the most beautiful natural sight I had seen in India. The heavy rains of the monsoon had raised the level of the Kanger River to a prodigious flow, and the tumbling water gave up a gentle roar that echoed down the deep, tree-choked valley. Reaching the top lip of the falls, the river plummeted 300 feet down the nearly vertical stratified rock. The short breaks between one layer of rock and the next gave the impression of hundreds of steps on a quite steep staircase.

A couple of us edged out onto these natural steps to sit and relax, letting the cool water flow over our heads and drench us. At one side of the falls, flooding had carved out a cave behind the falling water, leaving enough space for one person. By climbing over the slippery rocks and boulders, I was able to squeeze behind a section of the falls and be completely hidden within the cave. The ledge was just the right size to sit and not get washed down into the pool at the base of the falls, thirty feet below. The rushing sound of water, combined with the refreshing mist, was like a drug. Any tension or worry I had evaporated into the drops of moisture hanging from the cave ceiling.

Fearing my compadres might mistake me for drowned, I abandoned my cave and rejoined them on the bank of the river for photos and requisite rock-skipping contest. Two hours of wading and soaking later, we headed back up the steps, on guard for any monkey mischievousness, arming ourselves again with Man's first weapons, sticks and rocks.

Reaching the top, we walked stone by stone to the sharp edge of the falls and peered down as the rushing torrent fell from beneath our feet. There were no fences or barriers; unlike many natural wonders in developed countries, these falls were not barricaded to protect people from themselves.

We rested on the rocks by the river bank, cooling off from the climb and munching on snacks in a protective circle. A few of the braver monkeys edged nearer and watched us closely from adjacent trees, waiting for their chance to plunder. If they ventured too close, we nailed them with a pebble or raised our sticks, sending them scurrying noisily back up into the branches.

With a few final photos, we climbed into the car and set off for Jagdalpur. Along the way, we came across a liquor shop, and beer was proposed. Not fearing open container laws out there on the back roads of Chhattisgarh, I seconded the motion. Halfway back, we noticed large groups of villagers in the woods just off the road. Feeling neighborly, we braked, did a three-point in the road and edged off the shallow shoulder, parking beneath the trees next to three or four other vehicles. Out of the hundred to two hundred people there, most must have arrived at the spot by more traditional methods, like walking. We stepped out and heard intermittent cheering and shouting from groups of the villagers gathered in circles.

Walking closer to the assemblage, we saw, inside a makeshift ring, a flurry of feathers and blood. It seemed we had invited ourselves to a cockfight. One distressed old rooster had seen enough of his adversary and was bent on retreat, trying to run away only to be caught again and again by his human chicken wrangler. The wrangler grabbed his worried warrior, retightened the skinny, three-inch blade tied to the rooster's leg and, ruffling his feathers in an attempt to make him angry, placed him in front of the other fowl gladiator, trying to provoke him to fight. Eventually, the champion got the better of the reluctant feathered fighter; covered in blood, he succumbed to wounds. Next stop for him, a bowl of masala.

We were urged by the group to place bets on the next fight, and one of my Indian colleagues did. But, not entirely digging the action, after a while we all melted back to the car. It had an unruly mob vibe and the homemade brew was being passed around. Hearing horrible tales of brain damage, comas and even death caused by the poisonous hooch, we did not go near it and thought it was a good idea to get moving before the alcohol took its wild effect on the jungle people.

Reaching the guesthouse in the early evening, we went inside looking for Beebu to fix us up snacks and grub. We were slightly vexed when the loyal and omnipresent cook was nowhere to be found. But what we did find was disturbing: broken window glass and blood splatter in the kitchen. It looked like a crime scene. Our feeling of frustration turned to concern as we all wondered what our jovial little buddy had got himself into. We started making phone calls and found out the bad news.

Even though houses in Sun City were relatively new, the absence of running water was common; it could have been broken pipes or a shortage from the water department, we didn't know, but from time to time we would have no water. Usually, the hundred gallon black plastic water tanks on top of the house would help in cases like that, having stored sufficient water for two or three days. However, at times we would run empty and have to go with an alternate plan: ordering a tanker truck full of water from the fire department and having them deliver it to our rooftop tanks. Beebu was the guy tasked with climbing to the rooftop and snaking the hose from the fire truck up and into these tanks. The house had run low on water that day, and he had ordered a tankful.

With the rainy weather and wet roof, Beebu was too close to the edge while pulling up the hose. He slipped and fell, clattering down the side of the house. The twenty-foot fall was bad enough, but on the way down, his careening leg went through the double windows of the kitchen and caught on the frame while the rest of his body continued downward to the ground. He had multiple lacerations and a broken leg. The driver of the tanker truck and a couple of neighbors were able to drag him out of the dirt, into the kitchen and then on to a doctor. He had lost blood and was lucky to be alive. We rushed to the hospital, but he was sedated and sleeping.

Beebu was from Bhubaneswar, and that's where most of his family lived—including our cook at the guesthouse there, Banda, who was Beebu's brother. In no condition for house chores, it would take weeks before his leg healed and he was back up and around. After a couple of days, when I received a call to return to Bhubaneswar for an upcoming mission, it was suggested that Beebu return with me for a quite different and more deserved type of break.

33.

Around the Horn

While I sat in the barber shop waiting for a trim, in through the door walked a man growing a horn from his forehead. From an early age, I was taught not to stare—it was impolite my parents told me. Roger that, I get it. I despise being stared at, but upon seeing this man-unicorn, it took determination not to examine his coat hook-shaped sprout more closely. Not being able to stop myself, I did a double take. Indeed, it was not fake or some crazy body art. I would never have imagined it possible if I hadn't seen it, but somehow an extra appendage wasn't too surprising in this bizarre land of India.

Centered in the middle of his forehead protruded an upward curving, three-inch-long by one-inch-diameter horn. The way Indians stared at me most of the time made me feel as if something was growing out of my head, but the other shop patrons did not take a second glance at this chap. Perhaps they were more used to seeing horned men than foreigners; they continued what they were doing without missing a beat. Unicorn man grabbed a newspaper and, taking his place in queue for the next haircut, sat down.

I was back in Bhubaneswar, having flown in with a broken Beebu a couple days prior, and in need of a haircut. Anika and I had come to the barber shop together since she knew the owner and had said that she would wait for me. Her predictable restlessness soon took hold, though, and five minutes later, she found an excuse to leave.

"Michael, my sister called, and she'd like me to come over." Grinning, she added, "Will you be alright? Can you get back without being run over on the street?"

"Aren't you the spunky one?" I said. "I'll manage. Go, if you need to. I'll take a rickshaw, but if you don't hear from me, check the street gutters before the dogs have me eaten."

"Oh, how right!" she laughed. "You're like an exotic delicacy on their menu!" Flashing her heart-thumping smile, she waved and out the door she went, every man in the shop watching her exiting hourglass figure. Then they all turned and stared at me, like I had sprouted a horn or something.

Once the barber had finished barbering the customer before me, he paused and asked him a question. The customer nodded in the affirmative and the barber strapped an ancient-looking metal device onto his own hand. He flipped a switch, and it started vibrating and buzzing as he ran it back and forth over the customer's noggin. At first, I thought it was a type of hair clipper, but seeing the skin on his head jiggling back and forth, I figured it was a massager of sorts. Later, after my haircut, he held up the same contraption and asked me in Hindi if I would like a treatment. Suspicious, I hesitated, especially since the barber probably had not washed it or his hands all day, but seeing that the last guy survived, I nodded yes.

He slipped the scalp massager onto his hand, flipped the switch and my head and hair follicles were immediately immersed in bliss. While he ran it over my scalp, I was sure I could feel my hair follicles multiplying. He moved it behind my ears then, a part of my anatomy usually reserved for more intimate acquaintances, and I felt tension drain away, the same near-hypnosis dogs must go through when we scratch them behind their ears. The tension returned when I considered that the barber's filthy hand was invading previously germ-free territory on my cranium. I envisioned thousands of germs and bacteria building new homes on my scalp. When he deemed my dome done, I stood up from the chair, paid the man and walked out. I was in need of a hot shower, maybe bleach.

Deccan Aviation was a large-sized company chartering both helicopters and fixed-wing aircraft across India, and on a mid-August day a mission came up utilizing both our companies' aircraft. Their main hub was in Bangalore, but they had multiple locations across the country, and the Bell 407 that joined us that day came out of Kolkata.

The Bell 407 was a popular single-engine helicopter akin to the Astar. Crewed usually with a single pilot, it held seats enough for six passengers in its basic configuration, but with a VIP interior it held less. Power margins and speeds at the altitudes we flew were about the same between the two, but the edge went to their 407 that day; it was equipped with air conditioning. Upon finding out that one helicopter had air conditioning and one did not, the executives must have drawn straws to see who would have to swelter in the Astar with me.

The executives were from Vedanta Aluminum, a large mining and materials company headquartered in London. They had sites across India and other parts of the Eastern Hemisphere and operated bauxite and coal mines, aluminum smelting plants and electric power plants in both Odisha and Chhattisgarh, where there were abundant bauxite and coal deposits.

I met Captain Darpan from Deccan outside the Bhubaneswar air traffic control tower as we were both on our way to deliver our flight plans. He was hot-boxing a cigarette and looking bored. An unsmiling and serious man, he was a slender five foot eight, aged about fifty-five with graying and thinning hair. Like virtually all Indian helicopter pilots at the time, he was retired military.

I held out my hand, smiled and said, "Good morning, Captain." Referring to his cigarette, I asked, "Are you having breakfast?"

He shook my hand and stared at me with an icy emotional disconnect that left little doubt he was more capable of neck-punching me into a coma than telling jokes. Through a cloud of smoke, he said, "Good morning, Mike." Taking another deep drag and exhaling over his shoulder, he continued, "No, this is how I brush my teeth in the morning."

Our departure time from Bhubaneswar was seven o'clock, and our empty first leg was to Sambalpur near the Hirakud

Dam and Reservoir an hour away. Around thirty-three miles long, the manmade lake is formed from the pent-up waters of the Mahanadi River that flows near Raipur and Bhubaneswar.

We flew in loose formation, Captain Darpan insisting that I lead. I argued that he had the experience and should lead. Using the same argument, he said his experience and seniority earned him the privilege to fly tail and relax while I did the navigating. Argument over.

Overflying the Mahanadi and the huge, hazy expanse of the reservoir, we descended and landed at helipads on the water's edge. Captain Darpan claimed the closer helipad because he had the newer ship, air conditioning and the senior executives would be flying with him.

Vedanta had built luxurious company accommodations there for their top-gun executives. Backed up against the hillside were a number of white stucco bungalows with cherry-colored roofs for conventions or retreats from the grueling task of ripping bauxite from the Earth's crust. Manicured lawns and gardens with traveler's palms, hibiscus and bougainvillea lined the paths and driveways around the place. Across the dike from the helipads, hundreds of birds and waterfowl enjoyed the monsoon-provided surplus of water. Captain Darpan and I, along with our crew chiefs, had the chance to soak in the calming natural paradise for over an hour; we had an early start, and our passengers were a tad tardy.

At about nine-thirty, the passengers were ready and loaded for the flight to the aluminum smelting plant and adjacent power plant in Jharsuguda. Instead of flying direct, the passengers requested a sightseeing flight along the banks of the reservoir, then an overflight of their other site at Lakhanpur before landing at the complex. Flying toward the smelting plant, it appeared that we were headed toward a decent-sized city, its numerous tall smokestacks erupting out of brown landscape that, in turn, was slowly being smothered by hundreds of buildings. It was a bustling contrast to the tranquil gardens and river waters we had left in Sambalpur. Landing after forty-five minutes, we set down on immense concrete helipads that were large enough to accommodate an entire squadron of helicopters. The white, sunbaked cement sent up waves of heat and, after shutting down and climbing out, the glare forced me to squint hard enough to make my eyes watery.

The executives were whisked away to some far corner of the operation and, after securing our respective helicopters, we were whisked away to Vedanta's guesthouse. If the architects of their plant headquarters and guesthouse buildings desired to impress, they had succeeded. It seemed no expense was spared. From the spotless but treeless outside grounds to the polished granite and marble entryway, their three-story guesthouse building rivaled most five-star hotels, providing hundreds of neatly decorated rooms. There was even a swimming pool; the sun chairs around it were empty, though, and just beyond the screened fence stood industrial smokestacks.

Captain Darpan and I were given separate rooms to relax in while our two crew chiefs shared one, but they didn't complain. The plan was to wait until after lunch, then fly to Jharsuguda airstrip for barreled fuel. It was there that most of our passengers would board one of Deccan's airplanes. One would go with Captain Darpan back to Bhubaneswar, and one was going around the horn to Raipur Airport with me, to catch a commercial flight.

Jharsuguda airstrip was another World War Two airport with a single six-thousand-foot-long runway, a few rusting hangar shells, and four old, roofless thick-walled cement buildings. There were no other buildings or services, and our passengers had to stand in the shade of leafy trees while we refueled. The passengers flying in Deccan's waiting Beechcraft King Air wasted little time, and were airborne before we had the fuel drums opened and tested. I took the opportunity to walk around and explore the old airfield while BK and a few inexplicably appearing technicians refueled, but the distances were vast between the old hangars, buildings, taxiways and runway; there was too much to explore in my brief time.

I thought back to the war, when the airfield was filled with B-17s and B-24s. Or maybe they had been British Lancasters and a fighter wing of P-51s or Spitfires—I don't know as information on its history was hard to find, but I imagined warbirds warming up their engines and rumbling along the taxiway.

I tried to comprehend the logistical requirements of an airport like this at that time: not only the vast quantity of petroleum required, but bombs, bullets, beds, food and love letters from home. All of that and more had to find its way to this remote, desolate corner of the world, and this was only one of many wartime airfields throughout India, and the globe.

Someone shouted my name. Refueling was finished, and my passenger was concerned he would miss his airline flight in Raipur. Putting an end to my contemplations, I jogged back in the hundred-degree heat. Captain Darpan had already started and was ready to lift and depart. I glanced at him to wave goodbye, but he was focused on his machine and ignored me. I climbed in my seat and after starting, BK gave a check on each side of the helicopter, hopped in and we were off. No tower to worry about, just a blind radio call to any airborne traffic in the area, telling them where we were and where we were going. Climbing to four thousand feet, I set course for Raipur an hour and ten minutes away.

The weather had been good for the middle of monsoon season, with partly sunny weather, but later in the afternoon, low clouds and rain showers meant that I could not maintain altitude. Halfway through the journey, we had to descend to two thousand. By the time we were twenty miles inbound to Raipur Airport, I was peering with concern out the windscreen, searching for the few open spaces between clouds. Adding to that frivolity, Raipur ATC had us hold and orbit for nearly ten minutes for departing aircraft in their usual absurd routing of traffic.

We were inbound from the northeast, the airplane was taking off on Runway 24 to the southwest, and once again I could not think of any reason to have a low-flying helicopter hold so far away in such a scenario. The passenger studied his watch while we circled a cloud and erased his precious airline counter check-in minutes. With rain tapping on the windscreen and the airliner departed, we were allowed to proceed inbound the final distance and land straight-in on Runway 24. By the time we crossed the runway threshold, the airliner was a hundred miles away.

In the end, my passenger was happy to be in time for his flight, BK was happy to be safely out of the rain once again and I was happy that it was payday. I looked forward to confirming the bank deposit using the Wi-Fi at Hotel Grand.

Later, feeling cozy from two shots of rum and sitting at the desk in my hotel room, I was absorbed in the glow from my laptop when I noticed movement on my periphery. Glancing up, a rat had come through the crack at the bottom of my door, and I watched as it happily skipped across the floor and disappeared under my bed. I froze, glancing around left and right for a weapon with which to defend myself against this Happy Rat invasion. Armed with a jungle boot in each hand, I prepared for battle.

I waited for it to reemerge; not wanting to ruin its happy day, but there had to be boundaries. Just when I thought I'd have to get down on my hands and knees and wrestle it out from the bed, the furry vermin went skipping joyfully, playfully, without a care in the world, out the way it had come. Understanding why housekeeping left so many extra towels in the bathroom, I used two of them to plug the rat-sized gap beneath my door.

34.

Uneasy Rider

The frisky reggae beat and bassline of my favorite daybreaking music alarm chased my dreams away, and through semi-conscious thoughts, it induced a slight upward tug at the corners of my mouth. Due to some partially buried ocean-side reminiscence, visions of gently waving skinny palms on white sandy beaches flooded my waking mind every morning I heard that reggae-rock ditty.

After the first or second verse, I unburied my muddled head from the pillows and cracked a confused eyelid open, surveying the strange surroundings.

Where am I?
This ain't a beach bungalow.
India, son.
Oh. My.
Ah, that's right. I fly a helicopter here.

To advance further into wakefulness, though, I required caffeine, and on the occasions that I awoke at the Hotel Grand in Raipur, had taken to ordering not one but two carafes of their sweet milk coffee. The sugar and caffeine were not healthy on an empty stomach, I'm sure, but I was an unstoppable junkie. By breakfast time, I was a tad jittery, but my eyes were wide open.

We had parked the helicopter at Raipur Airport overnight, so I had a bit of legwork before taking off for Jagdalpur in the morning. There were landing and parking fees to pay and flight plan approval from the controllers in the tower. This being a smaller airport than Bhubaneswar, the runaround would amount to less, but it was still a bigger hassle than when we overnighted at Raipur Heliport, far from the goons of AAI.

There were a total of five security checks to get through the airport and one more to access the gate that lead to the control tower. That's where BK and I split up, him out to refuel the helicopter and me heading up the stairs to ATC. There was no Meteorology or Communications office as with Bhubaneswar, so on my flight plan, in lieu of an official signature, I was allowed to write, "Self Brief," which streamlined the process.

Introducing myself to the two controllers and the omnipresent chai wallah up on top, I exchanged pleasantries with them while they calculated my landing and parking fees. It was early in the morning, and their only traffic was an inbound Air India flight from Delhi, twenty minutes out.

I accepted the little cup of chai offered me and then, seizing the chance to voice concerns, said, "I have a question for you gentlemen."

One chap continued writing, but the other looked over his shoulder at me, "Yes, Captain, how can we help you?"

"I was wondering... is it necessary to have me hold and orbit twenty miles out whenever there is landing or departing traffic?" I asked. "It seems excessive, no?"

They both looked at each other but offered no comment.

"I'm at 500 feet AGL nearing Raipur... surely I wouldn't interfere with these airliners if I continued inbound?"

"Captain, those are the guidelines we must follow. If the airliner must go-around, we need room for maneuvering."

To that, I was thinking that if an airline pilot found himself at 500 feet in any situation other than landing or taking off, he was having a bad day, and a small, agile and low-flying helicopter would be the least of his worries.

"Please consider the helicopter's slow speed," I said. "Yesterday evening, we were held twenty miles northeast in worsening weather for traffic taking off and departing the area to the southwest. By the time we were allowed to continue inbound, and still miles from the airport, that traffic was fifty miles away."

Gathering steam, I reached my point. "I fail to see how we are a threat cruising at the treetops like we do."

"We're sorry, Captain, but those aircraft separation protocols were established by Airports Authority of India," said the one tallying my fees. By his tone of voice, I didn't think he was sorry at all and did not appreciate being questioned from someone in the peanut gallery.

The other chap, who was using binoculars to scan the runway, pulled them from his eyes briefly and said, "But since you think our aircraft holds are excessive, we will do what we can in the future to expedite helicopter traffic."

From his tone, also, it was hard to detect exuberant sincerity, and the control room took on a certain chill. But I didn't push my case any further or wear out my welcome; it was a work in progress. From that point on while flying, I did notice improvement, though nearly imperceptible, but improvement.

Taking off from Raipur, the skies were a high, gray overcast. We called ahead to Jagdalpur, where they said it had rained all night but had stopped in the morning. Monsoon season showed no sign of relenting, and mid-morning was perhaps the ideal time to fly. If we were lucky, the sky had drained itself by raining all night and would not be saturated again until afternoon, when the day had warmed.

I followed the Raipur to Jagdalpur road, where there were plenty of places to land if the weather blocked us in, and the further we flew from Raipur, the worse the weather became. By the time we were thirty miles inbound to Jagdalpur, the cloud ceiling forced us down to a thousand feet AGL. It was misty, with visibility deteriorating. The countryside was a soaked sponge, standing water everywhere, rice paddies inundated. In places, the only patch of ground not underwater was the slightly elevated highway.

Getting on the ground in late morning, before the visibility diminished further, I detected a slowness from the Jagdalpur crew. They would never be confused with a group who possessed alacrity, but there was no spunk or the usual laughter-filled gossip, and the few technicians that appeared on the ramp shuffled around, scraping their feet zombie-like with a clinical case of The Slows. The wet, gloomy weather had them half-asleep, or perhaps, with the helicopter out of town for a while, their weariness was caused by too much partying the night before.

When on a mission from Bhubaneswar such as that, I carried only one small overnight bag; just room enough for my laptop and an extra pair of socks. If my uniform became smelly, I washed it at night. It was washed often. Also keeping cargo shorts and a t-shirt for downtimes, I changed into these in the back of the helicopter and set off down the runway, my favorite jungle boots splashing through the puddles. Rabinesh had given me the Indian-made footgear from his IPS inventory; they were lightweight, durable and I would rate them the most comfortable boots I ever wore, an extension of my feet.

The crew did not stick around long; they threw the cover on the helicopter and disappeared. BK said they would be back in the evening to finish, then climbed into the company car and was gone. Everyone was in so much of a hurry to get back to their all-day nap that no one bothered to ask if the captain needed a ride back to the guesthouse, which was where I would be staying for this duration. No problem, that. I'd walked the twenty minutes before without dying.

The tarmac was soaked from the daily rains; the stray dogs that called the airfield home were stretched out in different places along the pavement, only able to find a few semi-dry spots to lie down. Motoring along the runway, my tired, out-of-shape legs and I reached one end only to glance up and see a dark cloud sneaking over the tree line and start to spit rain. It was not a matter of if I would get wet, but how much. The raindrops were cold and cup-sized, and I could hear the advancing wave of the downpour crashing through the trees and brush. In seconds, the squall line enveloped me, the water hitting the pavement with violent splat-ocity and exploding into trillions of clear beads.

There was no wind or hail, only gallons of water, and I jogged until the rain fell into my eyes and obscured my vision. Fully soaked, I continued walking, resigned to my wet fate but refreshed and content, even more so when a cold trickle of water found its way down the back of my shorts.

To my rescue came a lad on a motorcycle. Someone must have been keeping tabs on me because I was hidden at the far end of the runway. The airfield had been deserted after my crew left, except for the usual IPS hanging around, and when the rain started, they were probably taking refuge wherever they could find it. The motorcyclist raced up alongside me and braked hard, skidding slightly. Squinting from the rain behind water-spotted spectacles, he asked if I'd like a ride.

He was a kid of about fourteen, wearing drenched but decent clothes and having a neat haircut. His English was good, and he appeared educated. Raising my voice over the buckets of rain coming down and his revving engine, I asked, "Sun City, do you know it?"

"Yes, sir. You can trust me, sir," he said.

"I can, can I?"

My ability to trust had never fully developed, but I took the perch behind him and we took off through the rain, way too fast. He revved through the gears like he had something to prove. When we reached the parking ramp at the halfway point of the runway and our turn off, he downshifted and stomped on the rear brake, setting us into a fishtailing slide. Overshooting, he made a shaky 180 degree turn until we were pointed in the right direction off the runway, and then we fairly flew past my parked helicopter.

He knew all the shortcuts and side trails in town and Evel Knieveled through them with just a bit too much enthusiasm. We went around one small alleyway and slammed on the brakes again when we came face to face with a frightened herd of buffalo. In India, you should expect herds of buffalo in alleyways. They stopped in their tracks, half rearing on their hind legs, all bug-eyed and frightened. I was a little bug-eyed myself at that point, but my fearless driver was unflappable and weaved unsteadily through the smelly bovine obstacle course they presented, both of us putting our feet down to stay upright and vertical.

He seemed to think he was doing me a favor by going as fast as he could through the pouring rain. With the bumps and potholes knocking the words from my diaphragm, I told him, "Hey! I'm already... Soaked... Not... Any... Drier... With the... Throttle... Wide open!"

He ignored my shouting and did not relent, perhaps looking to impress me with his speed and agility. Splashing through every mud puddle he saw, we drove straight up to the guesthouse in a matter of minutes. I climbed off, eyeing him warily.

"Thanks," I said. "How'd you know the house where I stay?"

"My Dad's IPS, you flew him before, and we all know where your quarters are," he said.

I didn't know if I liked that.

He added, "They watch you sirs, closely."

If that was to make me feel warm and fuzzy, it did not. But, I thought it was better than being ignored. He looked at me expressionless, gunned his engine and in a cloud of muddy spray, drove off.

35.

Vertical Tsunami

The welcome mat was out, and there was a vacancy to be had at the Jagdalpur company guesthouse. I was hanging my sweat-stained cap there for an indefinite stay. Since our debatably successful day trip to Gadchiroli a couple of weeks prior, the company had been warming up to anti-Maoist flights around Jagdalpur once again. The lure of rupees was strong, and the lack of revenue flights elsewhere precipitated an openness to fly in the combat zone when able. However, we were waiting for the monsoon to clear out, and it would continue for at least another month, only rarely offering good flying weather.

While I had gone for a run, BK had brought my gear from the airfield and set it in my usual room. Arriving via the uneasy rider, I found the house was quiet with everyone napping, no one showing concern for the missing and saturated captain. I peeled off my soaked clothes, took a hot shower and wrapped up in a towel, feeling brand new. Feeling hungry as well, I went on an assault of the kitchen.

Opening the door, the kitchen smelled like a cow barn. Not daring to walk in there with bare feet, I had put my boots on, but still stepped gingerly around various multi-colored puddles and piles of goo. Finding half-warm khichdi on the cooker, I knocked the ants out of a sauce bowl, filled it up, grabbed a bottle of beer from the fridge and walked out. They had a rug in front of the kitchen door and I never saw it used by someone walking into the kitchen—only coming out did you need to wipe your feet. What fetid life form you might pick up on your boot while in the kitchen was a concern.

Vertical Tsunami

The IPS had requested a mission, but it was on hold until the weather would allow us to fly. During the several days' wait, India Independence Day came and went, and the government put on a large production at a nearby Jagdalpur park. Not a park really, just a brown, grassless area that was mostly used for playing cricket by ragtag groups of locals. They put up colorful decorations and banners for the commemoration, school kids sang songs and the IPS and CRPF marched. The chief minister flew in on his high-flying Beechcraft King Air and gave a speech; a few of us checked it out, but we didn't linger long in the midday humidity.

A few days later found me recovering from my fourth bout of acute food poisoning since arriving in India. The bubble pack of loperamide I had brought with me from the USA was long gone due to multiple bad food foul-ups and I just wanted my guts to toughen up already and get over it. I was losing weight, and had to cut an extra notch in my belt.

In Sun City, the sky showed deceitful signs of clearing as I convalesced with my old standby of ice cream and 7-UP. The mission that had been on hold was deemed worthy of an attempt. There was a new Dantewada district superintendent for the IPS, and he was eager to fly to the communities and camps under his charge for meet and greets. The prior superintendent had finished his posting in the district and was being transferred to Bilaspur, sixty miles north of Raipur.

I flight-planned the mission, warning Rabinesh that the weather was still in a monsoon pattern and we might not reach all requested destinations. Also, that we might have to cut the mission and ground meetings short at any moment and fly out in a hurry if the weather turned ugly, like it seemed bent on doing. The superintendent was keen to fly, though, and excited to meet his new constituency. I received the okay to launch.

We took off at eight o'clock the next morning for Dantewada. There were broken clouds, but there were also patches of blue sky, and I felt optimistic that we could get at least halfway through his program. Still, there was a good chance that the afternoon landings would be canceled.

Nine days out of ten, Rabinesh would be wearing civilian clothes instead of his uniform, or a casual mixture of both, but with the new brass around he was dandied up in full uniform. With the big smile stretched across his face, he came out to shake my hand and said loudly over the helicopter noise, "Hello, my friend! Good to see you again... Back to stay?"

"Good to see you, Rabinesh," I said. "I'll stay as long as no one shoots at me. Deal?"

"You got it, buddy," he laughed. "Those problems are all taken care of!"

In a shouting introduction, I met the new superintendent, and he climbed in back. He traveled with two bodyguards, and BK was on the ground ushering them aboard, trying not to get poked in the eye by all the rifle barrels being flung about. The superintendent had two sidearms and an AK47, plus a briefcase, and his bodyguards showed no lack of firepower either. These were serious and sour looking dudes carrying AK47s and enough spare magazines for a sporty firefight by the looks of them. They were well fed and fit, not the average jungle troopers whose physiques varied from soft and pudgy to that of skin and bones.

Our first stop took us past the Kirandul mines to Jagargunda, thirty miles south of Dantewada. The IPS stationed there were awaiting us and lit a smoke canister as we flew overhead. Being very much in Maoist-Naxalite territory once again, I made a spiraling descent to their well-cleared, razor-wire-encircled helipad.

The little village held no more than 500 people, but it was the largest for sixty miles between Kirandul and Konta. Jam-packed, cobbled together tin shacks and mud huts lining a tepid and algae-covered pond made up the local landscape. The most permanent structures were the three cement buildings for the IPS barracks and office. No snack shop, beer shop or any type of retail shop. No schoolhouse, either, though the government was trying to change that.

We spent two hours there, the superintendent introducing himself and listening to the villagers' concerns with local projects.

Throughout the first hour, I watched the weather deteriorate; the blue patches of sky that held promise earlier were surrendering to gray overcast. The day of flying from village to village that he planned was about to become abbreviated. Wrapping up the village meeting, he found it hard to pull away. There seemed to be far more concerns and complaints than hours in the day.

Walking through the wire gate and back to the helicopter, I discussed the options with the superintendent. In order to get back to headquarters in Dantewada, we would have to fly through the Kirandul mountain pass. Low clouds and rain would form there first, and we could see that it was the darkest area on the horizon; I told him weather probably had it impassable already. He wanted to press on to Chintalnar, though, our next stop only ten minutes away. I warned him that if we didn't fly back to Dantewada immediately, he might not be able to sleep in his own bed that night. He grinned, slapped me on the shoulder and said, "Wouldn't be the first time, Captain!"

Taking off in a spiraling climb, reaching four thousand feet and finding the correct heading to Chintalnar, I saw that Kirandul was no longer an option. Looking over my left shoulder to the north, the pass was obscured with dark, apocalyptic clouds and occasional lightning. I pointed out the window and the superintendent turned, gazing out the same direction. Looking back at me, he grinned and gave a thumbs-up. I did not share his happiness in seeing this great wonder of nature, but liked his enthusiasm. I still knew we had an *out* east of the rain-choked pass, but for how much longer was the question. From the flyable, splotchy sunshine of the morning, the weather was becoming pear-shaped in a hurry.

Arriving over Chintalnar, an even smaller batch of hovels than Jagargunda, I took several good looks around the horizon before descending. There was another front moving in closer from the south, but I thought it was slow and that we had time. Once landed, I shut down and caught up with the superintendent, who was rapidly walking away, focused on his next meeting. I warned that a storm front was moving this way and asked him to keep the meeting short. Knowing that time was only a number and not something real to these guys, I told him fifteen minutes until next take off; that way, he might be ready in thirty.

Ten minutes later, thunder rumbled. It was getting closer, and I was getting anxious. I did not want to spend the night in Chintalnar. Neither did my company want their helicopter to spend a night so deep in bad guy territory. If we were socked in it might be days before we could fly out again.

After twenty minutes, I felt the first raindrop and told BK to tell the guards that we were leaving and that, if the superintendent wanted to fly, he had better come. Not waiting for a reply, I started the helicopter. I figured, and correctly, that if he heard his ride leaving, the superintendent would be along shortly, and soon after finishing my after-start checks, he and his bodyguards came jogging up. Apologizing to him, I pointed at the now abundantly dark and spitting sky, then shouted over the turbine, "We have got to go!"

The usual easy smile had disappeared from BK's face as he checked the helicopter and then climbed in. I thought at that point he might have had his share of monsoon flying and was considering retirement. We took off in a swirl of raindrops, climbing too slowly for my blood pressure, then I pointed the fun-ship to the northeast and Jagdalpur; that direction was still relatively light compared to the rest of the dark horizon.

From the south, a bank of rolling, dark clouds were engulfing Chintalnar and the surrounding area. Due north to Dantewada, the mountains of Kirandul weren't even visible, buried within clouds. Our only choices were to return to Jagargunda, which would itself be veiled with rain in minutes, or head to Jagdalpur and hope it wasn't storming at our home base. If weather became too dicey, there were other IPS and CRPF camps along the way, although they would not offer much better accommodation or protection than Chintalnar.

Flying around clouds and through light rain, it took us forty-five minutes to reach Jagdalpur. Half the sky was rain squalls that we had to deviate around, covering more ground and burning more fuel. By the time we were on short approach to the airfield, a large squall had developed from the northeast and it was inundating one end of the runway, and moving slowly over the entire aerodrome. Foul weather was trying to shut the door on my airport once more.

Aiming for the parking ramp, I flew in a little hot and landed crosswind just beyond the hold-short line as the oversize raindrops began their pelting drumbeat. By the time I had hovered to our parking spot and shut down, the squall was upon us in sheets, pounding the fiberglass of the cockpit, drowning out the sound of the turbine and drenching our ground crew. Luck was on our side again as we barely beat the wall of rain.

An arc of lightning hit the Earth just off the end of the runway, followed immediately by its crackling, ground-shaking thunder. Despite his program being wiped out, the rookie superintendent was all smiles and thanked us for what we had done and landing safely. He jumped from the helicopter into the drenching rain and walked around to my door.

"Captain," he asked, shaking my hand, "when do you think we can get airborne again? Half an hour?"

I looked at him as raindrops dripped off his earlobes, then took a sweeping look around at the vertical tsunami we were immersed in. "Sir, it may be longer than that."

36.

The Big Time

During monsoon season, the mountain range paralleling India's east coast and lying between Chhattisgarh and Odisha states, the Eastern Ghats, proved time and again to be a deadly place to fly helicopters. During one helicopter-grounding, soggy afternoon in the guesthouse, I noticed my crew talking more excitedly than usual amongst each other. There was always gossip going around, and I didn't pay much heed to their blathering until they said that a helicopter had gone missing. Not just any helicopter, but a twin-engine Bell 430 belonging to the state government of Andhra Pradesh, Chhattisgarh's bordering state to the south.

It had taken off from Hyderabad in the morning, with Chief Minister YSR Reddy, his two assistants and two pilots aboard, with the intention of flying to a city named Chittoor, near Bangalore. Shortly after departure, ATC had lost contact with them.

Weather had been miserably wet for days in eastern India, keeping us on the ground for most of them. With no reliable weather service available, the closest we could come to a weather check, besides looking out the window, was a four-hour-old satellite picture published online by the India Meteorological Department. Day after day, it showed solid clouds from the Bay of Bengal all the way across India to Mumbai.

After the helicopter went missing, shockwaves of distress spread across the country. A colossal search operation was mounted with thousands of ground troops and low-flying Air Force helicopters and airplanes. Sami from our head office called and informed us that even we should prepare to search. That idea didn't thrill any of us. Joining an emotionally charged search operation, with an untold number of aircraft flying low-level in poor visibility, seemed like a good way to get hurt.

We were able to avoid it when, the next morning it was confirmed by the Prime Minister of India that YSR Reddy had been killed. The crew from an Air Force Mi-8 helicopter located the wreckage in the thick jungle of a hillside and winched a couple of men down to search for any living and identify the dead. There were no survivors.

In the aftermath of his death, I heard different media reports saying that over 120 people died of shock or committed suicide upon hearing the grim news. Many of these were his young supporters or those who benefited from his social welfare programs. During his tenure in office, he had offered schemes such as free electricity to farmers, cheap rice and free health care, among other programs designed to benefit the poor. His constituents were distraught and emotional for sure, but to hear that so many people committed suicide because of his death blew my mind.

The sparsely populated forest area where they crashed was within the Red Corridor and considered to be a stronghold of the Maoist-Naxalites, but it was soon ruled out that they had brought down the helicopter. An investigation based on evidence from the Cockpit Voice Recorder (CVR), concluded that factors causing the crash included a problem with the transmission oil pressure that distracted the crew from the worsening weather. It was noted that the pilots never discussed the bad weather or returning to base. It appeared that once they departed with the VIP, even with the weather deteriorating, the lifesaving action of turning back was not considered an option.

Only a year prior to this and within a hundred miles of the chief minister's crash site, another Bell 430 had crashed during heavy rain. All four occupants were killed, two pilots and two engineers. They had also taken off from Hyderabad and were about thirty minutes into the flight when ATC lost contact. CVRs were required equipment in India on bigger helicopters like the 430, especially VIP aircraft. The recording from that crash, when it was found, revealed no malfunctions from the aircraft. The pilots had flown controlled and level, but likely blind due to heavy rain, into the side of a mountain. Though both the Air Force and the owner of the 430 were involved in the search for the aircraft, it took over three months before that wreckage was found. This was due to poor weather but, perhaps most of all, to the fact that the helicopter's Emergency Locator Transmitter (ELT), had malfunctioned and hadn't sent a signal.

I had yet in my career to feel enough pressure from VIP passengers or frothy bosses to continue flying through poor visibility. Turning back was something I was not afraid of. There could be a certain feeling of failure, or possibly an undertone from the boss that I had been untruthful, but if the weather didn't look right, I would turn around. That's not to say that I was some prophetic, weather-reading wizard, it only shows my intolerance for nil-visibility-induced heart palpitations.

I knew the worst that could have happened to me was to be fired and forced to find work elsewhere, or in a new country, or back home in the USA. Not the easiest thing to do given the pilot job market at the time, but with my FAA license, I had options. Indian pilots, holding only the less internationally recognized Indian DGCA license, had only two, and that was to fly in their own country and compete for the limited pilot jobs, or get out of aviation. Perhaps they felt more pressure to fly through poor weather.

During the aftermath and investigation into the Reddy crash, we were recalled to Bhubaneswar to fly Bollywood movie support. Upon hearing this fascinating news, we unanimously agreed that being movie stars was where our futures would lie. But stymied on our first attempt leaving Jagdalpur, we had to turn back after hitting a wall of rain and clouds in the foothills forty miles to the east. BK was tired of peering through the windscreen looking for a hole to fly through. I could see him shaking his head out of the corner of my eye.

"Cap'n, 'dis is terrible weather," he said, in slow but steady English. "It is not worth the risk to continue more. Let us return to Jagdalpur for chai and coffee... Try tomorrow."

Not in the mood to push it either, I said, "BK, let's get outta here." I tilted the cyclic to the right and, after a 180 degree turn, headed back to the airfield.

A day later, we were better off and made it safely to our hangar in Bhubaneswar. A big crowd had gathered, excited by the news of the movie shoot the next day. After getting the helicopter post-flighted, Mahesh, BK and I drove to the movie set to meet with the producers and inspect potential landing sites. They were using the campus of KIIT University downtown for shooting the scenes, and after we agreed on a likely landing spot, the producers explained what they wanted from me. This turned out not to be much; in fact, the helicopter would be sitting static as a backdrop mostly, except for a couple of scenes when I would have to high hover.

No car chases, aerobatics or rooftop landings. I only had to sit and look like a pilot—something I'd been practicing. They certainly were not offering to give me any lines in this Hindi language movie. Nevertheless, I allowed myself a few seconds to entertain delusions about a movie career and breaking into the Big Time.

Monsoon season doesn't last all year long, and in September, the rains become less intense, with days of rain and days of sunshine. The day of the movie shoot broke clear and sunny, but the air was heavy with humidity. There was just no way to stay dry. The moment after walking outside, I was drenched with sweat. Wearing my washed and pressed uniform shirt with black tie, borrowed black trousers and borrowed black dress shoes, I was uncomfortable—but looking stellar.

Confirming with the producers that plans had not changed, BK and I took off for the short ten-minute flight to the university and landed on the lush green terrace of the campus. There were tall royal palms on one side and a three-story glass building on the other, plus an elevated walkway and a number of antennas and small towers that we had missed during the walk-through the evening before. It was a tight fit, but we were light and I came to a spot sixty feet above our landing zone and hovered straight down to the grass. BK jumped out and helped me coordinate with one of the producers, who wanted the helicopter turned just so. After three pick-ups and set-downs, the man was satisfied with my positioning, and I shut down.

So far, so good for my movie career. No one was killed or maimed from my landing, and someone even offered me one of those cool director's chairs in the shade and a bottle of water. My tie didn't last long. Within the first thirty minutes, I peeled it off and buried it deep within the helicopter. Normally, I wore the more sun-friendly khaki trousers in the hot sunshine, and the difference in temperature compared to the black pair I was wearing had me concerned about my ability to produce offspring in the future.

There were a number of gorgeous actresses and extras there, and I was able to strike up a conversation with a Japanese exchange student who played the villain's girlfriend. For her costume, she was wearing a black leather vest and shorts. I was uncomfortable in the heat, sure, but at least I wasn't wearing leather. Although what she wore amounted to no more than a belt, anyway, and showed a lot of her creamy white skin.

Her name was Kazue'e, she spoke good English and I was happily surprised that we could carry on a light conversation past "Hello" and "Konichiwa." We had lunch together from the masala takeout that was delivered to everyone, but later one of her suitors showed up and interrupted our getting acquainted. Not before I got her phone number, though!

Before any flights in the helicopter, they wanted it only as background in a few shots. The producer asked, "Could we just have the big fan on top turn... No engine noise... Could you do that?"

"How do you want me to make that happen?" I replied. "Should I stand beneath the rotor blades and blow?"

He didn't catch my attempt at humor, but we sorted out the shot with BK turning the tailrotor, causing the "big fan on top" to slowly rotate, and I sat in the cockpit looking important, or tried. After the static shots, I was asked twice to start-up and lift to a high, fifty-foot hover with the hero and villain fighting and wrestling on the landing skid, half in and half out of the left side of the helicopter. They did not use stunt doubles, the actors themselves were hanging out of the helicopter, but they were strapped in good with safety harnesses. Still, I hoped they would not end up dangling from the rope with all the cameras rolling, and focused on keeping the helicopter as stable as possible.

It was the part of the movie where the bad guys were winning; the third time I lifted, we came to only a short hover, and the villain fought off the hero, who fell to the ground. Shouting and laughing hysterically, the villain sprayed fake bullets out of his fake gun at his fake innocent victims below. I hovered higher and higher until we were over the treetops, then the villain and I flew away with the sinister intent of taking over the world.

That was it. That was my big premiere. Flying only a small circuit around the campus, I returned to our landing site and, while shutting down, the villain was let out of his harness.

I was thoroughly disappointed when no one yelled, "Cut!" or "That's a wrap!"

After that last, climatic getaway scene, the energy left the set. The extras had faded away, and Kazue'e disappeared. Actors were getting out of their costumes and taking off makeup. The film crew hung cigarettes from their lips. They had that look of relief workers get when they know they are done sweating for the day and they only need to secure their gear and wrap things up.

Indeed, it was late in the afternoon, and although I hadn't done much other than broil in the sunshine, I was worn out from my movie star debut. I was ready to tuck the helicopter back in the hangar and search for a talent agent.

37.

Old Wicked Ways

During the excessive wetness of the monsoon, Maoist-Naxalite activities had tapered off. Damp conditions, flooding rivers and muddy trails probably tempered the fervor of their campaign and made activities and travel difficult. The same went for the rest of the jungle-dwelling citizenry. The monsoon had been dissipating day by day, though, and travel by foot across the jungle was becoming easier for the insurgents and they were getting up to their old wicked ways.

To remind us of that, we received a hot call late one evening to return to Jagdalpur soon as possible the next day. We were to evacuate a trooper who had been injured when insurgents had triggered an IED. He and his mates were near the highway when it happened, and they had immediately raced away to Jagdalpur, seeking aid. We were not given details, but missing limbs were likely. The small hospital in Jagdalpur had him sedated and the bleeding slowed, but they could not help beyond that and had requested his transfer to the better-equipped Raipur hospital.

Early in the morning, we attempted to launch into the fog and haze but were halted on the ground by Bhubaneswar ATC. They said the visibility was less than fifteen hundred meters, and would not allow me to start, even after requesting Special Visual Flight Rules. For single-engine helicopters, fifteen hundred meters was the least amount of visibility DGCA allowed pilots to fly through while in controlled airspace. SVFR for twin-engine helicopters, meanwhile, allowed pilots to operate down to visibility no less than a thousand meters.

With precious time being erased, later in mid-morning, the unseen sun was able to melt away a bit of the fog, and we hurriedly launched. The sky remained thick and soupy until we approached the Eastern Ghats, and I half expected to turn back upon reaching the foothills. Instead, the further west we flew, the better the visibility became. We reached Jagdalpur in fine weather not quite two and a half hours later, deviating only a few times for low clouds.

Since BK and I, and the helicopter, were all running on empty when reaching the airstrip, and time was of the essence, the IPS brought us lunch in tiffin boxes while we refueled. We were given a stack of three each. One contained hot roti, and I quickly stuffed one of the irresistible chunks of flatbread in my mouth. Another held rice, and the third, aloo gobi, a spicy cauliflower and potato dish which was one of my favorite vegetarian meals.

Silverware was a luxury and not part of the option package for this hectic happy meal, so scooping up the aloo gobi by using an edge of the roti, I stuffed it into my mouth Indian style. Yummy. But I wolfed it all down too fast, and soon it sat in my gut like a brick. Since this type of lunch box was ubiquitous throughout India, insurgents often used them to plant IEDs and were referred to as tiffin bombs in the media. I had the good fortune not to experience any of those explosive devices, but sometimes the tiffin containers held volatile ingredients ready to explode in a more personal way, once introduced to my stomach.

Initially, we hurried with our meals and refueling, being that the trooper was in critical condition. But then we received word of a delay; the doctor wasn't able to stabilize the patient and would not allow him to be transported until he was. We waited, revising the flight plan multiple times until AAI asked us to fax a new one. Nothing had changed but the departure times, and we explained our situation regarding the critical care patient, but AAI did not care to hear our bloody business, they wanted a shiny new fax because they had run out of room to scribble their amendments on the goddamned original.

The weather had remained calm throughout the day, with broken and scattered patches of clouds, and the sun wasn't shy about blasting our little airport with its sizzling, ultraviolet death rays. Time went by though, and it was creeping on into the late afternoon, nearly to the point where I was concerned that the "no-flight after sunset" rule would bring any rescue flight to a halt before we were even off the ground. Talking to the IPS officer in charge at the airport, telling him I had to go soon if the flight was to be that day, he went to work on his police radio and, half an hour later, the patient arrived by ambulance.

He was unconscious, and his right leg was unnaturally shorter than his left. The bandages on both damaged legs were red with blood. Still lacking any proper stretcher for the aircraft, we had to lay the young man on the floor as delicately as possible. The doctor was holding the IV bottle, and he, along with another attendant, squeezed into the back seats to accompany the lad to Raipur. The trooper had many well-wishers to see him off, and BK cleared them away from the helicopter before I started. We took off with little daylight to spare and set course for Raipur. En route, with the smell of blood filling the cabin, I checked over my shoulder with the passengers and patient from time to time, but they remained calm throughout the flight.

Fifty miles from Raipur Airport, I gave ATC my usual call to let them know I was swooping into their airspace with an emergency medical evacuation to land at the heliport. They acknowledged me, told me to proceed inbound and that no other traffic was around. The flight seemed to be going smoothly until they asked for my FIC/ADC clearances. I gave them the last numbers that I had fought for and received from AAI.

"Helicopter, Alpha Bravo," ATC radioed, addressing me with the Astar's partial call sign, "Your FIC/ADC numbers are not valid... How do you wish to proceed?"

I rechecked the numbers on my flight plan and had read them correctly.

I radioed back, "Raipur Tower, we received the latest FIC/ADC before departing Jagdalpur. I request direct routing to Raipur IPS Helipad on an emergency medical flight."

"Raajjerrrr…" he trilled. He paused for a moment and then said, "Alpha Bravo, the FIC/ADC clearances provided have expired, you will need a new flight plan. How do you wish to proceed?"

There was a mix-up somewhere, but I had indeed given him the latest clearances I'd received and grew impatient.

"Sir, I have a trooper aboard losing a lot of blood, and missing one leg. Not long ago he had two."

Repeating my initial call, I continued, "This is an emergency medical evacuation, I wish to proceed direct to Raipur Heliport."

A few silent moments passed before he answered, "Alpha Bravo, I will handle FIC/ADC from here. You are cleared direct to Raipur Heliport."

"Direct Raipur Heliport, Alpha Bravo."

News of the blast had reached Raipur, and cameramen and journalists had staked out prime spots next to the heliport to video the landing. Nothing attracts a crowd like a crowd, and there were hundreds of citizen gawkers at the heliport with them. Upon setting down, BK quickly jumped out to keep heads and hands out of the tailrotor, a grave concern always when landing near an overwrought crowd. Troopers swarmed the helicopter, helping the doctor get their wounded comrade unloaded and into the waiting ambulance. Journalists and cameramen tried to swarm in also, flinging their cameras about and squeezing off shots over their heads, trying to win a Pulitzer; they were all pushed back by lathi-baton wielding IPS. Shouting, pushing and shoving, it was pandemonium on the heliport as I shut down.

With police escorts and every siren wailing, the ambulance barreled away down the narrow street with journalists in trail. While the sirens faded in the distance, so did the tension from the heliport. Order was restored, and the place became quiet. Most onlookers faded away after they had an eyeful of the helicopter and the ambulances, but a few hung around for a bonus gawk session. BK and his gang of mysteriously materializing technicians started wrapping up the helicopter while I walked around it for the post-flight inspection.

Delayed by our hotel driver, it was way past sunset before a ride was sorted out and we were transported to our Raipur home, the Hotel Grand. A job fair was being held, and rooms were hard to come by. BK was lucky, and he and his mob of technicians shared a room, a few sleeping on the moldy carpeting around the beds. I was apparently given the hotel's last room, and it had seen better days. The window glass was cracked, letting noise and mosquitoes in, and the shower had only cold water. There was no air conditioning and the temperature was stifling, but I figured it was survivable with only the ceiling fan. Switching it on, however, produced troubling gray smoke from behind the switch panel. A call to the front desk imploring for better options only resulted in rejection—there were no other rooms available.

"Please say you have cold beer," I said, just looking for an affirmative answer.

"Jee, jee, saa," the man said. "Yes, yes, we have many spirits available, can I send something to you room?"

"Thanks, I'll take it at the bar."

The dark bar was packed, and multiple TVs were broadcasting cricket. The patrons, all male, were focused on the match and shouting at the TV screens. I had a beer and was shoveling down the hotel's tasty dish of grilled fish and watching the cricket match.

Halfway through the meal, I received a call from Mahesh informing me to shift back to Bhubaneswar. There was an upcoming mission regarding one of the chairman's investment projects up in the hills.

"No problem," I said, and thought a bit of ferry time with the promise of no blood and guts on the other end would suit me just fine. In fact, if I never saw another teenager with a bloody stump where his leg had been would be quite alright.

In no mood for flight planning, but enjoying the spirited shouting from the crowd, I watched cricket late into the night. A turban-less, but patka-wearing bearded Sikh sitting next to me struck up a gab session of small talk, trying to explain the rules and the process of scoring runs. It began to make sense in my slightly buzzed mind, but I was far from becoming an ambassador of the game.

I eventually bid him a good evening and retired to my holding cell on the fourth floor. About having a heart attack from the cold shower, I shivered myself back to warmth and then tried the ceiling fan once more. Alas, no little elves had come to fix the wiring while I was gone, and smoke poured out of the wall once again. With one eye open and on the lookout for electrical sparks, I tried, but mostly failed to sleep.

38.

Middle of Nowhere

The beasts, numbering over a dozen, would not let me out of their sight. I had picked up my pace through the knee-high, lush green grass and weeds, temporarily gaining distance from them, but they soon closed the gap. I could hear weeds and brush getting trampled behind me. I could smell their breath and belching from the meal they had left behind in pursuit of me. Glancing over my shoulder, I could see that their eyes were fixated on me, ears pricked forward, noses extended out in front of them, trying to catch a whiff of this delectable creature who had stumbled through their herd. I reached the relative safety of a tree line, putting a massive Jujube tree between them and me. The cattle stopped, sniffed and stared at me wide eyed. Nature had called.

I remember, as a youth, being in the same situation on our neighbor's farm. Cattle are curious creatures, and if they see a lone biped walking across their pasture, they will come to check out the trespasser. It quickens the pulse, being trailed by big, lumbering animals snorting and kicking up dust, especially if the only form of refuge is a briar patch. You're fairly sure they won't hurt you, but the close proximity to a herd of animals that each outweigh you by 900 pounds or more sets off primeval warning reflexes.

We had landed in a remote meadow on a forested mountaintop near the tiny village of Malangtoli, Odisha. Hard to find on any map, it was a hundred miles north of Bhubaneswar and fifteen miles south of Barbil. Soon after landing, I developed a coffee over-capacity warning, and there were far too many villagers milling about near the helicopter for private work, so I had set off across the meadow where the cattle were grazing to find peace of mind. I wasn't bothered by the cattle so much, but a pack of thirty or so village kids found me amazingly curious as well, and I had to bend in close to the tree for adequate screening. As I leaned toward the tree, the evil-looking red ants that were climbing it began to perceive me as a threat, which led me to worry about where they intended to climb next.

We had taken off from Bhubaneswar mid-morning and flown forty minutes or so to this spot in the middle of nowhere. It was typical of places found in the middle of nowhere: tall green grass, tall leafy trees and graveyard quiet, with nary a paved road or manmade structure for miles, other than mud huts. It had friendly villagers and friendly cattle, and the added bonus of no Maoist menace nearby.

I had brought the chairman's daughter, herself an executive of the company, and three potential iron ore mining investors from Singapore to this idyllic spot. Now they were planning on how best to blast it to pieces.

The headmen of the local village were happy to greet us after landing, bringing garlands and gifts and singing songs, but it is likely they didn't know what a gargantuan strip mine would do to their mountaintop. Dynamite would soon be ripping apart the very meadow where their tail-flicking bovines were casually licking the windows on the helicopter. It would be a rude awakening for them when the project went through.

From somewhere, lunch was put together for BK and me, and we munched not-so-quietly on the spicy chicken curry and all the rice and roti we could eat. I was smacking my lips from the chilies and gulping water out of a pitcher. It wasn't bottled water, and the source was dubious, so I held back from drinking at first. But my mouth and tongue could not take the spice, and I soon drank with passion, trying to quench the flames incinerating my uvula.

The braver cattle grazed around the homemade chairs that the villagers had set up for us in the shade. One young heifer put her glistening wet nose on my arm, testing the limits of our relationship. The Indian cowboy-in-charge responded with a well-aimed pebble to her ribcage, and she tore off in a snorting, slobbering, head-shaking cloud of dust. I tried to tell the villagers that it was alright and didn't mind the curious cows—that I was an *All Creatures Great and Small* kind of friend to all species—and the cattle were not bothering me. Something was lost in the translation, though, and they stared at me like I was a freaky alien from another planet. They then alternated between throwing pebbles at the grazing cattle and having minutes-long gawk sessions at me; a few of them must have been thinking it would be fun to nail the foreign guy with a pebble or two, if I judged their pointing fingers and subsequent laughter correctly.

We spent five hours on top of the mountain, the businessmen discussing plans with regional contacts and villagers. They had spread out several topographical maps on the grass in the shade, holding them down with rocks and kneeling at their edges, pointing at different spots with twigs and making marks and notes with a red Sharpie. Twice we started up and went for short flights to get aerial views of the terrain. One spot was near an immense cliff and, with the midday updrafts, it was a little bumpy.

They requested that I slow down and hover over a rocky escarpment adjacent to this cliff, but it was quite hot and, with the gusty winds around the vertical terrain, the power margin just wasn't there to hover fully loaded like we were. I could only go back and forth over their areas of interest as slow as possible, and that led to more bumps and yawing. One chap's stomach did not care for that, and he let up his lunch into one of the helicopter's rare and endangered sick-sacks that I had swiped from a seat back pocket during an Air India flight.

Back at the mountaintop meadow, it was late afternoon before they began wrapping up their meeting. The cattle had moseyed off somewhere out of sight, but most of the villagers were still huddled around us in the lengthening shadows, staring. When not flying, I had stayed occupied with reading a book and getting up for short walkabouts. The village kids thought it their duty to keep an eye on me and would accompany me along the dirt paths. A few ran off in front of me, clearing the way of cattle with sticks and rocks, while others strolled alongside, looking up and watching me. I might have been the first white man they had ever seen. It's doubtful they had regular access to television or internet, and I figured they would remember for the rest of their lives the day a flying machine came to their mountain. Especially if, shortly after, bastards started blowing it apart and put a goddamned mine there.

We loaded up the maps, charts, notes and investors and cranked up for Barbil, only a short flight away—short by air, but a day or two journey by land over the deep rocky cuts and heavily wooded terrain. The village kids, laughing and waving, ran after us as we lifted off the meadow. I think a few of the little shits were chucking rocks. My passengers, even the one who had lost his lunch, wanted one more look at the potential mining sight. This being late in the afternoon, the thermals had dissipated, and I was able to offer a smoother ride for them, but they had seen enough after one final pass and I headed north for our evening destination.

Fifteen minutes later, we landed in the red Martian dust of Barbil. BK and I helped the passengers carry their gear and overnight bags into a couple of mud-splattered SUVs, and they rushed off. Waiting for the two of us was an ear-bejeweled, tallish, skinny and thuggy looking young dude. With one foot up on the bumper of the last SUV, he spat paan juice and glared as if we were the source of all problems in his woebegone life. BK said something in Hindi that sounded friendly to me, but the punk only grunted and looked impatient.

Satisfied that we had all the holes plugged and delicate helicopter parts covered, we grabbed our already dust-coated bags and climbed in with Thuggy Guy. No sooner did he have the engine started than he dropped the clutch and careened out of the parking area, narrowly missing our helicopter with kicked-up mud spray. BK and I shouted at the same time to slow down, him in Hindi and me in English, but the delinquent just grinned and laughed.

Instead of the company guesthouse, we would be staying with our passengers at the Lucky India Hotel, but the way this idiot drove, we would need luck to reach it in one piece. Against our continued protests and shouting, he continued driving way too recklessly, even for India. At every corner, the tires were chirping and squealing. BK slapped him in the head, but that only made the little prick more insane.

Careening into the hotel parking lot, he came sliding to a stop. We hadn't stopped berating him throughout the ten-minute ride, but the kid just wore a dumb smile. I wanted to break his jaw and then watch him smile. The calm and cool BK was thinking along the same lines, and he reached over the punk's arm, turned off the engine and took the ignition key. Once the car was immobilized, BK calmly climbed out and walked to the driver's door and, before the rambunctious snot could lock it, flung it open, grabbed his skinny neck and wrenched him out and down to the gritty pavement. I was out of the car as soon as it stopped and watched the events unfold with somewhat sadistic satisfaction. I hoped the young brat learned a lesson before someone, besides him, was hurt.

After getting our rooms sorted, I went for dinner at the brightly lit and modern looking hotel restaurant. I was pleasantly surprised to find such a nice place in Barbil, especially after my last stay in town at the poorly maintained company guesthouse. The investors, having dinner on their minds as well, invited me to their table for a cold beer and, when it came time to order food, the lemon chicken was a delicious choice. We shared a bit of small talk, but they mostly wanted to talk specifics about the mine and other deals they had going on. So, after the meal was over, I excused myself, stood up and tried but failed to cover my share of the tab. The group politely refusing to let me pay. Thanking them, I bid them goodnight.

Craving a smoke, I walked out the front lobby and saw our ex-driver moping on the steps. His clothes were dirty where BK had planted him, and he had bruises on his throat and a swollen eye. He glanced at me but quickly looked away. He had been crying.

As George Bernard Shaw said, "Youth, it is wasted on the young."

39.

The Shining

I didn't know for how long we would be recalled to Bhubaneswar area, but if the company wanted to keep running us back and forth from Chhattisgarh to Odisha, that was fine with me. It was a good scenic two-and-a-half-hour flight either way. Both places had their pros and cons. Jagdalpur had more flying and freedom from the hassles and illogical procedures of the towered airport, but Anika was in Bhubaneswar, and the positive aspects of that were indisputable. In the end, it was not my call. I would go wherever the company needed me and do whatever I could to earn the paycheck.

Right then I was in neither place, but flying from Barbil to the company's steel plant in Jajpur, Odisha, with the chairman's daughter, Nima, in the co-pilot's seat and BK sitting with the same three investors in back. It was another suffocatingly hot day, and the passengers looked uncomfortable and crowded, especially with BK taking up the fourth seat. Politely, he had leaned forward as far as he could on the edge of his seat to allow more room for the guests. Still, air conditioning would have made the experience more enjoyable, and I again felt the need to mention that over the intercom. Nima agreed that it'd be worth it and promised to press for the retrofit once she was back at the company HQ.

Nima was an attractive woman in her late thirties, university educated in the UK, married with two kids, and had been following in her father's business footsteps for years. She also held a pilot's license and was eager to talk about all things flying and plied me with questions regarding my experience and background. It was forty minutes of uncontrolled airspace between Barbil and Jajpur, and we had plenty time to cover all the main points.

Reaching the steel plant, it wasn't quite as vast and expansive as the others I had flown to in recent weeks, but it was still a monstrous operation that covered over a square mile. There were hundreds of buildings, conveyors and railroad loading facilities that all looked to be rust covered but in fact were only coated in the fine, red dust from the ore. Nima asked me to do a couple slow orbits around the whole facility for the benefit of the investors and, while at it, I searched for the helipad.

Once spotting it, I wasn't sure it was the right place. The pad was engulfed with head-high scrub brush and bushgrass, and it looked in quite poor condition. But judging from all the SUVs parked nearby, I figured this was the spot. Checking the torn and faded windsock, it hung limp as wet laundry. A little headwind would have been nice with all the weight I carried, but I was able to set down into a cloud of tumbleweeds without breaking anything.

Nima and the businessmen left for the steel plant, and after BK and I had the helicopter wrapped up, we clambered into our own SUV and were taken to another of the company's many guesthouses to relax and wait. Pulling off the road and making our way down the winding driveway, we could see that the guesthouse was enormous and extravagant, at least at first glance. But getting out of the car near the front lobby revealed that a coat of paint and a few weeks of TLC were in order. There must have been at least 200 rooms in the expansive three-story building, but as far as I could tell, BK and I were the only people around besides the ancient caretakers. It felt abandoned, haunted. It reminded me of the massive and empty hotel in Jack Nicholson's movie, *The Shining*, minus the snow and, I hoped, minus the psycho.

We were shown to our rooms and, after dumping my gear inside, I decided to explore. There were no other buildings that I could see within miles, and it was eerily quiet for India, where usually a television was blaring or Bollywood music was pumping somewhere. Even the traffic could not be heard as we were about a mile off the highway. Out the backside of the building was a junk-strewn mess of rotting construction materials and trash. In the better-maintained front courtyard, attempts were being made to give an appearance of upkeep. It was then that I noticed a small army of women stretched out over a part of the shaded lawn, trimming the grass by hand. They were making the tall grass short with no type of cutters, but by just ripping the sprouts up by handfuls and throwing them in a pile.

Judging from the weathering, I would have guessed the building itself was ten years old, and walking around the quiet and empty top floor, I discovered the project had never been completed. The dark and dusty corridors and hallways leading to the numerous rooms showed that all were in various stages of completion. It was so spooky quiet that it would have taken strong will to sneak around there at midnight. Walking down the darkened staircase, I eased back to the main floor. There, at least, were a few live humans and a stray dog near the lobby. An old man had scrounged up lunch for us from somewhere and had been looking for me.

Over lunch, BK and I made small talk about my upcoming mini-vacation. I had struck a deal with Sami to give me a one-week break from India in the coming weeks and in the morning, before takeoff, I had confirmed with him the dates that I would be allowed to leave. After so many months of Indian food and culture, I needed a respite. I wanted a real cheeseburger and, after months of filth, only wanted to be buried in sand on a white beach and then soak in the sea all day. And I wanted all that in a place where every set of eyeballs was not staring at me. After a little research, I had decided to head to Boracay Island in the Philippines, with the added bonus of a one-night layover in Bangkok.

Lunch over, the driver came to take us back to the helipad. Reaching there with plenty of time before the passengers arrived, we approached the helicopter to find an invasion taking place. There was a thin, dark line of ants moving from the edge of the cracked concrete, across the helipad to the helicopter skid and then up the cross tube, disappearing somewhere within the airframe. We cautiously set our bags down a safe distance from the tiny marauders, and BK flung open the doors to see what carnage they had created.

The passengers had received homemade sweets from our mountaintop villager friends the day before, and one of them had left his delectable gift underneath the backseats. How those tiny, six-legged buggers detected the sweet goodies way up inside a sealed helicopter and had it invaded and occupied within minutes of landing deserved a university grant for study.

Going on the offensive, BK first grabbed the bag of sweets and chucked it into the surrounding tall grass, accumulating several of the feisty critters on his arm in the process. Digging a small broom out of helicopter's cargo space, he began sweeping away their line of reinforcements that was trekking across the cement toward the skids. Having no Raid Insect Fogger available but, weirdly, finding an ancient can of hair spray beneath the backseats, I began spraying them with fluorocarbons and Aqua Net. Soon we had turned the tide of battle and had a sticky line of flailing ants stuck to the landing gear.

BK swept most of the remaining sweet-toothed ants out of the cabin, and we had it tidied up by the time the passengers arrived. After a brief explanation for the missing candy and the noxious smell of Aqua Net in the air, we loaded up and prepared to fly back to Bhubaneswar. The helipad was tight, and I had to hover up and out of ground effect for the takeoff in order to clear the vegetation. It seemed the passengers had picked up more souvenirs, books and other goodies from the steel plant, which bumped our weight even higher. I told BK that if we didn't have the power margin at the helipad, he would have to get out and I would pick him up at a more open space, like back in the parking lot of the haunted guesthouse.

He grunted and said, "No problem Cap'n. *You* can do it."

It wasn't as if I was flapping my wings trying to fly—I pulled one lever and pushed the other. If the gauges read that the engine was maxed out before we were flying forward, someone was going for a walk.

The Shining

We had just enough power for lift and flew out at maximum weight; Nima instinctively raised her feet to keep them from getting tangled in the treetops seemingly inches below us. The satisfying shudder of the aircraft passing through Effective Translational Lift (ETL), accompanied by the subtle bump into the air told me we were on our way.

40.

Ambushed

Just when I thought the monsoon was drained out, we flew to Jagdalpur in perhaps the worst weather we'd seen. The visibility, according to Bhubaneswar ATC, was sixteen hundred meters, but I would have guessed it much lower than that. The haze and mist around Bhubaneswar turned to low clouds and rain the further I flew, the exact opposite of my most recent flight that way. BK was again shaking his head while we went scud-running up the valleys, but I made sure we always had an *out* and that the valleys never became too narrow for us to turn around. We could literally turn the helicopter on a dime within a narrow valley if need be—if the dime was as big as a volleyball court, that is.

The boss was sending us back to Jagdalpur for an indefinite period, and the way they had been talking at the head office, the move was to become semi-permanent in the coming weeks. There was a lot of work coming up, and whenever the monsoon cleared, we would have consistent flying. There were tons of supplies to haul out to the IPS and CRPF camps, replenishing their food stocks, kerosene for the electric generators and replace equipment that had become unserviceable during the rains. If not supplies, personnel were always in need of transfer. The roads were being used more, but air travel was preferred for obvious reasons.

Reaching the familiar surroundings of Jagdalpur, I parked the helicopter and shut down in a light mist. There were no pressing missions at the time and, with the weather uncooperative, we were not anxious to fly anyway. But if the weather did improve, several IPS sorties awaited.

With rain and mist gently falling outside the door, even the guesthouse and Sun City could have a relaxing atmosphere.

Following lunch, the crew spread out on the worn and faded furniture throughout the living room, rubbed their ever-expanding bellies and gossiped incessantly—everyone at once, of course. Never were they serious discussions, but always accompanied with jokes and good-natured ribbing. After months of living, eating and sweating together, the guesthouse was becoming more like a frat house.

Except for a run late in the day, there wasn't much to do. I rechecked the in-limbo mission plans, but the skies were sodden and thick with clouds before nightfall. The chances of them clearing, and me flying, were nil.

Waking in the morning to a loud and strange Hindi conversation coming from our living room, I dislodged my ear plugs and could tell the voices belonged to several men who were obviously upset. Walking out of my room rubbing my eyes, we were being informed by the IPS of an ambush on the streets of Jagdalpur during the night. A popular politician's two sons had been targeted and gunned down by motorcycle-riding Maoist-Naxalites as they walked to a temple.

Emotions were running high throughout the IPS ranks and several officers came to the guesthouse, imploring us to take off quickly for an emergency evacuation. We were told to medevac them to Raipur, or at least one of them. The other was in quite critical condition and not stabilizing, near to death. With the popularity and political connections of the victims came an extra sense of urgency from the IPS, and I smelled trouble.

In answer to their question of when we could depart, taking a glance out the window told me all I needed. Heavy mist in the air, thick raindrops falling off the eaves, and low, unmoving, gloomy clouds. I knew it wasn't flyable. They insisted, though, seeming to think that somehow I could magically part the clouds and rain and fly the wounded to Raipur. As much as I wanted to help, I wasn't about to endanger my life or that of my crew. The clingy, low clouds were nearly brushing the roof tops.

I asked them to wait for the weather to improve, but they did not want to hear that and looked at me with sad, plaintive eyes. I politely reminded them of the numerous helicopter crashes due to poor weather around Chhattisgarh and the region, especially the recent crash and deaths in Andhra Pradesh with Chief Minister Reddy.

They didn't want to hear that either. They just wanted me to fly the helicopter and begged me to reconsider.

"Please do something, Captain..."

"We will do this," I said, gently as possible but trying to sound firm. "We will keep watching the weather, and the moment it improves, we will launch."

They relented and left the house. Not long after, however, I was forced to take calls from a great many people, most of whom only spoke in Hindi. All were asking us when we could fly. The IPS had given out my phone number to people who thought they could do a better job of convincing me: relatives and friends of the victims, plus politicians. I was glad no one else came to the house besides the IPS, but we were expecting unwanted visitors at any minute, and it was one of the rare times we closed and bolted the front door during daytime.

After an hour, the weather was even worse, with bigger raindrops coming down and slapping the pavement. It was one of those weather days where the system would not budge. Still, the phone calls came, and the pressure mounted. Sami waded into the fray, worried about the image of the company, telling me to be careful but to fly whenever the chance came. I assured him I would.

Then, thinking we would not hear the end of the phone calls and worried we would be perceived as cold-hearted backsliders who weren't even trying, I came up with a different solution: I proposed a short flight for a more accurate weather reading, although none was needed from my perspective. And to provide an objective view and second opinion, I would take one of the airport IPS troopers, Paavak, with me. He was the senior officer at the airport and one of those who had come to our house early in the morning. Once I had flown him a few minutes or so, we would return to parking and report if the weather was flyable or not—I knew it wouldn't be, but at least we would have tried and the pressure would be eased.

I gathered my gear together, put on my uniform, and told the crew the plan. BK did not like it and said it was too dangerous. Telling him no one would fly with me but Paavak, I persuaded him that I would not be gone long: just over the treetops and back to parking. Even so, I went through the motions of filing a Jagdalpur to Raipur flight plan, but we didn't tell the IPS and would not tell Paavak until we were ready. No need to have their hopes raised or, worse yet, give them a chance to do something foolish, like move the wounded from the hospital to the airfield expecting miracles.

We loaded up the car and drove to the airport, stopping next to the helicopter. Before we even set foot out of the car, every guard's cellphone shot up to his ear, each wanting to be the first guy to tell his boss that the pilot had showed up. BK and the crew settled them down, but more and more of the IPS and, then, civilians starting showing up. I emphasized repeatedly not to bring the patients, although they were demanding to. My fear was that the patients would be brought and their condition made worse on the way to the airport, or back to the Jagdalpur hospital after we could not fly them.

The mist had turned into a steady rain, and the dark gray overcast clouds looked low enough to poke with a stick. The crew asked about fuel, which I declined; it would have been difficult to add without water contamination from the rain. After a wet and dreary preflight, I hurriedly jumped in and started up. By that time, cars and people were streaming into the small airport and I was worried that the ambulance carrying the wounded would be next.

Giving a signal to BK, who was standing next to Paavak, he gestured toward the helicopter and told him to climb aboard. At first, Paavak's eyes grew twice their original size, looking at me and BK. He hesitated but, realizing that fellow troopers were watching, gathered himself and strode purposefully toward the helicopter. BK reminded him to remove his cow-pie colored beret before it was blown away in the downwash.

Climbing into the left seat, we strapped him in and placed the headset on him, making sure he could hear me over the intercom. Then I lifted off the ramp and taxied to the runway. I could barely see the end. Doing a 360-degree pedal turn, I scanned the surroundings for the most likely-looking hole. There wasn't one, so I headed straight down the runway until my airspeed was twenty-five or thirty knots and climbed slowly to treetop level.

"Do you see any place I can get through, Paavak?" I asked.

"N-n-no, saa," he sputtered.

He had one white-knuckled hand gripped to the seat, and the other was braced against the door frame. His eyes were a little wild, and his head was on a swivel, looking all around, out the side window and behind. Leaning forward closer to the windscreen didn't help his eyesight either, the clouds and rain were just as thick.

Turning south over the airport perimeter wall and open field, I saw nothing that I liked. Between the rain on the windscreen and the clouds, visibility was poor to say the least. The ceiling was an optimistic 200 feet and assuredly lower in places. It would have been suicide to continue. I finished my abbreviated traffic pattern, landed at my parking spot and shut down. Swinging my door open, I waved my arms in front of me and shook my head for all to see.

Paavak was out the door and on the ground nearly before my landing skids were. He shook his head emphatically and held up his hands like he was patting someone's back, trying to calm down the people who ran to him. The debate raged on, but the short flight had the desired result of showing one of their own that indeed the weather was hazardous. It deflected pressure away from us and onto Paavak, who I had made a believer.

Still not satisfied, several relatives and friends approached and begged me to fly. They were not belligerent but, rather, pleading mournfully. They had tears in their eyes and clasping their hands together, let out great shrieks of anguish as they kneeled down in the rainwater beside my helicopter, trapping me in the pilot's seat and imploring me to do the impossible.

Ambushed

After emotions tempered, the senior officers I talked with told me that the brothers had died. One of them had already passed before we reached the airport, and the other died soon after. The doctors could do no more for them.

41.

Carnival of Life

As my vacation days drew nearer, the call for flights out of Jagdalpur into the jungle became a steady stream. Depending on the weather, sometimes we could launch, while other times we were held on the ground due to poor visibility. The weather-grounding days were becoming rare, though, and with the number of flights picking up, the tone from Sami suggested the company was not happy about my break. He even implied they might cancel my vacation and reimburse me for the reserved flights and hotels. Before that drastic measure was taken, fortunately, Chatterjee was called to my rescue. He would take over any missions during my absence.

On the last day before I departed, a short program was requested to Konta, Bheji and Dantewada. I was concerned there would be a wall of clouds over the hilly breaks on the way south out of Jagdalpur to Konta, but it was good conditions for flying. Great, in fact. There were only low, wispy clouds at three thousand feet when we took off in the morning. I climbed through those and cruised on top of the scattered layer at five thousand feet in blue skies. Searching every horizon, I could not see any sign of convective activity and, in a rare occurrence, there was no haze. Instead of the usual milky white that diminished the horizon to nothingness and obscurity, I could see clearly for miles.

Flying to Konta loaded with four troopers and a few bags of rice, we unloaded and took on three more troopers and several boxes of ammunition for Bheji. At Bheji, the three troopers unloaded the ammo and exchanged places with three of their comrades rotating out. They had the yellow pallor of malaria, a common problem among both troopers and villagers after monsoon season with the amount of standing water.

Landing at Dantewada, Rabinesh was there to welcome us, and after shutting down, I joined him for coffee and biscuits while BK handled the refueling. It was a magnificent day in India by any measure. The skies were clear, with just a light breeze rattling the leaves. Even the temperature was moderate, not past the eighty-degree mark. The work finished for the day, we sat in the shade of the trees bordering the helipad, loitering and talking about my upcoming short holiday to the Philippines. Rabinesh gave me orders to bring back a pair of Havaianas sandals. In return, his wife would make me real, American style, chocolate chip cookies, so he said.

It was one of those days where everything clicked and the world was on my side. The people surrounding me were top notch, and I was living an adventure. For all the danger and potential violence lurking in the jungle at the time, I could not have imagined flying anywhere else.

Even so, I was looking forward to my spell outside of India. Chatterjee had arrived in Jagdalpur and, after flying back, he and I spent the afternoon catching up. I briefed him on the latest happenings around Jagdalpur and Bhubaneswar while he extolled the Mi17 and life in Shimla. We had not talked since my brush with death in Kistaram, and his eyes were the size of pies when I showed him the gaping hole in the tailrotor driveshaft that we had replaced. He was a consummate professional, but I could tell he was not pleased to be back in the jungle. Before bidding him farewell at the Hotel Devansh, I promised to be back as soon as possible.

I would be flying Raipur to Bhubaneswar on a commercial flight and, knowing the best time to travel is early in the morning, I set out of Jagdalpur at sunrise with a driver in his Tata. Making good time with our early start, it was still over half a day before we reached the Raipur airport; but the miles, bumps and cow jams on the road were not able to affect my good mood.

I was on vacation and feeling good, knowing a beach was only hours away, but anxious too, worried my company would change their mind at the last minute and cancel my leave before I fled the country. It had happened before. Or, worse yet, that something might happen to Chatterjee while I was out playing.

I relaxed when, in the departures lounge, they called for my flight to Bhubaneswar. With one free day before setting off on my journey, Anika and I had plans with Vihaan and his wife. They promised to show me a bit of ancient India, something I was not completely thrilled about, but looked forward to any time spent with Anika.

With Vihaan at the wheel of our borrowed car, we struck out at nine o'clock the next day, his wife riding shotgun while Anika and I were nestled in the back seat. Both girls were dressed in tight blue jeans and kurta tops with dupatta scarves. I had on a short-sleeve button down and my cargo pants with flip-flops. The sun was out and blazing, but we were comfortable in the air-conditioned car.

A half-hour later, we reached Pipili and turned left off the main road, headed for a temple in Konark. By that time in India, I had seen enough temples and didn't care to see another one, but my friends said that this particular temple was unique and should not be missed.

Vihaan said something in Hindi, then, that made the girls giggle. With a blushing smile, Anika told me that the ancient temple we were going to visit was adorned with hundreds of human-size sculptures that would not fail to impress me. Although having never been there, I had heard about the erotic rock sculptures of Khajuraho in Madhya Pradesh. Reading between the lines, I realized what type of temple my companions were taking me to.

We pulled into the parking lot, opened the doors and were immediately hit with the stifling heat and humidity. There were hundreds of people about but not as many as I'd thought there would be, and I was the only foreigner in sight.

Wandering over to the scraggly vendor stalls in search of bottled water, a shady-looking dude with no-good mischief on his mind noticed me and seemed intent on an ambush. Making my purchase of the water, I tracked him out of the corner of my eye when he sprang up from the dusty curb he was squatting on and made a beeline for me.

To loud protests and shouting, he grabbed a drinking cup from one of the vendors, shouted back at the man, emptied the contents in the dirt and arrogantly shoved the stamped aluminum cup below my chin. He stared into my eyeballs without shame or conscience, like I genuinely owed him.

"Get lost, dude," I said, pushing his arm out of the way and walking on.

"Jee, saa, jee... Yes, saa, saa!" He followed me and put the cup on my chest, begging.

Hoping just to be rid of the indignant turd, I dug out a one rupee coin and dropped it into the cup he had pilfered. He reached in, grabbed it and held it inches from his face like he expected it to bloom into a gold brick. Saying something clearly derogatory in Hindi, he glared at me, which ticked me off. I should've ignored him and walked away, but the shameless dirtbag really grated my nerves. I reached out, snapped the rupee out of his fingers, stuck it back in my pocket and said, "Go to hell, Gandu." *Gandu* being the only naughty Hindi word I knew.

Rejoining my gang, we walked to the entrance. My Indian friends were let in with a ten-rupee charge, but for just being a foreigner cost me 250 rupees. It was highway robbery, but I shelled out the cash and walked through the gate anyway, my fiscal sensibilities anguished.

The Konark Sun Temple was built in the thirteenth century and, at that time, it was located directly off the Bay of Bengal. The sandy beach and waves would have been where we parked our car, according to the information I'd seen, and ancient sailors had even used it for a landmark. In the present day, the ocean had receded, and the grounds sat about two miles back from the coast. The temple was in a slightly crumbling condition when we were there, and scaffolding had been erected to facilitate restoration work. It appeared no work was actively being done, but just erecting the scaffolding itself, which was mostly bamboo, looked to be a massive engineering feat, and perhaps a work stoppage and siesta was in order.

When I first approached the temple, it looked like the thousands of other temples spread across India. Walking closer, however, the shapes and figures of what the artisans were trying to depict became clearer. Simply put, it was thirteenth-century pornography. Although there were the usual sculptures of elephants, tigers and mythical beasts, the most numerous depictions by far were of sex and erotica. There were hundreds of life-sized statues that graphically showed an array of tantric sexual positions, sometimes involving one, but usually multiple partners.

The female likenesses were sculpted with immense breasts, and the males were also given an exaggerated profile—that is, unless they had available a form of ancient and powerful Viagra. Human and divine characters were shown engaged in the full spectrum of the "Carnival of Life" as the tourist literature stated.

I was almost speechless while we strolled around the outside of the structures, as were my friends and the other tourists. There were many opportunities for crude and adolescent jokes and I, astoundingly capable of inserting my foot into my mouth, did so multiple times. My companions were mostly quiet, though; maybe they were memorizing a few of the positions for future endeavors. I know my imagination was running a bit wild.

Perhaps that was the intention of the builders—to stir imaginations. Was it primitive sex education, or was it simply an ancient, gaudy tribute and monument to carnal pleasure? The tourist pamphlet went on to say that it took twelve years and over twelve hundred artisans to complete. That begs the question: Were there human models available during the sculpting?

We spent an hour and a half walking around the site, taking pictures and making crafty observations. I was broiled and soaked in sweat; all of us were. We found a decent shady spot under the trees near the six-foot berm that led down to the temple and, not worried about ants or stains, we sat in the soft, thick grass to relax and cool off.

The light breeze was the definition of bliss, but it did little to evaporate the accumulated moisture on my back and chest. All of us were ripe smelling. In India though, the use of deodorant was limited, and by that point I wasn't exactly a basket of mulberry-scented potpourri either. Never mind and nevertheless. Our thoughts were elsewhere.

42.

Puri Beach

Having seen all we cared to see of ancient erotica and taken photographs for future reference, we helped each other up from the matted grass where we rested, brushed off and walked to the car. Vihaan and his wife walked in front of us, giggling and whispering into each other's ears, no doubt of what was going through their minds. Anika was chatting on about something at her work, but my mind wandered elsewhere, and I wore an immovable grin. I heard her talking, but was distracted with the way her hair curved around her face and didn't comprehend a word she was saying. Noticing my crooked smile, she looked at me, stopped what she was saying and blushed.

"So, Captain Mike," she said, giving me one of her knee-weakening smiles, "What do you think of our ancient sculptures?"

"Magnificent," I said. "Looks like those ancient guys worked with hard tools."

Her smile getting wider, she reached up, poked me in the forehead, and her eyes narrowed. "Don't you get any crazy ideas up in there!"

We decided on a quick lunch in Puri and, afterwards, to hit the beach. Driving the forty minutes to town, we parked next to the sea, near the place I had brought my motorcycle months before. Helping Anika out of the car, we walked across the light traffic to a small restaurant, where the four of us were blessed with functioning air conditioning. The restaurant was vegetarian-only, but I was hungry enough to try their aloo gobi. My friends rattled off their own menu requests in rapid-fire Hindi and the beverage of choice was Thumbs Up cola. A Coca-Cola wannabe that tasted more like sugar water filtered through an engine crankcase than anything that would be approved by the FDA.

After the spicy, sinus-clearing lunch, we walked back across the street and down to the beach. There were more people out walking in the sand than the last time I'd been there, but it wasn't crowded. We took our sandals off and rolled up our pants. I was sorry I hadn't brought swim trunks or shorts, but looking up and down the beach, not a soul had proper swim gear on, except for a skinny dude who fancied himself a lifeguard. We knew this because he wore an odd-looking, white pointy hat that read "LIFEGUARD" in large red letters.

Widely scattered along the beach were a number of sun shelters for hourly rent, and they were just the right size for three or four plastic chairs. Vihaan hailed the proprietor of one and negotiated a deal for us all, but I didn't feel like sitting when there was a seaside to explore. I walked down the shallow incline to the water with Anika alongside, bumping into me unsteadily on the loose sand.

Snapping photos and walking through the sand in tight blue jeans on a steamy beach might have looked out of place with someone else, but not her. Even if she'd been wearing baggy coveralls, she would have been the most gorgeous woman on the Bay of Bengal. An elegant chin lifted toward the ocean, the breeze molding her kurta around each well-proportioned curve, a hand raised, shading her slightly squinting eyes, and long black hair blowing gently over her shoulders... But what I would've given to see her in a bikini.

The lifeguard followed along faithfully, carrying his emergency equipment—a small patched-up inner tube—and he appeared deeply concerned that a pasty foreigner like me might be swept away and lost during his watch. He tried to maintain an arm's-length distance. I guessed he was about fifty years old, five feet tall and eighty-five pounds. I've never been mistaken for a horse jockey, but I am not a big guy by Western standards, and I still outweighed him by at least double. The only way he could have rescued me was if he had a good arm and an accurate throw, and managed to ring the inner tube around my neck.

The vast majority of people on the beach were sitting or standing in their street clothes, content with merely watching the waves. Some, like Vihaan and his wife, were enjoying the scene from the shady protection of the sun shelter on the plastic lawn chairs. There were a few adventurous types who splashed around in the shallow water where the waves petered out coming up the beach, but all were modestly dressed, especially the girls and women, who kept even their legs covered with sarees or leggings. I think I saw not a dozen men or boys wearing shorts, and no one bared their torso.

I could not resist the urge, though. The crashing waves were four-to-five footers, the sea-scented mist filled my nose and I needed to get wet. Pulling off my shirt, I apologized to Anika for my immodesty and asked if she would hold it while I went for a dip. She giggled and continued to take photos, perhaps hoping to document the last minutes of the captain's life before he was swept away to Davey Jones' locker.

"Wait, I'm gonna give you my trousers too," I said, pretending to undo my pants. She let out a little scream and covered her mouth, running back a few steps, laughing.

Standing at the water's edge with one hand holding his inner tube, the other scratching the sparse hair on the back of his head, a new level of worry rose up in the lifeguard's eyes, and he said something in Hindi, pointing out to the ocean.

"What'd he say?" I asked over the sound of a frothy wave rushing up the sand.

"He said, you should be careful!" Anika shouted back. "Something about riptides all along here, Michael!"

I put my thumb and finger together. "Got it!"

With the lifeguard keeping pace behind me, I waded into the water up to my waist. The waves were gloriously powerful and nearly knocked me off balance every time they rushed in. I turned my back and let them crash over me, then leaned with all my strength toward the beach as the water sucked backwards, sand underneath my feet being vacuumed away, making it hard to hold balance. It was quite a workout, and I was panting like a lapsed marathoner after fifteen minutes of this Maytag action, but it was so deliciously refreshing. Though knowing I'd be crusty with salt afterwards, I felt more and more sanitized with each pummeling wave. Like the months of sweat, dust and filth, the food poisoning, anxiety and dried blood were being scrubbed from my pores and cleansed from my spirit.

After thirty minutes, I was starting to wheeze and reluctantly came out of the surf; a noticeable relief flooded through the lifeguard as my shaky legs walked up the sand. He stuck with me the whole time and flashed his wide, vacant-toothed grin. I smiled back at him. In fact, I'd been smiling like the Joker since my feet first touched the beach.

I slapped him gently on the back and told him, "Thank you, bhaiya."

"Jee saa, jee, jee, jee," he said, and then rattled on with more Hindi that I didn't understand.

Anika had bailed on me and retreated to the sun shelter with the other two. After I survived the first ten minutes, she figured the sea would not take me and, getting blasted by the sun, she stole away. I walked back to our group and, when the lifeguard followed me there, I fetched my wallet from Anika and gave him fifty rupees for his troubles. He was delighted with that and then, spotting one of his comrades further down the beach leading a camel, called him over.

I was slowly catching my breath, my heart pounding hard enough to send ripples beneath my left pectoral. Vihaan pointed that out and laughed, "Shall we call a doctor, Captain?"

"No need," I gasped, winking at Anika, "but someone be ready to give mouth-to-mouth resuscitation."

The girls scrunched up their noses and made sounds of "Ewww!" and "Auuuw!" simultaneously. Anika said sweetly, "I think we'll call the doctors first."

I put my shirt back on, feeling the sticky and scratchy salt all over my body. The camel jockey pulled up with his brightly decorated dromedary and stared at us, mainly me. Knowing an easy mark when he saw one, he pointed and demanded, more than asked, "You saa, you want ride camel."

Normally, I don't do those types of rides. I fear that, too often, the animals are exploited and abused. Perhaps not true in all situations, but that's my perception. Nonetheless, I'd never been on a camel, and the chances were slim the opportunity would come around again. So I bargained for a price and took my turn as a camel cowboy. A ladder was provided to mount the beast and, settling my bum onto the hard square seat, we set off down the beach.

The camel was so heavily garlanded and decorated, especially over her head and eyes, that I didn't think she could see well. I did my best to steer her left and right to avoid the other beachcombers, but we had a few close calls. The camel herder walked alongside but was lost in his own thoughts; his pinky finger plunged deep into his nasal cavity on a research expedition. Finding something of apparent value up in there, he would fish it out with an aggressive twisting of his head and hand, give it close examination and flick it into the sand. Some lucky sand-crab's hors d'oeuvres later.

Returning to our starting position next to my friends, I bailed off the camel and nearly knocked myself breathless in the process—should have waited for the ladder. A few more photos were snapped with the camel man and lifeguard, then they wandered off in search of their next customer. My shirt was so itchy and scratchy that I took it off again. Anika had been a real sweetheart and bought a cheap towel from a vendor along the street and then tried to scrape the salt off my skin— which only made it worse until a vendor came by with bottled water.

We watched the waves for another hour or so but, before leaving, I implored my mates to come down to the ocean and feel it. We walked closely together down the shallow slope as a foursome. Vihaan's wife was anxious and euphoric, she had never been so close to ocean waves before and was elated when the misty breeze blew over us and the waves rushed across our feet, up past our knees. She and Anika screamed in cute innocent-girl harmony while holding on to our hands to remain steady. It was an exquisite moment.

Walking back up to the car, the sky had clouded up, and I could smell rain in the air. There was a breeze that swirled around and blew sand into our faces. The girls used their dupattas to cover their mouth and eyes while Vihaan and I protected our faces with hairy arms. The breeze felt good despite the stinging sand and helped dry my damp pants and chaffing skin. Taking a last, squinty look at Puri Beach, we climbed into the car.

My companions had one more stop on their itinerary in Puri: the White Pagoda, or Jagganath Temple as it was better known. I wondered if this would be a temple like the one we had just seen. "No," they told me. "It's a more family friendly temple and quite strict religiously."

It was so strict that after we parked and walked to the entrance, I was forbidden to enter. It was Hindus-only admission. Apologizing for the temple's apparent intolerance of a backsliding Catholic, my friends asked if they should skip it; telling them not to worry, I went to wait at the car.

Sipping on the coconut a street vendor had viciously hacked open with his machete, I befriended two root-beer-colored stray dogs with a bag of soggy sour-cream and onion potato chips. They drooled a small puddle in the shade of the car and panted from the heat, but not for long. As I draped my leg over the open car door, daydreaming about bikinis, Bangkok and a beach on Boracay, the sky opened up and out fell cool raindrops equal in girth to my sand-encrusted big toe.

43.

One Night in Bangkok

Returning late at night to the Bhubaneswar guesthouse, my old whistle-blowing friend, the soggy security guard, eyed me warily as he let me through the gate; Vihaan and his wife had returned earlier while Anika and I had gone for dinner. I walked the dark stairs and halls to my room, anticipating a good night's sleep before my outbound journey the next day.

To my dismay, a visiting mid-management type from the mines, who stayed in a room adjacent to my own, had his television cranked to maximum. And though it was way past sleepy time, the sound waves reverberated along the walls like it was matinee time. I envied his—and apparently the rest of my housemates'—ability to sleep through a hundred decibels of ear-splitting Bollywood action, but I wished to toss his TV out the window. I have no idea how anyone can sleep like that. Another good case for a university study grant.

Evidently, no one was losing sleep from this inconsiderate and hard-of-hearing clown, although I knew I would. After I bathed and was ready for bed, the din continued to knock plaster off the walls. Banging on his door, I received no answer but the croaking and cackling TV. Taking the matter into my own hands, I grabbed a flashlight and finding the circuit breaker box at the end of the hall, switched them off one by one until the one powering his idiot box was cut. All was blessedly quiet then, and silence was to rule until dawn. Feeling a bit spiteful, I snapped off the one labeled "Water Heater" too.

I didn't have a lot of time off, about a week, and between the airfare, hotels and meals, it was not the most practical way to spend money at the time, but I figured a break from India was well deserved. I'd had enough of the stares and gawking, the chaos and grime, the lack of hygiene and the

Russian roulette with food poisoning at every meal. I wanted bikinis, beer and beaches. I wanted to fill my belly with cheeseburgers and pizza, and wallow through the gutters of casual decadence.

A lot of time, too much, would be spent in airplanes and airports, but that was just another price to be paid. From Bhubaneswar to Kolkata, Kolkata to Bangkok for one night, Bangkok to Manila, and Manila to Boracay Island. While waiting for my connection to Kolkata the next day, I figured it would all be worth it. I took a couple more phone calls from Sami, my heart stopping every time he rang, fearing the worst—canceled vacation—then switched it off, chucked it in my bag and boarded the plane. I would be in Bangkok by nightfall.

Kingfisher Airline was delayed in getting off the ground at Bhubaneswar, so I arrived late in Kolkata and had to sprint from the domestic terminal to international departures at the next terminal over. Along the way, money-grubbing, self-appointed porters from off the street tried to take my bags and carry them the hundred-yard distance. They stared at me with hostility while I ignored them and brushed through their groping, outstretched hands.

Making my way to Immigration, I chose the line that looked to be moving the quickest and, as usual, it came to a standstill the moment my feet stepped into queue. It was suddenly held up by the immigration officer fielding calls on his cell phone. When he did get to me, he spent my precious minutes chatting on his cell-phone in tones varying from cheerful to wrathful. Ending the call, he smiled and took his time explaining how his teenage son had a flat tire on the way home from school.

"The boy's an idiot," he said, shaking his head. "Didn't know how to operate a car jack."

I smiled back but was not appreciating this insight into Mr. Immigration's family life.

Arriving in Bangkok at sunset, I took a taxi to my hotel, which had been booked earlier online; it was close to Suvarnabhumi Airport but still close enough to the nightlife the city was famous for. I had an early flight the next day and didn't want to be caught in traffic far from the airport. After checking in and dumping my bags, I hailed a taxi to take me close to Patpong, where a cheeseburger and Heineken awaited me at O'Reilly's Pub.

Wake up was too early the next morning, and then I was back in a taxi on the way to the airport, at least during that time of day, the brutal traffic that incessantly choked Bangkok was light. I checked in through the airy, well-lit airport and then to the Burger King inside the terminal for coffee.

Tired, I'd had little sleep the night before. There's much to see, and Bangkok is a bustling mob filled with friendly smiles and beautiful people. Thai women are particularly gorgeous, with an air of femininity that escapes many other cultures.

The Thai Airways flight to Manila departed on time and reached there after lunch. I was to meet a friend of mine, Amy, at the airport and then she and I, along with two of her friends, would fly together down to Boracay. I'd met Amy years before while she worked as a nurse in a small town near Minneapolis. She had since returned to her native Philippines to help care for an ailing father, both of us staying in touch over the years.

Manila had a confusing set of domestic airport terminals that, depending upon the airline, could be on the other side of the airport from where a traveler lands, as was my case. It took me a while to get sorted and find the correct terminal, but our flight to Kalibo wasn't until later in the afternoon, and there was no need to rush. Reaching where I was supposed to be, it was about an hour before Amy and her friends showed up, and we checked in with Cebu Pacific airline with time to spare.

Amy was a bespectacled and slim girl in her early thirties, as were her friends. They all worked in the medical field, and their initial shyness faded while Amy went through introductions and ice was broken. I was glad to have their company, and they were glad to be going to Boracay Island again. It was a popular destination that all three of them had been to before, and they promised to be excellent tour guides.

When researching our trip to Boracay, I found that the usual, closer airport to the island was in Caticlan; but that airport was closed due to a couple of mishaps with the airlines. Prior to our visit, there had been two airliners that overshot the short runway, and the Filipino government had closed the airstrip to review landing and takeoff procedures. That left travelers like us with the only option of landing in Kalibo, then taking a ninety-minute bus journey to the boat jetty in Caticlan.

After landing at Kalibo, we boarded the bus with other tourists for the jostling ride through the darkening, tree-lined countryside. The switchbacks and curves had me and the others close to carsickness. The entire bus cheered as we pulled into the parking lot across from the jetty, where the boats were tied up, bouncing in the waves. With dusk giving way to night, we were herded onto a long wooden boat that held thirty or more people and after the captain had double checked with the bus driver for any more riders, started up his diesel engine, and deckhands cast off the lines.

It was only a short rocking ride, not ten minutes to reach Boracay from Caticlan. The ferry nudged its bow gently into the sand, and we jumped into the surf and walked up the beach. Palm trees were leaning from the brisk wind, and Amy nearly lost her straw hat as she chased it over the sand, laughing. The deckhands and hotel porters collected our suitcases and luggage from the top of the boat and stacked them near a half-dozen waiting minivans.

Boracay had hotels. It was hard to believe there were over 300 to choose from on the tiny island. We were headed to Willy's Hotel, and they had sent transport to pick us up.

In another ten minutes, the van pulled into the narrow driveway of the hotel, and we went to check in. My friends had booked their room with double beds and giggled like schoolgirls while they settled in, talking excitedly in their native Tagalog. Splurging when I'd booked mine, I chose the big suite on the third and top floor. Throwing my gear on the king-size bed, I swung open the balcony doors and looked down between the palm trees to the dim beach, seeing white foam from the waves where they rolled up on the sand. The strong breeze blowing in off the ocean tousled the curtains around my door, and I stuck my foot out just in time to catch the door before it slammed into its frame.

We had picked Willy's because they claimed they were far enough away from the all-night action for some peace and quiet, but still within easy reach of good food and entertainment. In the distance, I could faintly hear the music and thumping from a disco, but as advertised, it was calm around the hotel. When we were all properly attired, me in cheap Billabong knockoffs and a T-shirt, the girls in bikini tops and shorts, we walked out to the dark, lightly-crowded beach and headed toward the bright lights and music.

We spent three all-too-short days on Boracay, but we crammed as much as we could into each one. During the days, we rode ATVs and tried our skills at kite surfing, among other activities. I was sunburned crab-red after the first day due to lengthy snorkeling action. There were dozens of little sailboats lining the beach that could be rented, with crew, by the hour or day for exploring around the island. The water was amazingly clear; at twenty feet deep, you could still make out details on the ocean floor like it was only twenty inches. Jumping off the boat and feeding the hundreds of multicolored fish, the girls screamed with delight when the fish nibbled on their skin.

We rented a sailboat and crew for a day, sailing to the as-yet commercially undeveloped and quiet Carabao Island to the north. The beach was covered with broken coral and rocks, as if all the coral and beach detritus from the white and smooth Boracay beaches was vacuumed up and deposited there. The boat crew told us they would buy a couple of chickens from the locals and grill them on the beach for late lunch while we explored. There were no shops, stores, discos or any type of tourist-related development on the island, and it gave us an idea of what a paradise Boracay must have been before being *discovered*.

There were a few small but sturdy houses and one narrow, paved road just up from where we beached the boat. One enterprising old timer offered us two beat-up motorbikes out of his lean-to shack for cruising around on. The bikes did not look reliable at all, but the price was right, so we set off on a one-hour ride-about. It was a different world compared to Boracay, undisturbed and peaceful, with only a few locals around, no tourists except for us, the jungle still firmly in control. I suppose it was only a matter of time before a hotel or two went up, though, and the sleepy little island would be discovered too.

Returning the motorcycles and heading back to the beach, the boat crew had the chicken barbecuing on a makeshift grill over driftwood coals, and it smelled delicious. The word *delicious* is a woeful understatement. There is no word in the English language to describe the incomparable smells and taste of beach-barbecued chicken. Sitting in the shade of a giant old jackfruit tree, burning my fingers on a grilled chicken leg and sipping an ice cold bottle of San Miguel, life was indeed good. The scene was travel-brochure quality.

The crew spoke in Tagalog mostly, except for the captain, who spoke good English. The girls made the young teenage crewmembers nervous by asking questions about the islands. The boys answered shyly and studied the sand at their feet or the roasting poultry on the fire, grinning self-consciously at being the center of attention of the beautiful opposite sex.

Every night we would bum around the D-Mall area. That was the entertainment center on Boracay where, from the hundreds of shops and market stalls, a person could buy all the touristy trappings a suitcase could hold. It also held plenty of restaurants and bars. We had a superb evening at the Hobbit Hut with T-bone steaks, live music and wine. The girls had just enough of the latter to stand up with the band and sing along to UB40's version of "Red, Red Wine." There were many pizza joints, cheeseburger stands, Italian food and French restaurants. They had it all. Even an Indian restaurant, which I duly avoided.

44.

The Sky is Crying

The morning of our departure from Boracay, we had a delectable breakfast of bacon, waffles, a small mountain of fruit, and because it was bacon, I ordered an extra heaping dish of it—sorry piggies. Reversing our inbound course, we took the hotel van back to the beach, shuffled ourselves onto the boat and putt-putted across the narrow strait to Caticlan; there we loaded on another van, which took us to another bus, which drove us the ninety minutes to Kalibo Airport. Journeying is tiring, especially if you're already bushed like the fifteen or so backpacker types aboard, worn out from the all-night Boracay party action.

I watched the scenery slip by the window while the girls dozed next to me. Peaceful rural Philippines passed by, mile after mile, offering views of tree-smothered hillsides and patchwork rice paddies. The local carabao looked identical to the water buffalo of India and were being used similarly as beasts of burden. Many rice paddies that we passed interned a carabao or two doing the needful toil. At Kalibo, we boarded our turboprop to Manila, landing there in the afternoon. It was a bit of a hassle getting into and out of Boracay, but worth every mile.

I checked in for a one-night stay at my hotel, changed clothes and grabbed a taxi to meet Amy in a part of the city known as "The Fort" for dinner. The area was redeveloped with walking streets, boutique shops and modern office space, and the urban planners had done the project right. Amy was eager to show me Murray and D'Vine restaurant, a kicky little pub known for delicious, heart-shaped cheeseburgers and their extensive racks of wine. After seeing it, I knew that if heaven had a restaurant, it would be identical to this one.

I would be headed west in the morning, back through Bangkok—again for one night—and on to India. In the meantime, I went from beach mode to urban mode in Manila. Although big city cruising was not on top of my favorites list, tromping through a sea of humanity and bar hopping was not a bad way to spend time when on the verge of tromping through the cow-pie lined streets of Jagdalpur once again.

At times, my airline and travel schedule lined up ideally enough that no sleep was lost, no stress was caused and a leisurely breakfast could be enjoyed. Such was the case the next morning before my departure from Manila and, though it was a working day, Amy made arrangements to join me for the breakfast buffet at my hotel.

It was a pleasant setting, listening to the tinkling of silverware and juice glass refills. The subdued conversation of the restaurant patrons and even rowdy kids causing a ruckus was a relaxing way to end my short sojourn into the islands. The few days of sun and fun restored a bit of civility, neutralizing some of the more unwanted and wild jungle adventures.

Bidding adieu to Amy, I tossed my bags in the taxi and headed for the airport, and Thailand. The skies were lead overcast leaving Manila, and waving goodbye to Amy made my mood dip into mope mode, the feeling not improving much throughout the journey. It was helped in no way by the soggy downpour that greeted me upon arrival in Bangkok. After clearing Immigration, finding my luggage and walking outside to the taxi, the sky was still crying and unhelpful to my disposition. Adding to the somber atmosphere, the driver had his radio tuned to an English-language station and the mournful playlist seemed to encourage more rain to fall. REM's "Everybody Hurts," Enya's "Only Time" and when Simply Red's "Holding Back the Years" came drizzling out of the speakers, I was looking for a bridge to jump off.

I needed to cheer up soon or the Thai police would be pulling another unidentified body out of a polluted canal, and after checking into my hotel, I boarded the Skytrain and rode it to the Saphan Taksin train station on the Chao Phraya River. I caught the water taxi heading upstream and filed off with other tourists near the River City pier, where there were a number of restaurant choices on the water's edge. Choosing Sala Thai café, I ordered a Singha and chicken cashew.

Falling into a rain-induced daze, I studied the boat traffic on the river and started plotting a plan to let Bangkok take away my blues. This was the Land of Smiles, after all, and good times could be had just around the corner.

Late in the afternoon the next day, I was dropped off at Suvarnabhumi Airport to continue the journey. My sour mood had reversed course through the night-life and lights of the previous evening and was on an upward arc. That is, until taking my place in front of the Kingfisher Airlines counter with a helter-skelter mob of Indian travelers. Most of them, every group it seemed, were pushing baggage carts loaded down with box after box of flat-screen TVs. No other tourists were trucking hundreds of flat screens through the airport; apparently they had missed the fire sale as I did.

The minimum order appeared to be two, others had five or even six boxes piled on, and they didn't mind running the cart up the back of my ankles while arguing on their phones or with their mates over the best way to stack them and get them through Customs.

In need of one last beef fix before heading into sacred cow country, I stopped at Burger King and ordered a double cheeseburger, then one more for the road. I planned on smuggling it into Kolkata for dinner that night, but ended up munching it down while waiting near the gate when the flight was delayed for two hours. By the time we reached Kolkata, the shadows were long. Filing through Immigration, the officer seemed to scrutinize my paperwork, trying to find a way, an issue—anything—to keep me out of the country. Half of me hoped he would.

In Kolkata for just one night, I stepped out of the terminal and took a hard slap from India and its blanket of moist heat and filthy air. The familiar smells of exhaust fumes, urine and body odor, along with the sound of car horns assaulted my recently refurbished senses.

I had chosen a hotel in the New Market area, where there's a street bazaar every evening, and it was in full rage when I stepped out of the taxi and slipped through the waves of pedestrians to the hotel lobby. A cute bellhop smiled shyly while unburdening me from my bags as I checked in, her small frame wrestling with my suitcase. One of its wheels had become a casualty somewhere over Burma—surely busted off by a flat-screen TV—and she continued struggling even after multiple attempts to help her. Showing me to my room, she pointed out the instant coffee and water boiler and, before I could stop her, she went about fixing me a cup. Not in the mood for hot coffee, I had rather planned to hit the streets and find something more refreshing and cool.

Cruising the bazaar, I had to turn sideways often while walking through the bustling throngs of people. It was more of a side-stepping shuffle than a leisurely stroll. The frenzied bazaar had shops and stalls selling mostly food, but a person could find almost anything he was looking for down the streets and alleys. Surrendering and retreating from the swarm, I had a beer on the rooftop bar where I was boarded for the night, Hotel Lindsay. A good respite from crowds, the restaurant and bar still offered great views of the thrumming city.

Back again to the airport in the predawn. The early morning streets I passed through were strikingly barren compared to the night before, except for the street dogs and street sweepers, who spoiled the air with their little trash fires along the road. The flight to Bhubaneswar took an hour; I spent more time in the terminal than flying through the air. Once on the ground, Mahesh met me at the airport, gazed into my eyes, and surprised me with my further itinerary: there were no flights available from Bhubaneswar to Raipur, he had booked me on a train.

I had seen the overcrowded conditions of India's trains and lost track of the number of train wrecks reported by the news. I was less than overjoyed with the travel arrangements, but there was no practical way around it. A flight to Delhi and back to Raipur was cost prohibitive and time consuming. The train would be the most efficient means in getting me to Raipur on my journey back to Jagdalpur to relieve Chatterjee.

Alright, I figured, *no problem. I'm in India, might as well experience the famous Indian train system.*

Mahesh claimed the train ride was only eight hours. Once seated in the train, however, and chatting with my three compartment-mates, they chuckled and said it was more like fourteen.

"There are many stops along the way, young man," a gray-haired but balding man told me.

He was wrapped in what looked to be a green, king-size bed sheet. Shaking his head, he continued, "Your friend was mistaken. The time the train moves is perhaps eight hours... but so many stops."

Mahesh would have been tickled to hear himself referred to as my friend.

My traveling companions were cheery enough. One was a paan-chewing professor, another was an ex-government minister of sorts and the third we never found out. He kept darting in and out through the curtain on our compartment, restlessly walking up and down the aisle with multitudes of other fidgety travelers.

It turned to night shortly after we started moving, and there was not much sightseeing. The window was perpetually fogged up from the arctic air coming from the air conditioning vent anyway. The train moved twenty to thirty miles an hour, not more, because there appeared to be a train stop every mile or so. Just when we were smoking along and making good time, brakes would squeal and we would come to a stuttering, twenty-minute halt, the faint glow from a train station's lights penetrating the condensation on the window glass.

Mahesh had given me chicken tikka takeout before departing and, after gulping it down, I wrapped up mummy style in the train-provided blanket and, remarkably, slept like a baby the whole night through.

Upon waking, I peeked out from my blanket and saw three strange new pairs of eyes peering intensely back at me: a stoic but bedraggled looking mother with two runny-nosed kids. My mates from the night before had been replaced. I felt a little less than human, but after two cups of chai tea and a walkabout through the car, my circulation crept back to normal and brain function was restored to an approximate Neanderthal level.

Reaching Raipur at midmorning, I shuffled off the train and hired a bicycle rickshaw to take me to the Hotel Grand. Sami was in town, and he offered his room so I could freshen up. Taking a near-scalding hot shower, I wished to steam out my sinuses and lungs to cleanse away the mutant bacteria that had been blasted there all night from the train's air vent. I gulped down coffee along with idli and chutney for a late breakfast, and while Sami was out buying gifts for the upcoming Diwali holiday, I did burpees on the room floor.

We'd be heading out for the long, rumbling trek to Jagdalpur in the afternoon, and my journey back would be complete. Chatterjee was waiting on the other end and was anxious to get out of the jungle and back to Shimla.

45.

Happy Diwali

Cloudless blue skies early in the morning, Jagdalpur's weather appeared to have finally cleared up. After the long monsoon season, we were expecting the IPS and CRPF to increase the amount of flights to resupply their camps and rotate personnel. When I relieved Chatterjee, however, he said there had only been three flights during my entire break.

I wondered if that was due to poor weather or a reluctance to fly; I knew there was flying to be done and was ready to be back at the controls any time. I was restless and had the urge to fly.

We also realized that the holiday season of Diwali was approaching, and the IPS tapered off their workload whenever a holiday arrived. Diwali was one of the biggest yearly celebrations in India. It was a time of gift giving and feasting, comparable to Christmas in other parts of the world. The company had instructed the jungle-visiting Sami to come up with a list of important IPS officers—officers integral to our continued business in the region—and deliver gifts to them. Depending on the officer's influence, the gifts ranged in value from a box of sweets to whiskey to mobile phones. Looking for something to do, I joined the self-styled "*Sami* Claus" on his gift-giving journey around the countryside.

Something added to the long list of peculiarities about India was the lack of driver's licenses amongst the crew. I shouldn't have found it odd, looking at it from their perspective; most were raised only on the ubiquitous and generally lawless two-wheelers. Cars were a luxury to a lot of Indians, so they had no practical experience with such things as steering wheels, stick-shifts and clutch pedals. Growing up a country boy, I was driving the back roads when just able to reach the pedals of the family's station wagon. Culturally myopic, I had mistakenly assumed that driving a car was as second nature as drinking water to everyone.

Having ridden with Sami previously, I knew he lacked basic driving skills and he liked to hit the bottle, "Because," he always said, "life's a party!"

But I thought we could keep it safe by keeping him off the sauce, and he was sober enough when we departed from the guesthouse; at least, he didn't smell of liquor. If his driving began taking a real dangerous turn for the worse, I thought there would be time to get behind the wheel, and then I could really scare the bejesus out of everyone.

Babeesh joined us and, with the Punjabi pop music cranked, the three of us rolled out to the highways and byways. Our first intended stop was Dantewada to see Rabinesh. We never made it there.

Driving only the first couple of miles, I immediately regretted volunteering myself for this charity tour. Sami's jerky starts were expected, but he drove too fast and recklessly for even middling comfort; with aviator sunglasses perched on his nose, he fancied himself Lewis Hamilton. We didn't get five miles out of Jagdalpur before, heading around a corner, he crossed the centerline and wiped out a motorcycle-riding chicken farmer on his way to market.

"Watch out!" I shouted, grabbing the dashboard and Oh-Shit handle attached to the door frame. It was the first time in many miles of driving that I'd had to use a handle like that along with its namesake exclamation.

"Saa! Saa!" Babeesh's hand shot up between the seats, and he pointed at the pending poultry pickle, as if we hadn't seen it.

Sami clamped his talkative mouth shut mid-syllable, and it's probable that his seat endured a little clamping as well.

The chicken rider, who had maybe fifty chickens strapped and dangling off his two-wheeler, understandably freaked out when he saw our Suzuki Maruti shoot out of the corner and barrel directly toward him. He barely had time to hit the brakes, then wobbled, skidded and swerved down into the ditch, ending up in the brush a bloody pile of poultry feathers and Honda parts.

Sami tried to correct our glidepath by cranking the steering wheel back to our lane, but it was too much to ask of the tires. The front tires went where they were pointed, but the rears broke loose and, in a howling squeal, the back of the car swapped ends with the front. We were lucky not to flip over and roll down the pavement. Momentum kept us in motion, and we plowed down into the opposite ditch from the motorcycle chicken massacre. Coming to an abrupt halt, we were nearly on our side with two wheels up in the air, pinned at the foot of the hill that was the reason for the curve in the road to begin with.

"Everyone alright?" I asked, after realizing I was still of Earth.

No answer from the other two; looking around, I saw they were both wild-eyed, but unscathed. The smell of burning rubber and whiskey filled the air as Babeesh floundered around amongst our Diwali gifts. Sami and I had our seat belts on, but he didn't. Still, he had managed not to be thrown through the open windows. My door was up against a bank of dirt, and the car body was tweaked, causing the other doors to be jammed shut. Still, we managed to crawl out and survey the vehicle damage.

Up on the road, splattered with blood, the chicken farmer stood in his torn robes like a crestfallen Statue of Liberty, glaring down at us. He was holding his right arm in the air with his left and both of his bare legs were bloody. White chicken feathers fluttered in his hair while more tumbled across the road in the breeze. Scratching and pecking in the dirt next to their fallen companeros, the survivors were oblivious to the afterlife they narrowly missed. Not waiting for us to climb the embankment, the farmer started screaming in quite heated Hindi as we stumbled up to the road.

The IPS arrived and, taking refuge in their jeep, I watched the proceedings from within. Showing solidarity with their chicken-ranching neighbor, about a hundred feisty villagers showed up, and there was no need to complicate matters with my foreign face.

The company head office rang me up, worried that their pilot was hurt and they would have to ground the helicopter. I assured them the only casualties were cluckers and that their helicopter driver was safe and fit; eager to get back in the air and away from the madness.

I hoped that insurance or the company bought the guy a new bike and compensated him for the chickens, which were probably a main source of his family's livelihood. There was the question of his medical bills too. He seemed vigorous and healthy enough when berating Sami's driving, but he was quite banged up.

The morning of Diwali came, and we all chipped in and surprised our house-cleaning ladies with gift envelopes containing cash. It was only a thousand rupees—about twenty bucks—but they acted as if we'd bought them a new car. Their smiles and laughter lasted for days.

We were ourselves surprised when a mission 140 miles northwest of Jagdalpur was requested. Duty called, and I had no problem with flying, but the crew was reluctant and dragged their feet, making excuses. They figured holiday time off was well deserved. Then I pointed out that the aircraft logbook showed no flights in over a week—they'd had plenty of time off.

Takeoff was delayed for an hour and a half while waiting for coordinates, and that gave the crew time to warm up their cricket skills on the runway. The weather had changed; daytime temperatures were a comfortable eighty to eighty-five degrees and the mornings were in the mid- to low-sixties. Local folks, more accustomed to the heat, wore winter jackets and ear muffs or lit fires to ward off the "cold" in the morning. They burned wood, plastic or tires—whatever was flammable. The smoke from the many trash fires was nauseating and diminished the otherwise better all-around air quality. Of course, I relished those milder temperatures, and it was a welcome relief in the cockpit.

The mission was a flight to Rajnandgaon. We would meet four officers from the ITBP, the Indo-Tibetan Border Police, and give reconnaissance to three areas of concern for them. The anti-Maoist operations were shared amongst the IPS and other paramilitary organizations like the CRPF, who we flew quite often. This ITBP mission was a first for us.

As their name implied, the ITBP's usual area of expertise was in the Himalayan region far to the north. They were trained in mountaineering and high-altitude combat and were probably surprised to find themselves in lowland steamy jungle.

I had little faith in another reconnaissance mission attempting to spot movement beneath the jungle canopy, but I wasn't questioning anyone. I was ready to fly. As were the ITBP officers once I'd arrived, but a shutdown was deemed necessary for further discussion, and we were welcomed with the usual coffee and biscuits while my passengers readied themselves.

Their fatigue uniforms were distinctly different from those of the other groups I had worked with. The camouflage pattern contained the usual browns and greens, but snowy white splotches covered the majority of the thicker, cold climate fabric. They looked sharp but perhaps a tad overdressed for the jungle.

A topographical map was unfolded, and they pointed out the areas of interest. I double checked the coordinates on my GPS, and we set off, overflying the designated spots as I had done earlier during the monsoon in Gadchiroli. But this mission was more productive. Spotting a well-used trail, they had me circle it for over five minutes while they discerned its purpose and made notes.

After returning to the helipad at Rajnandgaon, Babeesh set about refueling the helicopter while I chatted with one of the officers. He told me they had found what they were looking for, a trail they had previously suspected as being used by Maoists, and it was showing signs of recent heavy use. Now that they had an aerial view of the place and confirmed coordinates, they would be able to more safely investigate on foot.

Happy Diwali

"Happy Diwali, Captain," he said, smiling and shaking my hand. "Surely, by now, you know this Indian holiday?"

"I certainly do," I grinned. "My crew has been practicing their Diwali celebratory technique for days now... and I've survived in spite of them."

It was too late to return to Jagdalpur before nightfall, so I took off and pointed the nose toward Raipur, forty minutes away, still cutting it close for landing before sunset.

Indeed, dusk was upon the countryside by the time the city of Raipur showed up through our windscreen. Lights were already twinkling on. Then we noticed other, more disturbing lights. Diwali celebrations were underway, and the sky over the city was being crisscrossed with rockets and fireworks.

I wouldn't say it resembled London during the Blitz, but the high-flying pyrotechnics certainly had my attention. Babeesh was like a kid on the fourth of July, pointing and shouting while the troublemakers in the streets below intensified their barrage. They seemed to enjoy this new aerial target and adjusted their aim for my Astar accordingly. Arriving over Raipur Heliport, I dropped the collective lever to its stop and spiraled tightly down, juking and jiving with evasive maneuvers like I was out in the jungle heading into a combat zone.

46.

Bottle Bass

Across the narrow road from the Jagdalpur guesthouse, in the grassy and trashy vacant lot where the cows had their daily graze, were four fishing holes. Not the normal fishing holes you find in a stream or lake, but tiny, man-made holes about six feet square and less than four feet deep. In fact, the holes had nothing to do with fish or any type of marine life, except perhaps a foraging frog. They were dug before the monsoon in anticipation of pouring cement footings for a future building. The monsoon rains came, filled up the holes, and voila! The neighborhood had fishing holes.

The fact that there were no fish living inside did not stop several of the top anglers in the village from donning their fishing gear and lucky fishing turban to try their luck. They would spend hours squatted down along the edge, glowering into a pool of water not much bigger than a Motel 6 bathtub, patiently waiting for a lunker's tug on their line. Toward dusk, a few would gather next to their fishing hole and pass a bottle back and forth. Perhaps that was the main reason they were there, for the bottle bass.

Though I doubt it, they could've still been perched there one early morning when it was still dark outside and a wedding parade visited our lovely and tranquil little neighborhood. Indian wedding parades are not serene, understated affairs but energetic, brightly lit and loud, the louder the better. Even—or perhaps, especially—at four o'clock in the morning.

Once again, my earplugs could not keep out the level of decibels being forced past them. My pillowcase and bed sheets shook with each erratic beat of the drums. So much light penetrated the curtains that I could spot Bermuda on the world map hung on my far wall.

They didn't linger but kept marching and winding through the streets; from the first drumbeat piercing into my dreams until it once again became quiet, forty-five minutes had passed. Almost five o'clock. I rolled out and made coffee.

We had a flight to Raipur Heliport and then a mission with a government minister to Bhairamgarh village. I welcomed these VIP flights only because the landing zone and surrounding area were guaranteed to be more closely guarded, allowing my blood pressure to run lower and my aggressive, spiraling descent to be more subtle. The befuddling fact with VIPs, though, was that they held great disregard for the clock. A requested departure time meant nothing, and the VIP could arrive any time from a half-hour before to one or even two hours after. No big problem, that, we just had to plan accordingly and let our displeasure be heard if sunset, a storm or bad guys with guns were coming.

Cruising to Raipur was superbly routine. There were no air traffic delays, the haze was diminished—a rarity—and the temperature was warm but not demonically scorching. Landing at the heliport, BK and I were feeling pleased with life. We had plenty of time before the VIP showed up in which to relax, take fuel and gulp down more coffee. Shutting down, I did notice more cars parked around the hangar than usual, but didn't give it much thought, assuming they were part of the minister's posse, awaiting their VIP.

Our good vibrations were about to end, however, when an impeccably dressed, white-haired gentleman wearing a blazer and checkered ascot came out to greet us. I had sudden ascot envy and made a mental note to peruse a haberdashery sometime soon. Holding out his hand, he introduced himself.

"Good morning, Captain," he said, but I didn't detect a smile, nothing to suggest he believed there was anything good with the morning. "I am Colonel Mohan, from the DGCA."

BK was in my peripheral vision, and I noticed his shoulders slump. Still feeling high and intoxicated from slipping the surly bonds of Earth, I shook his hand vigorously, smiled and said, "Good morning, Colonel, how can I help you today?"

"Well, Captain, you can start by showing me your pilot license, FATA—your Foreign Aircrew Temporary Authorization—and your flight medical certificate."

"Oh, I see." Having nearly complimented his choice of ascot, I was surprised by his demands, and any compliments were put on hold. "You're here to give us an inspection?" I asked.

"That's correct," he said, studying my FAA license. "Captaaiin... Michael, is it?"

"Yep, ahh... Yes sir, that's me."

"It's your lucky day, Michael. My group is here to inspect Chhattisgarh state's operations," he gestured over his shoulder to the government hangar and aviation offices. "Since you were kind enough to drop in first, I'll warm up with you."

A team of DGCA officials had descended upon the Chhattisgarh government aviation unit to give them a thorough two-day site inspection. Those inspections included the records for the government's Agusta 109, maintenance and fuel logs and other administrative documents required in their day-to-day operations. Their helicopter hangar, of course, was next to the Raipur Heliport that we just landed on, and figuring we were a bonus to their fun, out-of-the-office time, the DGCA jumped at the chance to give us a good going over as well. We were easy prey, like flies in a spider web. Colonel Mohan pounced on us with little mercy when we dropped out of the cockpit and landed in his realm.

I carried my ID and all the required paperwork with me every time I flew. They were folded in a plastic bag tucked into a pocket on my kneeboard. Meeting his disapproval, though, was that my original FATA had been filed at the office in Delhi. The facsimile Sami had sent was barely legible. Mohan *tsk-tsked* loudly as he squinted at it from behind his wire frames, holding the corner with thumb and finger like it was an overused handkerchief. Begging forgiveness for my long list of shortcomings as a human being, I promised to carry a better example in the immediate future. Displeased, but seemingly satisfied, he dropped it on my pilot's seat and turned his attention to BK.

Colonel Mohan talked professionally polite with me, but when confronting BK, who was waiting with one foot up on the landing skid, he switched from English to Hindi and from polite to disdainful. With no desire to be witness to the carnage and bloodletting while the maintenance logs and BK's credentials were dissected, I walked the length of the tailboom like I was post-flighting and, as the decibels rose between the two men, just kept walking to the hangar and the pot of coffee.

So much for our routine and peaceful morning. BK took a beating, but in the end was able to convince Mohan that our maintenance logs were indeed in order—something I held in quiet disbelief. I was glad BK was the crew chief on the flight and not someone else; knowing he had more experience in handling maintenance matters and, especially, the prima donnas at the DGCA.

All the DGCA fireworks were over by the time the VIP arrived, avoiding any embarrassing flight delay caused by the paperwork being out of whack. Judging from the smaller number of vehicles in this minister's convoy, I guessed he ranked a little lower on the ladder than previous VIPs we had carried. I found out later that he was the Water Resource Minister for Chhattisgarh. Not a title that held a lot of pizazz, but a respected politician just the same.

Bhairamgarh is a 140 miles south of Raipur, the same distance as to Jagdalpur, but fifty-five miles west. Since our little disputation with the DGCA, BK had become thoughtful, and perhaps, a bit grumpy. His mind was elsewhere, though he still managed a smile at my jokes. His inflight entertainment—as he probably lamented daily—was my sense of humor and little jokes. From time to time, I came up with some witty stuff; usually, it was witty only to me, however.

Circling before landing in the small village, the landing zone was soon overrun and mobbed by tribal folks. There was a strong security presence, but for this political ceremony, villagers had been informed beforehand for miles around, and thousands showed up for the event. The sheer size of the crowd was a cause for concern; they were too emotional and pushed through the barriers in an attempt to get closer to the landing helicopter. Another worry was that, within the people milling about, there could be insurgents looking to cause trouble.

We circled for a few minutes, waiting for security to regain control. I could see the mob being chased off by lathi-wielding police, and guessed that more than a few folks went home that evening with a bruised backside.

The minister said something to BK in Hindi, which he translated and relayed to me over the intercom, "Captain, saa, the minister would like you to land, saa."

"Ah, yeah, I'm not up here sightseeing," I said. "Does he want me to land on his people?" I glanced at the minister and then BK. "Tell him I'm waiting for security to clear the helipad."

"Okay, saa." BK took off his headset and, twisting in his seat, translated to the non-English speaking minister. I think he translated, anyway. Perhaps he told the minister that this captain was crazy and liked to fly in circles.

Another couple of minutes passed before I set up to land. The minister was leaning forward in his seat and getting antsy. He divided his time between looking at the view out of the window and the looking at the side of my head. There were no more mob scenes on the helipad, thanks to the threat of a beat down from the ring of security, and we landed in a cloud of dust and swirling trash. The minister was then escorted away to his function amidst cheers from the surging crowd. I was surprised a water resource minister would have such an adoring fan base.

After getting the helicopter shut down and secured for the afternoon stay, we were shown to a small building nearby that made up part of the local school. The landing zone itself was the school's sports arena. Lunch was prepared for us, and we sat and ate while being watched with what seemed a thousand pairs of eyes. Villagers were eager and fascinated to see a foreigner. Smiling broadly, they offered greetings such as, "Hello, Uncle" or "Namaskar, Captain."

To my bashful astonishment, several older villagers bent down and touched my feet and knees. I had seen this unique greeting before, though never for me. In fact, it was the most common Indian gesture I had seen, other than the head bobble. Touching someone's feet showed respect to the one whose feet were being touched. I felt like a rock star.

A stage had been set up and, over the next few hours, a number of politicians spoke to the crowd. The villagers listened for a while but carried on mingling with their neighbors. Food stalls were set up, along with a few other shops selling clothing or trinkets, and it had that state or county fair feel from back home—minus the corn dogs, cotton candy and overcrowded beer tent.

This was where I first saw the traditional sport of kabaddi, a brutal mixture of running, wrestling and tag, described to me by one of the senior police on duty there as recreational combat. It looked to be heavy on the *combat* and a little lighter on the *recreational*, judging from the bloody noses and screams.

Bounded by a small court, one bare-chested man would dash across a line, attempting to tag one or more of his opponents and retreat back across the line before being wrestled to the ground. Usually he was quickly smeared into the dust, unless he was a bigger dude. The chaps getting flung around must've been the biggest sports stars from their respective villages and were quite beefy compared to the rest of the locals.

Hours later, the politicians wrapped up their speeches, and we flew back to Raipur at dusk, spending the night at Hotel Grand. The recent Diwali holiday meant that rockets and fireworks were in quite adequate supply, and night over Raipur was like a Super Bowl half-time show, filling the sky with the color explosions of a rainbow. Ordering a beer from the bar, I walked up to the roof and lit a smoke, sat down in a pilfered chair with my feet up over the edge and critiqued each volley of pyrotechnics.

47.

The General

As I approached my tenth consecutive day of duty, we had a flight carrying the IPS, Jagdalpur Region Inspector General, General Thomas, to Bijapur for meetings with officers and troop inspections. After the long and flight-restrictive monsoon season, he wished to be flown to visit as many of the outlying districts as possible and hold meetings with senior officers, bolster troop morale and show support.

We had become increasingly busy, and the flight requests kept coming in. There were limited days of consecutive duty and flight time allowed by the DGCA, however, and according to their FDTL, Flight and Duty Time Limitations, I would have to take a day or two off shortly. The crew was getting whiny from the nonstop operations tempo and, as much as I like to fly, I also looked forward to a small break from the action.

Although based in and living with his family in Jagdalpur, General Thomas was from the far northeastern state of Nagaland. It is one of the smallest states in India, lying east of Bangladesh and sharing its border with Burma. Nagaland's many tribes and people, including the general and his bodyguards, favored the appearance of Mongolians rather than what many perceive as South Asian. General Thomas, himself a powerfully built man, bore a close resemblance to Genghis Khan.

Each Naga tribe had their own traditional language, customs and dress, but two traits common to all of them were language and religion; English was the official language and Christianity the predominant religion—hence Thomas' Christian name—and two of the many things the general and I had in common. Always a gentleman, his professionalism and integrity were unquestionable, and he was one of the most practical men I had worked with.

Upon arrival at Bijapur, BK and I were invited by the officers to breakfast in their mess hall. When traveling with General Thomas, we were always treated with respect and politeness, always invited to join him at his meal—if there was one—and always given relatively comfortable accommodations to freshen up or relax. This is not to say that we were treated like dirt when flying with other VIPs, we were always well looked after, but flying with the general there was more *esprit de corps*.

After first arriving in India and during my initial days in the jungle, I tried to find excuses to avoid these shared meals, the general's and the other VIPs, but they would not take no for an answer and demanded I join them out of politeness and curiosity. I was the new one, the foreigner, the pilot from the USA, so every meal became an investigative interview. I really preferred to just sit back and listen. Answering questions from most everyone seated around the table left little time to scarf down the grub. After a while, I came up with automatic responses to most questions:

"Where are you from, Captain Mike?" The most common.

"From the American Midwest, near Chicago," I'd reply, figuring that was specific enough and easily identifiable.

"Ah! Chicago! Oh it's so cold there, Captain! Isn't it? You're a long way from home, aren't you?"

"How do you like India, Captain?" Another popular one, usually coming quickly after the first. And with that delicate query out there, everyone would stop chewing and slurping to glare at me, waiting for me to answer; as if I would dare answer in even a mildly unfavorable way, they would line me up against the wall for the firing squad.

"You know, I like India," I'd say with vigor, "It's a bit chaotic, but I can roll with it."

Many questions were about family and why I wasn't married. In a country where the average age for wedlock was twenty-four and most of those were arranged by family, a single professional was rare and strange.

"What does your wife do, Captain?" They'd ask, setting the trap. "Has she joined you here in India?"

"Oh, no, I haven't married yet."

"What!" Again, everyone would stop what they were doing to watch this odd and bizarre single man. "Really, Captain, you should be married by this point in your life. You're getting old."

It was impossible to get away from these shared meals without being boorish. Once, trying too cleverly to miss out on a breakfast invitation at the Dantewada mess hall, I told Rabinesh and the other officers to go ahead and eat, hoping they would just have their morning sustenance without me. I lingered at the helicopter. Refueling was complete, but I stayed at the helipad shooting the breeze with BK. Unbeknownst to me, thinking they would simply start to eat while I played hooky, all the officers waited. And waited. Then waited some more, just for me to show up.

Thinking I had outsmarted them, a while later I walked in the hall to fetch a quick coffee and herd our passengers to the helicopter. But all the officers were gathered around the table, half-starved and feisty, wondering why that pokey goddamned pilot was taking so long. I ended up eating with them anyway, only now the questions were more curt and testy, the looks more impatient and hostile. From then on, I figured that since I wouldn't beat them with my games, I might as well join them.

After our mid-morning breakfast with the general, we had an additional flight carrying a few troops and supplies to an IPS camp near the tiny and remote village of Pamed, forty miles to the south. The terrain we flew over was rugged and beautiful. Roughly paralleling our course was a jutting mountain plateau that ran the distance from Bijapur to Pamed and beyond. Along this ridgeline were at least three spectacular waterfalls with drops of 400 feet or more. After the rainy season, the plateau was still draining, and the waterfalls were at their peak flow.

As I flew by one after the other, I wondered how many people had seen these beautiful sights; not many, I guessed, they were way back and up in the hills. What little human civilization existed lived far below, they had no reason or, probably, desire to explore those ridgelines. There certainly wasn't any sign of human activity along the plateau, it was much too rugged to access for settlement. I felt lucky and privileged to see these rare natural wonders.

It took us twenty-five minutes to reach the camp. To travel by truck or jeep on the crude trail that snaked along the lowland would have taken a day, if not the better part of two, and this was prime territory for Maoist-Naxalites with hundreds of sites for hiding and potential ambushes. The IPS did travel by vehicle on that trail, but it was fraught with danger. Cruising along at four thousand feet was a welcome relief to any troopers lucky enough to fly.

We arrived over Pamed and the troopers below lit off a greenish-yellow smoke canister. Then, while funneling down to the tiny helipad, I took quick inventory and reckoned there were satisfactory numbers of troopers lining the perimeter fence. Again, I was doubtful there was any protection a kilometer and a half out, though the officers always confirmed there was, but at least a little security was to be had at the helipad. They all had their rifles poked through the fence and pointed toward the surrounding jungle, but every eyeball was pointed toward the helicopter. At one of the most dangerous phases of the mission for me and them, landing, they ignored common sense and a possible attack from the nearby trees.

BK was on the ground, helping to unload the supplies and rations. The troopers rotating out of camp ganged up next to the helicopter and were impatient to climb aboard. The door was closed in less than a minute, and I brought us off the helipad to a short hover, then we were off, circling our way to safe altitude. As the helicopter started to move again, the urge to stare was too strong, and our protection force gawked at our every movement until we were at a couple thousand feet. If an enemy sniper was around, he could have picked off any number of targets—including me—during the noise and distraction of helicopter operations.

Upon our return to Bijapur, we kicked out our passengers, shut down, refueled and then waited for General Thomas to finish his work. Hearing the horns and drums of a marching band, I went to give it my review. The troopers were decked out in their finest dress uniforms, complete with unique headdress: a navy blue, turban style cover with a red and blue pleated fan running down the center. Their shirts were olive drab criss-crossed by a red sash with rank insignia, and the trousers were a light khaki—not the best to hide perspiration, but more comfortable than dark material—tucked into white leggings on top of polished black boots.

Later in the afternoon, the wind picked up, and the skies became threatening and overcast, a stark contrast to the beautiful, clear weather we had during the morning. I was anxious to be airborne. The accommodations were safe in Bijapur, but I didn't want to spend the night there. Rare was the VIP who noticed such problems as impending bad weather and understood the consequences to helicopter travel. The general, having good common sense and also wanting to avoid a slumber party in Bijapur, noticed the darkening skies and sent a messenger to prepare us for an immediate departure.

He arrived at the helicopter as the first big raindrops drilled into the powdery dirt around the helipad, sending up tiny mushroom clouds of dust. I had the Astar fired up and spinning while he saluted and shook hands with his subordinates, then, without looking back, he climbed in with his Jet Li look-a-like bodyguard and gave me a thumbs-up for Jagdalpur.

48.

King of the Jungle

Early one morning, as the gray dawn turned to yellowish-orange, I was awakened by a slight, barely perceived movement and rustling near the window. Having anticipated rising with the sun, I had left the curtains open at this unfamiliar guesthouse before going to bed. We were in Nagpur, Maharashtra, at a particularly peachy government guesthouse where the IPS had quartered us the night before.

Adjusting my line of vision and peering through the window, I saw nothing but an appealing green expanse of well-manicured gardens and grass. The guesthouse was built into a slight hillside, with the front rooms overlooking the driveway and gated wall and the rear facing rooms, where I was quartered, looking back over this lawn. The building had been backfilled after being constructed, and the sloping lawn started just below my windowsill; I could see the morning dew in the lawn that stretched for about half a football field, ending abruptly at the jungle's edge.

Hibiscus and magnolia were planted around the building, and palm trees were spaced evenly throughout the lawn. It was the most agreeable guesthouse I had stayed in. And peaceful. It was the first night in as long as I could remember where it was quiet enough not to wear earplugs. To be billeted permanently out of this guesthouse would have been wishful thinking, though. We were only in Nagpur for one night.

Suddenly, a black-faced, Wookie-like monkey appeared and pressed his face against my window, fogging it up. I was drowsy, still lying under the sheets and, upon seeing this potential invader drool on my window glass, a startled and uncontrollable "What-the-hell?" rumbled out of my windpipe.

Realizing I wasn't being attacked in a *Planet of the Apes* parallel dimension, my heart rate relaxed, and I chuckled as three other peeping Wookies joined him at the window. They were looking for morning entertainment, but I had nothing to offer but the sight of my white bum. I learned later from the security guards that these were gray langur monkeys, not quite as common as the aggressive reddish-brown rhesus monkeys. The langurs were kept at places in India like this guesthouse, to be used as a deterrent to the marauding rhesus, which feared the larger primates.

The previous day, my company had sent us to Nagpur for another VIP mission: flying the Home Minister of Maharashtra from Nagpur to Chandrapur for a funeral. Nagpur was a couple hundred miles west of Raipur, and Chandrapur was even further. Both were far outside our usual area of operations, but Sami smelled a buck and offered our helicopter when he caught wind from his crony contacts that Maharashtra's own state helicopter was unavailable for the flight.

While in Chandrapur, with the home minister paying his last respects at the ceremony, I had sequestered myself at the local IPS officer's mess. Most of that time was spent on my back, counting ceiling tiles and stains, but I was roused from daydreaming by a vacant, bawling stomach. Showing disregard for culinary common sense, I tried to appease my hunger pangs with room temperature cucumber sandwiches. The menu had been militantly vegan and, in trying to stay away from the perceived gastroenteritis of gobi masala, I recklessly chose the cook's forgotten, day-old cucumber slices and bread.

Returning the home minister from Chandrapur to Nagpur late in the day and then being shown to the guesthouse, the local IPS rewarded me with a bottle of Hayward's 5000 beer. The bottle was covered with frosty ice and cool in my hand, but after pouring myself a glass, I could not finish it halfway before being forced to retreat and hover over the toilet. The overnight became a disturbing scene of hourly visits to the bathroom until right before dawn, when apparently, I strung together several restful minutes before being awakened by the long-tailed Wookie monkey monsters outside my window.

Our mission complete in Nagpur, we needed to get back to the action, but our return flight to Jagdalpur was giving me apprehension. Beforehand, when Sami had first tasked us to fly to Nagpur, we had been in Raipur on another assignment. In flying Raipur to Nagpur, we were able to follow, or at least stay within a few miles of, well-traveled roads and their relative safety in case of an emergency with the helicopter. However, the mission backlog in Jagdalpur was piling up, and it was a hard sell for Sami to agree upon a return ferry flight from Nagpur through Raipur to Jagdalpur; it would have added an hour's flight time and a fuel stop. He insisted we fly from Nagpur direct to Jagdalpur.

The problem with flying direct from Nagpur to Jagdalpur was that, for all but twenty of the two hundred miles, the route covered was rugged wilderness and the domain of Maoist-Naxalites. In *my* domain, four thousand feet above that, I had nothing to worry about, but in the event of aircraft trouble, we were a long way from friendlies. Even if we could find a helicopter-sized spot to set down in amongst the thick jungle and rocks, a survivable outcome would be a question, not a certainty. Nagpur airport had a control tower, so we could stay in radio contact until sixty or seventy miles outbound, but after that there was a lot of hazard-infested jungle where we would be on our own.

After I raised an objection to the company's desires, Sami fired back, "Captaaiin, it's alright, you take your helicopter direct to Jagdalpur and save all that time and fuel expense! I would never put you in harm's way," he safely stated from his desk in Delhi. "You are king of the jungle, man! No harm will come to you! Please, do this for me, bro."

Closing in on one year in India, but still a rookie when it came to dealing with the culture, I gave in to pressure from the company and flew direct to Jagdalpur. It was over too many miles of hostile territory that could have, and should have, been avoided.

As time went on, I started developing a head-office-bullshit gauge and used tactics to reduce risk where I could.

I would argue to take the safer, but perhaps longer route and, on several occasions, it saved our skin. On two of those in particular, when continued flight was hazardous—one mechanical and one due to bad weather—we were able to land within minutes at IPS/CRPF camps and call for help. If those emergencies would have happened thirty miles deep into Maoist-Naxalite controlled jungle, we could have expected no mobile phone service or friendly greetings from the locals carrying fruit baskets.

I pleaded for a satellite phone the entire time I was posted there, but the Indian government did not allow such devices to be owned by private companies; this I was repeatedly told by the head office, and my bullshit detector was pegged.

I would look out for the helicopter, passengers and myself the best I could, and the extra fuel burn be damned. General Thomas, for one, appreciated that. The crew did too and, after a spell, I was no longer questioned by the head office as to my route planning. In effect, I did become King of the Jungle.

Upon returning to Jagdalpur, there was an overcrowding situation at the guesthouse. The company's other helicopter was in town, and Zach the pilot, and his accompanying crew chief and technicians had invaded, making space limited. No problem, I took up residence with my friends at Hotel Devansh for the time being.

The Devansh was in the center of town and, when I had free time and was feeling brave, I would head out into the scrum on the streets for a walk. There was usually something new to see, I just had to avoid getting hit by cars and motorcycles, or crapped on by a cow. Since Devansh only had vegetarian dishes, certain evenings I'd walk to the Rainbow Hotel and Restaurant, where I could find chicken tikka masala or any other tortuously spicy meat dish; the chefs would see me walk in and commence to chopping more chili peppers, laughing maniacally.

On a late afternoon, when the temperature had been in the nineties, I decided during my street travels that swinging by the beer shop would be most appropriate. But upon reaching it, I found the metal gate slammed shut and no one around. By that time in the jungle, I'd become a borderline alcoholic and being denied a sudsy brew was akin to being told the Plague was upon us.

I returned to the Devansh sweaty, despondent and thirsty. Sahara Desert thirsty. I lamented to the desk clerk about the barley and hops dilemma.

"I'm so sorry, saa," he said, which he wasn't. He didn't even look away from the Bollywood flick he was watching. "Another round of elections start soon and selling alcohol is off limits until after the votes are counted."

"When will that be?" I grumbled.

"In three days, saa. Can I offer you chai tea?"

Chai tea wasn't going to cut it. I declined with a further grumble and headed to my room. Accompanying me and brandishing my room key was the hovering, shifty-eyed and shady-looking bellboy, who had watched my exchange with the clerk. Whenever he was around, which was most all the time, I kept him in sight; he had the look of a nefarious, backstreet-connected hoodlum. His twitchy eyes were always on my gear, my watch or my rear, and my trust of him did not go far.

Reaching my room on the third floor, he glanced up and down the hallway and, when he had my door open, darted inside. From inside my room, he frantically waved me in. I stared at him but cautiously stepped forward, and he closed the door behind me.

"Don't get weird, hombre," I said.

"You want beeya, saa?" he half whispered.

"Yeah man! Can you get me a beer?" I shouted, suspicion turning to elation.

"Saa, yes saa, quiet... Quiet, p'ease... You give me money." His open hand shot out, the sweat and dirt from how-many-days accumulated in his palm.

I gave him plenty of cash and held up two fingers saying, "Bring me two, bhaiya." He snatched the money and dashed out, slamming the door.

After fifteen minutes, a sharp knock from the hallway signaled his return with the contraband; opening the door, I was almost knocked over when he sprang past to put them in my room fridge. His bellboy hat fell off as he slammed the refrigerator shut. Putting it back on his oily head, he eyed me with a cool, thieving stare and held a finger to his lips, whispering, "Saa, must be quiet, thik hai?"

He didn't say another word, or bring any change, and he nervously left in an invisible wave of body odor. I peered down the hall after him, fearing that some kind of trench-coat-wearing, anti-alcohol Indian gestapo might be lurking in the shadows.

49.

Heart of Glass

Out at the Jagdalpur airport one late afternoon, Zach had joined me for a run, but his stride could be measured in yards and soon he tore off down the runway like a gazelle across the Serengeti, leaving me far behind in his wake. That was alright, we would spend a good hour at a more pedestrian pace after his Olympic tryout. The runway tarmac, great for landing aircraft, was also good for a casual, meditative stroll. During our walk, we had the entire world's problems solved, but our combined complaining used up more oxygen than if we had run a three-thousand-meter steeplechase.

Along both sides of the runway, the IPS was tasked with clearing the jungle-like vegetation that had been growing steadily for a year or two. But no one told them that brush cutters and mowers had been invented, and they'd hired bulldozers for the job. That seemed ludicrous. Instead of leaving a nicely trimmed grassy area on either side of the runway, the bulldozers scraped the vegetation away down to the topsoil, leaving dusty, bare dirt to blow around in even the slightest breeze.

Indeed, the bushgrass and scrubby trees were getting tall; the brown soil below held some fertility and, combined with the daily rains of the recent monsoon, the vegetation stretched over our heads by two feet. But scraping it into piles around the airport perimeter made as much sense as combing your hair with a pitch fork. To make matters worse, once the unearthed vegetation became semi-dry, the geniuses lit it on fire, leaving the airport and surrounding area enveloped in smoldering smoke for days.

After our gossip and grousing session, we boarded the car to take us back to our lodgings, the driver letting me off first at the Devansh and then delivering Zach back to the guesthouse. I told them so long and watched the car drive away down the noisy, cow-cluttered street. Feeling good and feeling energized, under the influence of endorphins from my recent run, I scaled the steps two at a time, up to the glass door leading into the lobby.

Lost in thought about my upcoming dinner, or beer, I vaguely noticed that the old, threadbare welcome mat in front of the door had been exchanged for a shaggy new brown replacement since I'd left for the airport. I grabbed the door handle and gave it a pull, much the same way I normally did, but instead of it opening gently, the entire glass door suddenly exploded and crashed into hundreds of pieces all around me. All that remained in my hand was the door handle and a few splintering fragments of glass.

When the staff had placed the new mat at the doorway, they didn't bother to check the door's clearance. I would have been fine if I had pushed-in rather than pulled-out, but the double doors were clearly designed to operate smoothly, opening in either direction. You would think common sense would've had them test the fit between the new mat and the swinging doors. The bottom of the door caught the top of the new, thicker mat that I was standing on barely enough to cause it to fracture and then go nuclear in my hand.

Standing in my cutoff cargo shorts and sweaty T-shirt, white legs glowing like oversize fluorescent light bulbs in the evening darkness, I looked around at the carnage created. The sound of breaking glass echoed down the lobby for what seemed half a minute. I took roll call of my little piggies and other appendages and was relieved to come up with the correct number, not losing any to door shrapnel. The clerk came dashing over, glass crunching under his shoes, while the shady bellboy cowered behind the desk. I froze in one spot, fearing any additional movement might cause something else to explode.

I waited days to be thanked by hotel management for being their official door tester, especially in light of the ongoing wedding season, but no thanks were given. I'm sure it would have been a bad sign if the door exploded during a marriage celebration. With my recent modifications to the entranceway, my fellow hotel guests weren't burdened with opening a door either. The hotel maintenance staff draped a white bed sheet in the opening. What I'd done was a favor.

The Devansh being the newest and perhaps nicest hotel—albeit minus one door—in Jagdalpur, it attracted many wedding parties. The traditional wedding season was late September through January, the period between monsoon rains and summer heat, and the hotel staff were gearing up for a busy time of nuptials.

Returning from flights to Sukma, Jagargunda and Gollapalli late in the day, a beehive of activity awaited me at the hotel's entrance. Middle-aged women wearing sarees and concerned looks were supervising the construction of a flowered wedding trellis. I didn't think my appearance posed a threat, but they were reluctant to let me pass. Perhaps they had heard how I make an entrance and were worried about further damage to their chosen wedding venue.

Being let out from the car and walking up the steps should have implied that I was a guest of the hotel and had intentions to enter the lobby. The herd of women were all talking at once, ignoring me, pointing and shouting instructions for the best way to put up a trellis, and they would not stand for any interruptions. The three beleaguered hotel staff tasked with the hard labor of putting up these wedding decorations glanced at me but were busy receiving an earful concerning their artistic shortcomings and deficiencies.

The women numbered about a dozen and had rolls of flesh peeking out the bare midriffs of their sarees, evidence that they were well-fed middle class—evidence that they were in need of full length mirrors—and, when walking up the steps, several glanced my way and regarded me as if I were a big, moist insect.

Not making way for me to get through, they only continued shouting and pointing out errant décor while I stood enveloped in their warmth.

"Excuse me, please," I said politely, but too quietly, as most paid no heed. "Would you mind if I came through?"

A few sniffed and huffed, then reluctantly shuffled back a few steps to let me pass, clearly intolerant of any interruption to their toil. I squeezed inward, but was expecting, and prepared, to wrestle my way through the rest of the sumo-sized madams at any moment.

It had been a long day, and I didn't feel like going anywhere. I sent the shady bellboy for brews, lawful brews this time, and had room service bring me one of their cardboard-flavored vegetarian pizzas. An hour or two after sundown, I was ready to call it a night; but alas, that was also time to call a start to the wedding festivities.

That meant music, and in line with any Indian wedding music worth its chilies, it was loud. The wedding party was on the first floor and I was on the third, but they could've been in the room next door for all the bedlam. Even if there had been thirty floors' separation, the ear-splitting ruckus would have reached me. I prepared my earplugs and myself for bed but knew it would be futile. A little relief from the racket was had late in the night, when the party left for the traditional parade around town. I listened as the loud marching band slowly faded into the distance, and hoping they were gone for good, I was able to catch a few winks of sleep in that beautiful quiet.

No luck, though. They were back in a couple of hours and, if anything, the decibels had increased. About midnight, with sleep impossible, I decided just to get out of bed and invite myself to the party. You can't fight 'em, so join 'em. All I had to wear was my sweaty white uniform shirt and khaki trousers, but I figured the ripeness of my apparel would not be worse than any of the guests'.

I found Indians were generally easygoing, especially when it came to partying, and assumed they would not mind a wedding crasher. But walking into the banquet area, I felt like a hooker in a church for being the only foreign, and uninvited, face at the wedding. That feeling was compounded when a stern, fortyish-looking man walked up and asked me bluntly, "What are you doing here?"

"Umm... well, I'm a hotel guest and only wanted to see the celebration that's keeping me from sleeping," I grinned. "And you know, that's a beautiful trellis out front."

"No, no man. Sorry, that came out wrong. What I mean is, what are you doing in Jagdalpur? In India?" He smiled and held out his hand, "My name is Kanu, and this is my niece's wedding."

Telling him my occupation spawned an hour of conversation. He was an IPS officer based in Raipur and had come with his family to the celebration. I had hauled a number of his mates to places around the countryside, and he became inquisitive and curious, asking questions about flying to the IPS and CRPF camps.

When he found out that I'd been the pilot nearly shot down at Kistaram, he gave me a whiskey and toasted my luck. He took me around like a prize pony to people he knew, getting around to the bejeweled bride and garish groom, who were happy to have a picture taken with me. I congratulated them and wished them much luck; they slightly scrunched their noses, and I could tell they didn't understand my English, but they got the gist.

By that time, and with flights coming in the morning, I was ready to give sleep another try and excused myself, heading back to my room, much to the objections of my new Raipur friend. The trellis-building ladies I had to fight through earlier, however, were glad to see me go, my compliments of their decorations notwithstanding.

50.

Chaos at Kistaram

The stench of alcohol was strong in the helicopter. We had just taken off from Kistaram on the first of two requested sorties originating in Dantewada, and the three troopers we had in back were hammered. Droopy eyelids barely hid bloodshot, vacant eyes, and their overall appearance was wretched. I asked Babeesh to crack open his side window to circulate more fresh air.

I didn't smell much better as, after waking up that morning, I had discovered that both water and power had been cut off to the hotel during the night. The front desk blamed the city street department, and they hoped to have it rectified by my return in the evening. Using a couple bottles of water, I rinsed what I could but during the preflight in the morning, a not-so-fresh manly scent began to develop.

We continued on to Dantewada, but something about the unruly crowd we left at Kistaram nagged at me. We were used to minor confusion at the jungle camp helipads. As usual, there was no one in charge—no improvement over the months—and routinely it was left up to BK or Babeesh to sort out who was coming aboard and who was not. We had been to Kistaram and other IPS/CRPF jungle helipads many times, and they knew the drill: no more than three or four passengers at a time. Still, it was common to see five, six or even more troopers watching hopefully while we landed. With traveling bags in hand and ready to dash to the helicopter once our door was open, they'd race, pushing and shoving, to be first in line to board.

I pleaded with Rabinesh and other officers many times to have the rotating personnel sorted before I landed. Promises were made, but the discipline remained dismal.

At Kistaram that morning, there had been a particular sense of disorder. That, combined with the inebriated condition of the troopers aboard—and our violent history with the place—should have been enough cumulative evidence to cancel the second flight there. Reaching Dantewada, we took fuel, and I spoke with Rabinesh.

"These guys are hammered," I said, pointing to the stumbling buffoons making their way off the helipad. "What's the security status at Kistaram?"

"Oh, don't worry, Mista Mike. These guys have been in the jungle a long time." He smiled his toothy smile. "They probably brewed up some homemade hooch and had a going away party last night to blow off steam."

"I'm fine with blowing off a little steam, but can the assholes wait until I haul 'em outta the jungle?" My coarse language checked his smile slightly. "If they're all drunk, who's guarding the camp?"

He went on trying to reassure me, but something felt not right. Nevertheless, after refueling, we loaded up three passengers and enough rations to put us at maximum weight.

Before starting, I thanked Rabinesh for the usual coffee and told him, "Listen, my man... we'll head back there, but if we see something we don't like, I'm not gonna land. These rations will be back here in Dantewada, and they can eat leaves and dirt."

"It's okay, my friend," he said, his smile back at maximum glow. "These guys at the camps love you, they'll watch out for you."

Of that, I'd never been convinced.

Arriving overhead Kistaram once again, I told Babeesh, "If you see anything... *anything* that looks out of whack down there, you let me know straightaway."

"Saa, yes saa," he said, with his eyes widened to dinner plate size. "I don't think we should be heeya, saa."

"Me neither, but let's get it over with. If you see something, speak up."

The troopers on the ground had depleted their supply of smoke canisters, so showing initiative and clever thinking, they lit a tire on fire. Clever, unless it turned out their only vehicle within miles now just had three good tires remaining.

We started our descent, and it all seemed okay. Armed troopers were forming a perimeter a few hundred yards out from the helipad, and as we neared the ground, there were several chaps standing by the camp wire with bags and rifles. The situation looked normal, and I committed to landing.

"All okay, Babeesh?" I shouted over the intercom.

"Okay, saa!" His head swiveled from side to side and front to back.

I set down in a dusty cloud of weeds and leaves and lowered the collective. I briefly glanced at Babeesh as he jumped down off his side of the helicopter and started unloading the passengers and rations. Then, looking back toward the camp, I saw mayhem start to unfold.

Joining the few chaps already waiting with bags were several more, and then, in a matter of seconds, a whole string of desperate troopers came spilling out of the barracks building like angry hornets from a kicked nest, some still stuffing loose clothing into their bags. It appeared most of the camp was bent on mutiny.

The first troopers already waiting saw this and did the quick math. They realized the law of the jungle was in effect and that they had better hasten onto the helicopter before the seats were all taken. A mob of fifteen or twenty rushed the helicopter before I could do anything. They pushed the three inbound troopers out of the way and, when Babeesh tried to stop them, they pushed him out of the way.

In a matter of moments, what I feared most—besides getting shot—was happening. With discipline in shambles, soon there were no less than eight of the hooligans scuffling around in the four back seats of the Astar, and more were trying to scramble in. With their drunkenness, I was afraid one of them on the outside was about to end up as dog meat from the tailrotor. Babeesh was back up on his feet and getting feisty, pushing, pulling and shouting his way amongst the swarm, trying to restore order. It was all happening so quickly that there was nothing I could do but sit behind the controls. I certainly didn't want to shut down, given the bloody history of Maoist-Naxalites in the area.

A couple of raging, ugly dudes who were stumbling drunk and carrying rifles shouted at me to takeoff. They pointed at me and then at the sky gesturing to fly away. And I wanted to, more than they knew. The Astar was a powerful machine, but taking off with that many bodies aboard was not going to happen, especially if half the scrum was hanging onto the skids.

I looked at the punks behind me and saw red. They were jostling around and still trying to fit more in, although Babeesh was slowly regaining control. There was shouting and wailing. They had tears streaming down their faces and refused to leave the helicopter. I turned and, reaching back, gave the closest deserter a slap across his face. Because I was strapped in the seat and at an odd angle, I didn't land it quite as hard as I wanted to. Still, it stung him, and he and the others quieted down, slightly.

Babeesh and I continued shouting for them to get out, the ugly dudes outside kept shouting for me to takeoff, and the group of mutineers in the back were shouting and bawling to stay aboard. It was a hazardous situation, made more so by alcohol and the extreme lack of leadership and discipline. And all the while, I knew the longer we stayed on the ground the chances of getting shot by the real bad guys grew.

Babeesh had stopped the onslaught from outside, but the dregs in back still would not budge. Shifting my buttocks in the seat and reaching behind me again, I went with a closed fist approach and bopped the closest one on the nose. I was pissed. I wanted to hurt those bastards who were putting me in a life threatening situation again.

They got the message then, and reluctantly let Babeesh pull them out of the helicopter and away to the side. I was relieved to see the two angry dudes with rifles start shouting at them instead of me. Still, they glared with drunken fury.

In the turmoil, a fifty-pound bag of rice that hadn't been unloaded was trampled upon and torn open. The back floor was covered in rice. Babeesh scraped out what he could onto the ground until I shouted at him to leave it. In his haste, the now-empty rice bag flew out and into the downwash, catching precariously on a wilted weed. The last thing we needed was to have that bag wrapped into the tailrotor or main rotor, but Babeesh climbed aboard, leaving it.

"Get that rice bag, Babeesh!" I pointed to it.

"It's empty, saa!" Babeesh, having much experience in the jungle, normally would have recognized the hazard, but he was rattled from the mob scene.

"Grab that fuckin' bag before it gets sucked in the tailrotor!"

He looked at me and out at the bag, not wanting to step foot on Kistaram soil again. He hesitated but jumped out, grabbed it, then put it on his seat and sat on it as he slammed his door shut.

My collective lever was already coming up, and the takeoff path was clear, mostly. One of the ugly dudes was staring at me threateningly, holding his rifle with one hand on the receiver and didn't move an inch while I accelerated past him. It looked like he was still deciding if I should live or die. Blasting him with dirt and weeds, I hoped the belligerent drunk wouldn't take any pot shots at us while we flew away, climbing up and back toward Dantewada.

Adrenaline was flowing, but I began to relax. The mob scene replayed in my mind. I tried to think how we could have handled that better or, even avoided it altogether. Nothing we saw before landing hinted that we faced trouble; the intoxicated troopers had all been inside the barracks, packing their bags and hidden, while we landed. But a little voice had been telling me something after our first flight to the camp, and I should've listened to it.

Babeesh's hands were shaking, and his eyeballs were nearly outside his skull. The interior of the helicopter again smelled like booze from the warm bodies in back. After the mayhem we had just left on the ground, the screaming engine and whirring rotor blades seemed like quiet relief.

Moments later, Babeesh shouted, "Saa, those guys we'e drunk!"

I glanced at my nerved-up junior crew chief in the left seat. "What gave you that idea, Babeesh?" Grinning uneasily, he looked over at me, and I said, "It's morning, but I could use a drink myself. How 'bout you, buddy?"

"Yes, saa! Dat's a fine idea!"

"Pass me a bit of that nasty paan in the meantime, my friend."

"Jee, saa!" He started to look around the floor and seat for his typically well-stocked stash of foul tasting, leafy fixings that he kept in a fanny pack. Not finding it, though, and getting uptight, he began squirming around, launching a full-scale search.

"I think it fell out!" he exclaimed.

Dropping the collective to its stop to reduce power and raising the nose to slow us down, I pulled a hard right 180 degree turn back toward Kistaram.

"Saa... uhh, where do we go?"

"I'm not leaving this jungle without your paan!"

"No, no, no!" The whites of his eyes were like empty white tea cups. "Leave it, saa! I don' need it! P'ease don' take me to Kistaram again!"

51.

Escape India

The morale of troopers in the most remote IPS and CRPF camps like Kistaram had been waning, as our recent incident with the personnel stationed there demonstrated. From time to time other, less serious incidents, such as the lack of a smoke signal or a trooper's tardiness at the helipad would come up, but those procedural discrepancies could be dealt with by telling Rabinesh to rectify the problem before I'd agree to fly there again. I also had immediate solutions to certain predicaments; in the case of a lack of smoke signal, I would not land, and if a trooper was tardy, I would leave him—unless the reason for his tardiness was that he was wounded. For safety's sake, every time we landed at the remote camps, I assumed an attack was imminent, that time was of the essence and didn't loiter on the ground.

If the incident was serious enough or happened too frequently, I'd write up a report and have it delivered to General Thomas. Returning to base at Jagdalpur the afternoon following our Kistaram moonshine run, I sat down and spelled out the odious actions of the miscreants. His resulting action was tough. The officers in charge of the camp were stripped of command and they, along with about a dozen troublemakers, were ordered to vacate the camp and return to Dantewada by road. Their replacements were also ordered to Kistaram via the road, a hazard-strewn distance of over fifty miles. I was relieved to hear that both groups had arrived at their destinations safely. I would have felt horrible if they were attacked along the way. Nonetheless, landing any time soon at Kistaram was improbable until discipline had improved.

The root of the problem was morale, however, and the government's solution seemed to be more troop rotation flights to and from the distant camps—getting them back home to family more often. This was at the peak of wedding season, mid-December, and a lot of the young men I was hauling had nuptials planned. Our flight requests from the IPS and CRPF were an everyday occurrence, and the number of sorties per day was increasing. Zach, who had spent most of the year flying candidates during election campaigning in other far reaches of India, was now in Jagdalpur as well and getting busy with the paramilitaries.

My busy days were coming to an end, though, at least temporarily. The company had decided to install an air conditioning unit on the Astar, and rumors were that we would be flying to Mumbai by the end of the year. There were other major inspections due on the engine and drivetrain, and the work involved would be hard to accomplish in Jagdalpur or Raipur. In fact, the DGCA would not give us approval for maintenance work in either place.

My mates and I were, at first, expecting a shift to Bhubaneswar again, but try as he might, Sami was told that even our hangar there would not suffice. DGCA demanded the work be done in a properly equipped maintenance hangar, and much to the disappointment of both Anika and me, plans were developing on the opposite side of the country, in Mumbai. The company had a monstrosity of a hangar there with the proper tooling, parts and equipment to please the strictest DGCA official. It had room enough for the company's Mi17 and quite a few other aircraft.

Also coming from the company head office was the rumor that I would be able to enjoy ample free time while the aircraft was grounded, with pay, perhaps even outside the country.

I'd been used to free time with no pay during other irksome stretches of my career, so the part about "with pay" caught my attention, as did the chance to escape India.

Before that time would come, we had many missions remaining. One particularly special mission for me had nothing to do with the IPS or CRPF. I would be in Raipur for at least one day having my Pilot Proficiency Check, or PPC, with the DGCA. Even with, and perhaps because of, the Astar's soon-to-be-grounded condition, the company wanted me current and legal before flying to Mumbai.

The DGCA was understandably reluctant to send any of their staff to such a remote location as Jagdalpur, so a check flight in Raipur was agreed upon. Remarkably, the company had planned and informed me about this PPC well in advance: about a week. A week in advance was exceptional.

I had told Anika that my trip to Mumbai instead of Bhubaneswar was imminent, but knew I would have at least one night in Raipur after my check. Soon after the company had set up the PPC, I asked her by phone, "Would you be willing to meet me in Raipur? How could you get there?"

"Ohh, I want to see yoouuu, Michaelll... I'd have to take the train, it would be such a long journey," she said, her voice managing to both coo and whine in the same breath.

"I know, it's such a brutally long journey, I've been on it... Well, are you even free from work for a couple days?"

"Yes, I do have free time... and I've never been to Raipur before," she said, slightly warming to the idea.

Then I brought out the heavy weaponry. "Once I'm in Mumbai, I don't know if I will see you again. I'm headed back to the USA."

"You won't come back to India, Michael?"

"I don't know yet. Next year's plans are up in the air."

"... Alright, I'm coming then. Give me the exact date you'll be in Raipur, so I can book the hotel."

The IPS, upon finding out that I would be traveling to the state capital, requested a stop in Naranpur on my way north to pick up an officer, as it was not far off my flight path. Normally, they would drive the highway to or from Raipur, but if they found out I was deadheading in one direction or the other, they'd come along for the ride. This wasn't a problem unless that particular officer could not tell time.

After landing in Naranpur and discovering that our passenger was not yet ready, I shut down and, along with BK, stood in the shade of a jujube tree. Naranpur, like Dantewada, was considered a safe camp. It was a place where we could shut down, take fuel and relax. While waiting for the tardy character, the security guards milled around, kicking at the dust and glaring at me, probably concerned that they'd miss breakfast if they had to stand guard around the helicopter much longer.

After a half-hour passed, I knew my appointment with Mr. DGCA might have to be postponed. I didn't have his phone number—didn't know his name—but wanted to call Sami so he could get in touch with him and beg for my forgiveness. Cellular service was down, though, and we had no signal. We were parked in the middle of this horseshoe-shaped barracks complex some distance from the main government offices, but I figured the rundown-looking stucco shacks nearby must've still held a landline phone or two.

I asked the guard in charge, who was leaning on his jeep, "Namaste, my friend... Say, is there a landline phone here I can use?" I made a vague pointing gesture that encompassed the nearby shacks, trying to be concise and wanting a reasonable estimate of the distance to a phone.

"Jee, saa, you can use a phone heeya, we have many," he said.

Assuming that, indeed, a phone was just a short walk away, I said, "Good. If our passenger doesn't show up in the next ten minutes, I'll have to use one."

"Jee saa." I could see gears turning behind his eyes. "I'll send the driver to check the passenger, saa."

With that, he joined us in the shade and sent his driver away through the dust of the parade ground.

What initiative the chap had, I thought. *That was mighty nice.*

Ten minutes later, there was still no sign of a passenger or vehicle, and I hate to keep anybody waiting. Being early is being on time. That's what I learned years ago, and of all people to be late for, a DGCA inspector was nowhere near the top of the list.

"Time's up, bhaiya. I need to use that phone now," I said to the guard and started walking to the nearest building, twenty yards away, where he suggested sat a landline phone.

"Saa, yes saa... Ahh, where you go?"

"To use the phone, you told me there was a phone here," I pointed a thumb over my shoulder.

"Jee saa, we have a phone heeya," he said. I stopped walking and looked at him. He continued, "Heeya saa, over heeya." He was pointing down the dirt track.

"You mean you have a phone, but not here, and it's down that mile-long dirt road where you just sent your jeep?"

"Jee saa!" he laughed and shook his head. "We don't have a phone heeya, saa!"

My mind-reading deficiencies aside, we reached Raipur Heliport, and I dropped down onto the landing pad in a swirling typhoon of sunshine. My tardy passenger was happier than a beef-cow at a vegetarian barbeque for avoiding the highway ride and was all smiles when he jumped to the ground. With a quick wave, he was off to join his mustachioed colleagues, who stood in awe of this great man from Naranpur, one so important he warranted a helicopter ride.

Mr. DGCA didn't seem happy, though, and I couldn't blame him. He was standing in a man-sized opening of the sliding hangar doors with his arms folded and brow furrowed. His glasses were dark, so I could not read his eyes, but the ascot he wore told me enough. It was Colonel Mohan, whom we had met many weeks before, when he had shown much displeasure for me, BK and the helicopter. I was still searching for a proper ascot, one that matched my eyes.

"BK, there's a good friend of yours," I said, grinning.

"Oh no, saa, he not my friend," BK said as I chopped the throttle and let the turbine wind down. "Dat's da same guy, he grilled me last time. He not nice to me, saa."

"Yeah, mate," I said, "and he looks pissed!"

I jumped down from the cockpit and, fearing the worst because of my tardiness, walked straight over to him and held out my hand.

"Good morning, sir, my deepest apologies for being late." He shook my hand, unsmiling, while I continued, "You see, the IPS called this morning, and they had an additional…"

He held up a hand, cutting me off, and shrugged. "No worries, Captain, it's alright. I talked to Mr. Sami in your Delhi office, and he explained the situation. I have all day in Raipur, and you're my only appointment."

That was good, and that was bad. Good that he was in a decent mood, bad because he had all day to grill me on everything from Alpha to Zulu.

"Excellent, sir," I said. "I'm glad Sami was able to reach you."

"Oh, yes. He promised that he'd take care of me, that my stay in Raipur would be comfortable. He even reserved a room for me at the Golden Tulip and hired a driver." The Golden Tulip Hotel was out by the airport and one of the most expensive in town. I wondered what other transactions took place between Sami and Colonel Mohan.

"Have you had breakfast yet, Captain?" he asked.

Surprised at his friendliness, I said, "Yep, yes sir, I filled up on egg roti this morning."

"Why don't you go have coffee and relax a while. I'm going to have a word with your crew chief out there."

I glanced at BK, who was directing the refueling and nervously watching us.

"Alright, sir. Thanks," I said, but hesitated as we started to walk in separate directions. "Take it easy on my friend out there, he's a good chap."

He laughed and said, "I know BK. He is a good chap. I'm gonna play with him a bit, but you guys don't have anything to worry about today."

52.

Anika

My proficiency check was a piece of cake. After BK finished both refueling and getting verbally roughed up by Colonel Mohan, we took off from the heliport for Raipur Airport, where we did a dozen takeoffs and landings. Mohan had a list of the maneuvers he wanted to see, and it covered the common emergency procedures, such as loss of tailrotor control and hydraulic system failure. The simulated engine failure and autorotations he asked for were no issue, not due to any exceptional piloting skills from Super-Ace Pilot, but more to do with leaving the power all the way up.

Grabbing a navigation chart that was rustling around in its pocket from the breezy vent, he stabbed his finger on a small town thirty miles away and told me to fly there without the aid of GPS. It was a town just south of Raipur, Dhamtari, and one I routinely flew over. Checking fuel and then requesting permission from ATC, we flew for fifteen minutes, buzzed in overhead and landed briefly at a helipad by Dhamtari's dam. He only wanted to see that I could handle the aircraft safely, competently and find my way around. We were done by lunchtime, meaning close to three in the afternoon.

Mohan and I filled out the usual paperwork and then, stamping it, he christened me SATISFACTORY for another six months of India flying bliss. The DGCA was finished with BK and me and, having no immediate orders, we drove to the Hotel Grand. There we would wait for the phone call from Sami telling us to either head back to Jagdalpur or make a flight plan for Mumbai. They did not know yet which it would be.

Waiting until the last minute was standard operating procedure for my company. It was even in the company's operations manual. That is, it had to be—I couldn't find it written anywhere, but with them ardently waiting until the last minute on *everything*, I just assumed it was.

Sarcasm aside, one could reason that the company wanted as many billable flying hours as they could get before a lengthy grounding of the machine. It was a matter of coordinating with the maintenance team in Mumbai and having the required aircraft parts on hand.

Arriving at the hotel, we found it overrun with beautiful young women mingling about in the lobby and in and out of the Grand's two banquet rooms. It was like walking into a beauty pageant. Forget about the rest of chaotic and sometimes-ugly India; when Indian women get dolled up in their flowing and glittering sarees, with makeup, styled hair and sparkly gold jewelry, their beauty is staggering.

There was a bit of a queue at the reception desk, and it was fortunate that Sami had booked our rooms in advance; the hotel was near to capacity, with both an engagement party and a wedding taking place at the same time, filling the Grand with vibrancy and elegance. We were content to take a seat on one of the settees, wait for the line to thin out and soak in the energetic atmosphere.

My phone battery was getting weak from taking calls: Sami in Delhi, Rabinesh in Dantewada and others of the IPS in Jagdalpur. The IPS and CRPF had a number of flight requests and were not happy to see me go.

It was finally decided that we would head back to the jungle and fly as many missions as possible before I would ferry the aircraft to Mumbai at the end of the year. We'd head to Dantewada in the morning for a mission.

"Should we check in, saa?" asked BK. Ten minutes had gone by while I was chattering on my phone. "Less people now."

"Yep, we should... Can't stay here all day," I said, glancing at a newly arrived group of alluring ladies.

"Nuttin' wrong wit' da view d'ough, is d'ere, saa?"

We stood up and went to check in. There were all those beautiful women, but none for me.

Anika was on her way from Bhubaneswar, though, and had sent a text message saying she was two hours away. With the usual delays, it would be sunset before she arrived. I did not envy her much, riding the train for over fourteen hours, but she didn't seem to mind. She had been riding crowded trains her entire life and seemed accustomed to it. I took a quick shower and had a bite to eat, then waited for our rendezvous.

Wiling away the minutes waiting for Anika, I found it hard to sit still in my fourth-floor room and traipsed about the hotel. The wedding and engagement parties were gearing up on the ground floor, the wedding especially. Music was being sampled, and the louder the better, of course. Working my way up from the ground floor, I stopped in the bar, where European football was on one TV and cricket matches were on all the others. The room was full of men and, after sitting at the bar briefly with a Thumbs Up, I moved on.

On the roof at sundown, I watched the big orange ball descend through the hazy sky until the horizon gobbled it down like an enormous Pac Man dot. On cue, the muezzin at the nearby mosque warmed up his speakers and started bellowing out the call to evening prayer. During his all-too-short interludes between wails, while he recovered his breath and filled his lungs, I heard a train whistle in the distance. Evidently, the muezzin heard it too, and fearing the railroad's whistle might drown out his tune, seemed to turn the volume up. The mosque's speakers rattled in their mounting brackets as distorted sound waves howled across the city.

Hearing the train whistle, I wondered if it was the one Anika was riding. I didn't wonder long as my pocket vibrated and then my phone began to ring. I read the caller ID.

"Hi, Anika. I was just listening to your train at the station."

"What? No, not my train Michael, I just arrived... argh, such a long journey."

"That's what I mean. I can hear your train's whistle arriving in the station. I'm on the roof of the hotel."

"What are you talking about, goofy man? I'm here at the Hotel Grand, JUST ARRIVED. It's so noisy! Where are you? What's that singing in the background? Are you at a mosque?"

"Ah, okay, I got it," I said, "No, no, I'M ON THE ROOF OF THE HOTEL, my dear... Never mind, I'll see you in the lobby in two minutes, two seconds."

A pause. I heard a sound like she was blowing out a candle.

"Roof... two... What did you say? MICHAEL!"

She was travel weary and tired; between the wailing at the mosque, the festive music blasting in the hotel and my hillbilly accent, she was thoroughly confused. And a little testy.

"I'M COMING!" I said, then clicked off and walked down, hoping to reach her before she chucked her phone against the wall.

Even with all that beauty bustling around in the busy lobby, Anika was not hard to pick out in the crowd. Instead of wearing traditional clothing, she was wearing something more travel friendly; she had on a pair of her usual high-heel shoes, along with skinny blue jeans topped by a loose-fitting white blouse. Her hair was pulled back into a ponytail, and it flowed back and forth across her shoulders while she talked to the receptionist. Her black locks appeared as soft and delicate as an artist's oversized paintbrush.

There was no shortage of goddesses inside the lobby, but when she spotted me and the smile lit up her face, she won the Miss India title hands down; no dispute, as far as I was concerned. She had finished checking in and, after retrieving her suitcase, greeted me when I walked up.

"Hello, Michael. We meet again after soo long... You're looking good. At least, I don't see any bullet holes."

"*You*. Are a sight. For sore eyes. Stunning. It's been far too long," I said.

"Could you get my luggage, Michael? My feet are killing me."

Taking her suitcase and bag while walking to the elevator, I said, "I'm glad you came. I didn't know when I'd get to Bhubaneswar again."

"I've missed you... and now you say you may leave India?"

"Well, ah, yes, there's a chance."

"But you're coming back, right?"

"Don't know yet. We can talk about it over dinner. I reserved a table at the Hotel Babylon restaurant. It's fairly crowded here."

The elevator chimed and the door opened, spilling out several partygoers and hyperactive kids. We stepped in, and I quickly punched the DOOR CLOSE button before anyone else could jump in and ruin our first brief moments of privacy in weeks.

She was staying on the third floor, and while she freshened up in the bathroom, I switched on the movie channel and watched *Mama Mia*. Raipur was even more conservative than Bhubaneswar and certainly more than Delhi or Mumbai. Just being alone in the room with her would have caused certain conservative Indians to be apoplectic if they found out, perhaps to the point of violence. An unmarried couple alone behind closed doors was frowned upon, but with Anika's independent streak and stubbornness, she wasn't bothered. I, on the other hand, was wary. It posed a challenge, but I made sure no gawking eyes were watching before I darted through her doorway.

Hitching a ride in an auto rickshaw, we rode through the noisy streets out to the Babylon and discovered it was as busy as the Grand. There was at least one wedding taking place, but perhaps several. The grounds around the building were mobbed with shiny, happy people, and a pulsating party was set up and humming along at full tilt in the adjacent grassy courtyard. Brightly colored decorations covered everything from the chairs and tables to the expansive, curtained wall that was erected to keep out interlopers like me. Music was booming to the heavens. Men were dancing with men, and women dancing with women. Dancing, again, looked to be a gender-divided team sport.

Anika and I were seated in the restaurant, and the menus were brought by an overdressed and over-starched waiter. The chap's uniform must've weighed fifteen pounds, five pounds alone in his glittery turban. A steaming platter of butter naan was placed between us, and I attacked it like a ravenous jungle beast. The doughy, flat bread was irresistible.

We talked over my future plans and, after her initial concern that I would not come back, she declared that I would.

"I know you'll come back to India, Michael. You've been bitten."

True, I had been bitten. I'd been bitten by a lot of things and was lucky to be alive.

"How do you know I'll be back?" I asked her. "Can you see my future? Are you a fortune teller?"

"A fortune... what?" She asked, her dark eyes narrowing. "No, Michael, just like I told you when I first met you in Delhi... That I'd see you again in Bhubaneswar? Remember? And that happened... You'll be back to India," she smiled. "I know."

Of that I was not sure, but talking about it was a mood killer, so I changed the subject. Giving her a flirty-eye-browed look, I said, "Shall I tell you about your future tonight?"

Wrinkling her nose, but blushing, she asked, "How will you do that? Judging by your frisky look, no. Don't say a word... And what's wrong with your eye?"

She shook her head no, dangling earrings catching the candlelight, but her smile said yes.

53.

Goat Rodeo

Upon hearing loud, guttural sounds, one of my eyes sleepily cracked open. Confused, I thought I'd heard a goat right outside my fourth-floor hotel window. Listening harder, perhaps it was more of a *goattural* sound.

Then, there it was again. A goat, surely, and that time another one answered it. It sounded much too close to be down at street level, and I wondered what strange sights India had in store for the day.

It was still dark outside, but getting out of bed and walking over to the window, I could see the graying promise of morning on the horizon. Hearing the goats again, I adjusted my gaze down through the windows of what I had guessed was a neighboring three-story apartment building for humans; but one of its occupants had the lights on in what, instead, looked to be the top-floor penthouse suite for goats.

A man appeared, the goat whisperer, and the reason for the early morning bleating became apparent. He was holding a long butcher knife.

Turning back to bed, I considered jumping under the sheets again and noticed dark splotches on my white pillow case. It was evidence of the bloody battle waged the night before against swarms of predacious mosquitoes. I had plugged the crack under the room door to keep the usual pests and rodents out, but a latch on one of the two windows was broken, and I could not get the bloody thing shut all the way. Even using my well-practiced MacGyver skills with a butter knife and ball-point pen, a two-inch crack to the outside world of goat bleats and ectoparasites remained. Legions of mosquitoes infiltrated and ambushed me. The slaughter was wholesale.

Anika and I had stayed late at the Hotel Babylon, enjoying the other happy couples' wedding festivities, and returned to the Hotel Grand after midnight. The partying in the Grand's own banquet halls was not even slightly easing up by that time, and the pounding music surely hadn't, making sleep an iffy business. Not that sleep was high on the list of priorities.

The day's mission called for an eight o'clock takeoff, but the bed linens beckoned with irresistible temptation. Digging deep into exhausted reserves of willpower, I avoided the bed, picked up the phone and ordered two carafes of sweet milk coffee from room service.

After I clicked off with room service, BK called, wondering how much fuel I wanted in the tank. Easy math with the Astar: a full tank still left plenty of weight available for passengers or cargo; neither of which we would have on the flight. We had only a little over an hour's flight to Dantewada, where we would have to take fuel again, but replacing fuel barrels at the hangar in Raipur was easier than replacing the fuel barrels in the jungle, so I took as much as I could while in the city.

Having a light breakfast in the hotel restaurant, Anika and I then found my driver, and we headed out to the heliport. I told her it wasn't necessary to join me, but she wasn't about to listen to that.

"Of course I'm coming to the heliport to see you off and say goodbye!" she said, getting feisty. "What sort of heartless man are you, Michael?"

"It's okay, Anika. I thought…"

"No," she cut me off, "You didn't think, and yes, I am coming."

Raising her nose for emphasis, she ended the short debate.

She'd be catching the train to Bhubaneswar in the late afternoon and, after waving me goodbye at the heliport, would head back to the hotel and wait for the city's two new malls to open. She had shopping on her mind, and I was thankful for not being able to take part in her mall conquests. Given the choice between flying to a place like Kistaram or shopping at the mall, I'd take my chances with the junglies in Kistaram every time.

When we arrived at the heliport, there was the usual crowd of onlookers, including school kids, retirees and others. Hundreds of troopers were doing morning calisthenics on the parade ground just yards from where my helicopter sat. The December temperatures were cooler; it must've been in the mid-sixties or low seventies. BK wore a sweater, and the guards wore jackets, but the temperature was comfortable to me. Despite the many smoky trash fires in the streets around the city, the morning air was pleasant.

BK had the refueling and his preflight finished, and Anika walked around the helicopter with me while I did my own checks. She was dressed casually but exquisitely in a yellow kurta top with white pajama bottoms and dupatta. Her hair was held in place by a clasp, with a few loose black strands brushing her cheek. She was happily chit-chatting away, and then, remembering that I'd been shot at, wanted to hear the story again and see where the bullets hit.

When I finished my babbling recount of the event, she said, "You know, that incident was quite unfortunate for you, but fortunate for me."

I rapped the tailboom that I'd been leaning on with my knuckle. "You mean this incident, where I was nearly killed by bullets and fire... that was fortunate for you?"

"Well, think about it... Because of that, you were based in Bhubaneswar for a time, and we came to know each other better."

I laughed, "Ahh, yes, the silver lining!" You have a point, don't you, my dear?"

Not much was left to do but fly away, so we said our goodbyes. I impulsively wanted to give her a hug, but there were too many people around—particularly the troopers, who were now doing jumping-jacks and shouting cadence in exercise formation. From their cultural point of view, physical contact like that implied that she was promiscuous. As with holding hands, hugs were only between people of the same gender, from what I had seen. It just wasn't done in the countryside, especially between an unmarried couple, and I wished no trouble for her after I had left.

Taking her hand, though, and offering a smile, I said, "Au revoir, my dear Anika, you will be in my thoughts."

"Oohh, French! Captain! The language of romance!" she beamed.

"Oui, oui, Mon Cheri. I've been studying for you."

"What else do you know?"

"About five words total... it's a work in progress," I said.

"Ha! You got that right! You are a work in progress!"

I turned, climbed into the seat and started buckling up. She reached in, tugged on my trousers cuff and looked up at me with those adorable dark eyes.

"I will always remember you, Captain. You are in my heart forever."

Putting on her oversize sunglasses, she turned to walk away, and I stared for too long, committing each of her beautiful curves to memory. Getting started and with my takeoff checks complete, BK jumped in, and I advanced the throttle to flight. The downwash was swirling, her clothes buffeted by the wind. She smiled like a movie star and wrapped the dupatta around her head with one hand while waving with the other. After a quick wave back, I brought the Astar to a hover, did a pedal turn and accelerated through the parade ground. A sea of troopers parted to either side like the final scene in a Bollywood movie. We flew away into the milky-white sky, and I was slightly distracted when keying the radio for Raipur ATC.

It was only BK and I headed back into the jungle. The IPS in Raipur had tried to amend takeoff for a ten o'clock departure to accommodate an officer who was headed back to Jagdalpur. Rabinesh, who was overseeing the main mission from Dantewada, would not have it. He had his own priorities and time requirements to worry about without factoring in an officer who had been late for breakfast. He argued that if the officer could not wake up early enough for the pilot's scheduled eight o'clock departure, he could travel the highway back.

The flight plan called for a stop at Dantewada, where Rabinesh had a crate of assault rifles to deliver to a tiny village named Badrakalli, lying on the banks of the Godavari River. From Badrakalli, we would carry three troopers back to their district headquarters in Bijapur. After dropping them off, we were requested to shut down, have lunch and wait for an officer there who needed a lift to Jagdalpur. It would be five or six flight hours unless an emergency came up.

Spiraling down and landing on the large, Mi17-sized helipad, I saw Rabinesh wearing his usual casual uniform and his usual big smile. He had an odd substance in his hair, and it resembled a cow-pie. Shutting down and jumping out, I went to greet my friend, eyeing the matter on top of his noggin.

Shaking my outstretched hand, he was beaming. "Hello Mista Mike. You're looking good, my friend!"

"Thanks buddy, you're looking good too." Gesturing toward his cow-pie-colored dome, I said, "Except for your new hairstyle." I chuckled. "What is that?"

He was chuckling too. "Don't be afraid, it's hair coloring."

"Hair coloring? You have gray hairs to hide, old man?" I grinned. We were about the same age. "I would never have guessed it. Normally, you look like a supermodel."

"You think so?"

"Yeah... Well, more like a footwear model... That'd be better."

"That'll be my new part-time job!" he said, reaching down to dust off his sandals. "But yeah, I do have a few gray hairs, it comes from dealing with deranged pilots."

"You have looked in the mirror today, right? You look like the deranged one."

"The gray hair doesn't bother me, but my wife... She can't stand to look at them... or me, at times. Come on, brother, let's have coffee. We have idli and gravy too, if you're hungry."

"I have a long day ahead. Maybe I should load that crate of rifles and be off. I've never been to this place called Badrakalli before," I said.

"Are you afraid you won't be able to find it?"

"No, I'll find it alright, tough guy. What I'm really worried about is if you made that disgusting coffee, or if a real cook did."

"Oh, is that why I hear you're leaving us again? My cooking skills?"

"Yep, I'm headed to Mumbai, gonna join the Bollywood scene," I smiled.

"Well, that you will have to tell me about. Come on, let's eat."

54.

Scarred for Life

Badrakalli village was so tiny it barely fit the description of a village; there were only a few shacks, partially constructed with corrugated tin, and three stout stucco buildings housing the combined IPS and CRPF forces. The village lay near the confluence of the Indravati and Godavari Rivers that formed the borders of Chhattisgarh, Maharashtra and Andhra Pradesh, and these rivers and their surrounding lands were much the same as the rest of the area: remote. Barring the northern Himalayan region of India, this jungle landscape that we roamed was probably the most far-flung in the country.

Flying in from Dantewada, we approached the camp overhead at four thousand feet. Everything looked in order, we received the proper smoke signal, and I started our descent. The two rivers, which had been running full and bank-to-bank during the monsoon, had drained off to a relative trickle inside their main channels. On each side of the sparkling, narrow ribbon of water were miles and miles of cream-colored sand. A group of villagers with a team of oxen were out on the dry riverbed, filling their cart with this sand, and they looked up and gazed at our helicopter while we spiraled down to the helipad.

I could see a number of troopers spaced around the perimeter, more so than I would usually see at my landing zones, and they were armed and attentive. Most of the troopers were wearing at least partial camouflage uniforms, and they were paying close attention to their surroundings, in contrast to the shirtless, vacant stare of the riff-raff found at places like Kistaram.

Hovering down to the helipad that sat on the edge of a twenty- or thirty-acre rainwater pond, I noticed that the pond was almost dry. Most of the surrounding land was flat, but there was just enough of a slope that the local people had long ago built an earthen dam on one end of the village to trap the runoff. It was only a couple of months after the monsoon, and I was surprised to see it nearly empty. Most of the rainwater ponds that we flew over on a daily basis were brimming with water, but theirs was already drained to less than the size of a baseball diamond. Judging from the villagers wading through the muddy water, it wasn't even knee deep.

Upon landing, BK and a few of the troopers hustled to offload the crate of rifles and ammunition, then they held a brief discussion just outside the throw of the main rotor blades. BK jogged back to the left side of the helicopter and shouted, "Passengers not ready, saa!"

"How long before they are?" I asked.

"Can you shut down, saa? 'Dey 'bout half-hour away... 'Dey still on patrol."

Shutting down in one of the farthest reaches of the jungle did not sound like a good idea. Still, I liked the look of the troopers; they appeared alert and well disciplined. I asked my trusty crew chief what he thought.

"What do you think, BK? The camp seems well patrolled and secure. What about the helicopter—can we trust that it will start up again, way out here?"

He looked around the perimeter, then back at me as he smiled and patted the doorframe with his hand. "'Dis good machine, saa, it okay to shut down."

I cut the throttle and pulled off my headset. When the screaming whine of the turbine subsided, all was quiet except for some gentle goat bleating and an occasional cow bell's chime. There was no wind rustling the leaves, no mechanical device of any kind to clutter up the auditory sense, nothing but the subdued talking of the troopers and the occasional jungle bird. The temperature was still moderate, and the usual heavy haze blocked out the sun's hot rays. It was beautiful.

Knowing that a promised half-hour of India time was optimistic and could easily become an hour or more, I grabbed my camera and went to investigate the sights of Badrakalli. BK and a few of the troopers stood by the razor-wire-topped perimeter fence and gossiped quietly in Hindi while the rifles and ammo were being carried back to the huts and shacks that comprised the camp. The usual onlookers hung around to see the white-skinned pilot, their first in a lifetime.

It was always peculiar shutting down at a new place like that, in front of hard-living and isolated villagers. The pattern was typical. Climbing out of the cockpit and down to the ground, a buzz started amongst the gathered crowd of gawkers, who lined up as close to the helipad as security allowed them. Taking off my hat to readjust the sweaty light brown locks of hair, they stirred even more, some of the old men pointing and chattering.

A few of the bolder kids gathered around me while I walked to what was left of their pond. They were full of piss, vinegar and smiles, jostling with each other to be the closest to me. They felt it vitally important to touch my arm—not a grab, just a small poke to see if my flesh was real or if I'd pop like a balloon.

The few villagers that I saw, perhaps forty, were gathered and began wading in the muddy pond. A herd of goats milling around in the drying mud outnumbered the villagers by about two to one, and apparently they were on the menu often; other than a few sparse rice paddies, there wasn't much for crops or vegetables around. The paddies and the pond were the only clear areas. Tall, green trees and jungle grew thick everywhere else. Being close to the river, I assumed fish were also a major portion of their diet, and they probably weren't the sticklers for veganism that most of their fellow countrymen were.

The pond water was shallow and dirty, the color of a chocolate milkshake. I didn't see how any form of life could possibly survive, but still they waded through it with fish nets. I watched for a while, and nothing resembling a fish was caught. The goats watched too, keen on them catching a good pile of fish; the more fish caught meant that less of their friends would end up on the dinner mat that evening, dinner tables being rare.

As I wandered around on the earthen dam, the reason for the low water became apparent; on both ends, water had washed away the corners, allowing most of the pond to escape. The monsoon rains did indeed fill up their catchment area, but nearing capacity, rainwater had started creeping around the sides of the dam. Having nothing but soft sand to hold it back, the water kept washing away more and more until only their current puddle remained.

The oxcart that had been out on the riverbed when we first flew over then came meandering along a trail through the trees, and stopped next to the washout. Men with buckets, some using only their hands, started scraping and shoveling the cart's contents into the gaping gully next to the dike. At that rate, they might have had it filled by the next monsoon, but with nothing to support the soft dirt and sand, they were likely to lose it all again. Perhaps I should have helicoptered out a cement mixer along with the crate of rifles.

Interrupting my newly acquired role as dam repair supervisor, a half-dozen kids came running out from the direction of the helicopter, all laughing and giggling as they pointed over their shoulders.

"Saa, saa!" they yelled excitedly and pointed back toward the helicopter, three-quarters of a mile distant. Seeing activity back on the helipad, my escort of munchkins and I started walking back, ready to get to work again.

The three passengers I was sent to pick up were the superintendent of Bijapur district and his two bodyguards. Reaching the helipad, though, I noticed a fourth trooper with the look of advanced malaria. The superintendent, dressed in camouflage fatigues and jungle boots, had an AK47 slung on his shoulder and a sidearm on his hip. He was a stoic and serious, mustachioed sort in his mid-forties. "Namaste, Captain," he said with no smile but a firm handshake. "How are you?"

"Namaste, sir."

Not waiting for my reply to his query, he continued, "Captain, do you have room for one more today? This man is quite ill and needs medical attention in Jagdalpur."

"Load him up, sir, let's go."

We had enough fuel to fly all the way back to Jagdalpur, so upon landing at Bijapur, we declined the offer for fuel but accepted the offer for lunch while waiting for the Jagdalpur-bound officer. The superintendent and his bodyguards were taken away by one SUV, while the malaria medevac, plus BK and I, were hauled aboard another and taken back to the barracks to relax and wait.

When we overflew Jagdalpur airport upon our eventual return, the crew was gripped in a cricket match taking place in my parking area on the airport ramp. Hearing and then seeing me fly overhead sent them all scurrying for fire extinguishers and coveralls. The ball got away from one of the chaps, who chased it along the runway into the dirt.

I landed next to Zach's Jetranger and shut down. The Bijapur IPS officer, who had finally shown up after a delay, waved a quick thank you and disappeared before I had cut the engine. Two of the rifle-slinging security guards helped the malaria patient hobble off the ramp and to a waiting ambulance. It was late afternoon, with the sun maybe an hour away from touching the distant trees on the horizon, and other than the faint, acrid smell of smoke coming from nearby brushfires, the conditions were ideal for a good jog down the runway. Zach arrived from the guesthouse in his jogging shorts and started stretching his giraffe-sized legs. Having my own running gear with me, I told him to wait while I changed into my shorts, using the backseat of the Astar as my locker room.

Babeesh, distracted earlier by tallying the cricket score, didn't realize that I was inside the aircraft or what I was doing and had started climbing all over it working on the post-flight inspection. With a passing glance inside, he accidentally got to inspect more than he cared to while I was in a disadvantaged state of undress.

The other crewmembers, guffawing like it was comedy hour, knew that I was changing clothes, but could not pass on a bit of odd humor and had let him approach the helicopter clueless. Seeing too much, Babeesh shrieked and jumped from the helicopter as if he had burned his hands. He stumbled and fell to the ground, twisting an ankle in front of the now-hysterical crew.

"Sorry, saa," he yelled, rolling on the pavement and clutching his leg, "I so sorry! I di'nt know you was there, saa!"

Knowing the crew and loitering guards were having too much fun at our expense, I popped open the left door and hung my ghostly white buttocks outside for the rest of them to view, assuredly scarring them for life.

55.

So This Is Christmas

MAOISTS ABDUCT 5 TROOPERS IN CHHATTISGARH

So read the English-edition newspaper headline in Jagdalpur one morning, and I wondered if that would mean an additional flight or two for us. I didn't wonder long; while perusing the article, a call came from Rabinesh requesting a flight to the area.

"Good morning, buddy," he said. "How goes it today, my friend?"

"Another day in tropical paradise, Rabinesh," I answered. "I'm in the middle of a bikini wax, can you call back in fifteen minutes?"

"What? A bikini what?" His voice went up an octave, "What are you doing with wax?"

The troopers had been headed to their homes near Naranpur on leave from distant and tiny Dhanora IPS camp when guerillas stopped the battered country bus they were in and forced them off at gunpoint. This, after troopers in the area had been instructed by their superiors to avoid backcountry buses when going on leave. The Maoist-Naxalites had warned that they would do such a deed if any troopers were found on the public buses, and the threat of abductions increased substantially further away from the main highway. It didn't seem the IPS had an alternate plan to transport their troopers heading out on leave, though. We were trying, but we could not keep up with the number of flight tasks requested. Covering hundreds of square miles, as we were, required a squadron of helicopters.

The mission called for a flight with General Thomas and his entourage to Naranpur district headquarters, with possible further flying if it was deemed practical to search for the missing men. The officers I talked with were disgusted with the troopers for ignoring warnings and orders and didn't want to waste time by looking for careless wrongdoers. They were concerned, of course, but frustrated. The Maoist-Naxalites strived for attention, and this incident provided plenty, being splashed all over regional and national news. It was the troopers' own fault that they were abducted, but the officers could not simply ignore the incident. A reluctant mission was proposed, and I started my flight planning.

We flew the general, his bodyguard and a government appointed hostage negotiator the thirty-minute flight from Jagdalpur to Naranpur, where several senior officers were waiting. A convoy of Tata SUVs rushed them away to a nearby guesthouse and, after we had the helicopter secured, Babeesh and I were taken to the same building. Considering the remoteness of Naranpur, there were a surprising number of journalists milling about at the guesthouse guard gate, snapping photos and taking notes while our identification was checked by the guards.

"You look like Mr. Bollywood, Babeesh," I said.

He was overdue for a haircut, and his oily, black bush of a hairdo was pointing into the air like a fuzzy-troll doll. He smiled his red, paan-stained smile, running fingers through his grimy locks and said, "Saa, pe'haps 'dey want my autograph."

The guesthouse was converted into a command bunker of sorts, with a bank of landline phones set up awaiting the hostage takers' demands. These, along with each of the officers' multiple mobile phones, which were lined up in front of them, rivaled the amount of communication circuitry on the space station. I was welcomed into the common area of the guesthouse, where the men had gathered and trays of finger food and drinks were provided, but I didn't stay long. Mostly, I relaxed in the private room offered me or paced in the shade of the tree-lined courtyard.

With the phones not ringing and nothing accomplished, a few hours later a reconnaissance flight was requested. The phrase "In doubt, fly 'em out" was coined by one of the officers, and the expression gained purchase; in a day of inaction, nothing screamed action more than a chopper hammering through the air. "Flying them out," however, seemed unlikely.

I took off with three officers and the general, leaving the hostage negotiator back with the phones. The last we saw of him, his eyes were closed, arms folded, and his head was bobbing up and down off his chest.

Dhanora was seventeen straight line miles south of Naranpur, and the passengers were in no hurry, so I kept the speed down to sixty knots while maintaining a safe altitude above ground and out of rifle range. We followed the dirt road where it snaked through the first rice paddies outside of Naranpur, then through the hills and trees as agricultural land quickly gave way to jungle.

The officers had their headsets off and were carrying on a chatty, shouting conversation with a few seldom and random glances out the window to the terrain below. I kept puttering along until we reached the speck in the road that was Dhanora. Pointing out the window and announcing to them that we were over the location, I heard them become silent briefly while they absorbed the view.

We flew on to Orcha, just another eight miles southwest and where IPS/CRPF Intelligence theorized the captives had been taken. Obviously, there was no sign of them in the midday sunshine, but as General Thomas explained, hearing the helicopter flying overhead would help keep the trapped troopers morale healthy, if they were in earshot.

Orbiting the tiny village half a dozen times, I felt my pucker factor increase with each turn; I was plenty high enough to be out of reach of conventional rifles, but that didn't stop the feeling that we were being tracked by a hundred gun sights. Puttering along the road back to Naranpur, we criss-crossed back and forth in order to saturate as much terrain as possible with our delightful chopper sound of music.

Back at the helipad, Babeesh helped the officers down while I cut the throttle.

"Good job, Mike. Do you need fuel before heading back to Jagdalpur?" asked the general while getting out.

"If you're finished, sir, we'll take fuel and prep for Jagdalpur."

"We're done for now. We gave the prisoners a glimmer of hope, but there's nothing else we can do but wait for the phone call... The fuckers probably want a prisoner exchange." He scowled, then checking his watch, said, "I've maybe two hours here yet... say, takeoff at five?"

"We'll be ready."

Unlike all my other VIP passengers, the general respected punctuality and meant what he said when he gave a certain time. At five minutes to five, he rolled up. It was only him and his bodyguard—the hostage negotiator and others were staying in Naranpur to finish their work.

Several days later, the hostages would all be released unharmed and would publicly receive an award for bravery. Back at the IPS base, though, they were drilled for not following procedures.

It had taken all of forty minutes to fuel up from the fuel barrels Naranpur IPS kept on hand. The rest of the time I'd killed inside the nearby barracks in front of a fan, reading a book. Babeesh spent the time telling stories with the troopers around the helicopter. The whole of India appeared to be champion story tellers.

General Thomas also liked to tell stories and gossip. Every time he flew with us, if he wasn't entertaining colleagues, he donned one of the headsets in back and chewed the fat with me. Being that his English was excellent, we covered a broad range of topics. After taking off from Naranpur and setting course for Jagdalpur, we had been talking over the hostage situation, but then it became quiet momentarily.

"By the way," I said, "I want to remind you that I'll be taking the helicopter to Mumbai for maintenance in several days... Zach will still be here with his helicopter, though."

"What?" He had been lost in thought, looking out the window. "Oh yeah, I saw a letter come across my desk to that effect. We're gonna miss this chopper. When are you coming back?"

"There's nothing definite planned yet. It seems the upcoming work will take time. Not only are we doing the required maintenance, but we've decided to install air conditioning."

"Oh, nice," he chuckled. "I'll request flights more often if that's the case."

"It'll be more comfortable, for sure... Also, I may head back to the USA during that time. I'm still waiting for the company to decide."

"Got it. But you're coming back to Jagdalpur at some point, yeah?"

"I can't answer that, either. My one-year contract is coming to an end soon and, if given a chance to fly back home, I may check out job options back there."

"I see," he said.

"This company wants me back, too, so I'll have to weigh my different options in the coming weeks."

"Right, right. Well, you'll have to do what's best for you, but we'd love to have you back, Mike," he said, giving me the warm and fuzzies.

Oftentimes while flying, if it had been quiet between us for a while, he would start humming a tune just loud enough for the voice-activated intercom to turn on. Since he was a fan of rock and roll, it was usually something I recognized, and even if it was a bit off-key, I'd still put forth my best guess.

"Sounds like Black Sabbath," I'd say, or, "Is that Tom Petty?" He'd hum for a while, his mind working.

We talked about the Maoists or flight operations, but our conversations covered everything from family to farming, the Foo Fighters to *Flags of Our Fathers,* food and booze to football teams. He was well versed in American pop culture and movies, and if nothing else clicked, the default topic would be music. We shared the same taste; although his favorites were more from the classic rock genre, he liked a broad range of hits. Once, he burned me a number of blues tracks on CD. Quite serious at times, he was also a fun-loving guy, and the troopers respected him.

On our way back to base, he asked, "What are your plans for Christmas?"

It was only a few days away, but I hadn't given it much thought. I figured it would be nothing special: Skype back home, an extra piece of chicken perhaps. I knew Santa Claus wouldn't find me in the jungle.

"No plans," I said, "Maybe a beer or two."

"We're having a little get together at my house on Christmas Eve, a few people for dinner. Why don't you and Zach come join us?"

"That sounds great. I'd like that. I'm sure Zach would too."

"We can have a few drinks, and my wife is making a feast, usually more food than any of us can eat. She's a great cook." His wide, stout girth was proof enough of that.

After we landed back at Jagdalpur, he reached over the front seat, shook my hand, smiled and said, "See you in a couple days, Mike."

"Looking forward to it, see you then."

Christmas Eve cocktail hour started at eight, and being the prompt individuals we were, Zach and I arrived at seven forty-five. General Thomas' government house was an immense, white, one-story building built during British colonial times. It was gated and guarded, with a spacious courtyard and ample shade trees, palm and eucalyptus being the most prevalent. Inside, the ceiling must have been twelve or fourteen feet high and, like the outside, whitewashed throughout. In his living room was an immense wide-screen TV showing a Van Halen documentary.

Dressed in a white cotton shirt and khakis, he greeted us cheerily at the door. We were the first guests to arrive, and while we exchanged pleasantries and small talk, his wife rushed out of the kitchen with a plate of hors d'oeuvres. She was wearing an apron over blue jeans and a Western-style blouse. In appearance and demeanor, she was the female version of her husband, albeit in a more elegantly feminine way.

She gave us a quick smile, then was all business. She thrust the plate under our noses and said, "Here, you guys try these." It was a plate of little chicken drumsticks, and it was more of an order than a suggestion. "You're the first here, and you have to tell me if they're alright."

They were dipped in a red, pasty sauce. Grabbing a drummie, I shoved it in my mouth and peeled off the meat like I was a miniature tree debarker.

"Careful," she said, "they might be a little spicy."

As the first molecules of chili paste erupted on my tongue and the nerve-searing spice spread across my gums, I held up a thumb and said, "Excellent! Wouldn't change a thing!"

We had not arrived empty handed—we gave him a bottle of Johnnie Walker, and from that he poured the drinks. We all clinked glasses, toasted each other a Merry Christmas, and settled into our chairs, waiting for the other guests to arrive.

"Don't you guys worry about flights tomorrow," the general said, while the whiskey began to flow. "Tonight is for celebrating, and tomorrow is for relaxing. You can have the day off."

Great idea, as birds would be singing the next morning by the time we left.

Several of the general's officers showed up, a couple local politicians from Jagdalpur, and a Dutch chap who worked nearby for Doctors Without Borders. When all of us were well lubricated and spunky, nearly ready to sit down for the meal, a familiar tune began to be heard over the din of our voices. The Dutch doctor looked out the door and said, "Carolers! There are carolers outside!"

Next door to the general's sat the Catholic Church. When Zach and I drove by it on our way to the party, we were surprised at the large congregation filling its courtyard in preparation for the Christmas Eve mass. Hinduism is by far the largest religion in India, but Christianity and Catholicism have deep roots there as well; Jagdalpur had its own diocese.

So This Is Christmas

The general told his guards to open the gate and let the carolers in, and without missing a beat, thirty or forty singers from the church walked through, lining up in orderly rows, singing "Joy To The World." It was chilly for India, in the mid-sixties, and most of the carolers were dressed in Christmas sweaters and scarves, just like a scene from *White Christmas*. They next belted out "Oh Little Child of Bethlehem," and if not for their strong Indian accents, I would have thought they were a close match to Bing Crosby.

56.

New Year

"Sorry, Captain, you'll have to wait for the regular collector to show up before you're able to take off. It's not my job." So said one of the air traffic controllers while he sipped chai tea and nibbled on a biscuit. "I apologize for his tardiness, but as you know, today is a holiday."

I was in the airport tower at Aurangabad, Maharashtra, on our way to Mumbai, and I had just inquired for the second time about payment of our landing and overnight parking fees. My stomach was unhappy with the way it had been treated the night before, New Year's Eve, and all I wanted was to be in my helicopter with the sun at my back and a cool breeze blowing through the window.

The company had waited until the absolute end of the year before giving BK and me firm orders to vacate Chhattisgarh. We had squeezed out as many flight hours and missions from the IPS and CRPF as we could, then had left Jagdalpur early on New Year's Eve with the intent of making it all the way to the company hangar in Mumbai by nightfall. Declining to fly hundreds of miles over vast jungle to our first fuel stop in Nagpur, I instead overflew Raipur and stayed close to roads and civilization, landing with only the legal reserve of fuel.

We were doing alright timewise up to that point, but then a lengthy delay on refueling at Nagpur put us behind schedule. All other commercial aircraft took priority over our little helicopter and we kept getting bumped down the refueling list by the likes of Kingfisher and India Airlines.

By the time we reached our second stop at Aurangabad and refueled, the day was waning and the likelihood of reaching

New Year

our friends at Juhu Aerodrome before darkness was doubtful. Sami, wanting to avoid any additional hotel and overnight costs, tried convincing me to push on. He did not understand the risks. Not the risks of flying at night—Mumbai is lit up like the bright side of the moon, and finding my way would have been elementary. The problem was that Juhu Aerodrome lay less than a mile from Mumbai International Airport, and the entire area is blasted with radar monitoring.

Landing after sunset at our secluded jungle base of Jagdalpur was one thing; while not particularly legal, it could still be accomplished without putting anyone in danger or the authorities going ape-crazy. But flying a Day VFR-only helicopter into the second busiest airspace in India at night would have been a quick way to get one's hinder in a sling.

"Captaaiin!" Sami prodded. "It's still early in the day, you should have plenty of time before sunset to reach Juhu."

"No, Sami, we can't afford the risk," I pushed back. "It's my license to fly we're talking about."

Specifically, it wasn't my pilot license that I would risk losing. Indian DGCA had no authority to take my FAA license; however, if I was found to have disregarded regulations, they could have revoked my Indian FATA, the slip of paper that was my authorization to fly in India. I did not want to leave like that, if I was leaving.

"But it's New Year's Eve, Mike. Do you want to spend it alone in Aurangabad, or with the crew in Mumbai? I know they're having a party at the hangar tonight."

Now he was just trying to make me feel bad.

"Looks like it'll be only BK and me here tonight," I said, "But we're gonna paint the town red, just the same."

"You're gonna paint... what?"

"It's an expression, buddy. Hey, do you think you could find us a couple of rooms in town while we secure the helicopter?"

"Alright. I feel bad for you guys, stuck out there," he said, relenting. "I'll make it up to you. Give me an hour, and I'll try to book the best hotel I can find."

I was a little concerned that what Sami called the best hotel he could find would end up being the cheapest hotel he could find, but he did come through for us and booked a couple of rooms at the Rama International Hotel. A quite gorgeous place, it must have been at least a four star. It was a six star compared to the places I had laid my head over the previous couple of years. They sent a uniformed driver in a vintage, but well-maintained, Hindustan Ambassador sedan to pick us up. He must have been the only driver in the whole of Maharashtra to pass his driver's exam honestly. He calmly maneuvered through traffic from the airport to the Rama's lobby entrance, and not once did he need or use his horn—a pleasant change of pace compared to the horn-honking dirt track racers that clogged the road.

Entering the hotel, we were greeted by a festive buzz through the busy halls and corridors as the other hotel guests and partiers prepared for the evening. The saree-wearing beauty-queen receptionist who checked us in explained that there would be a buffet dinner and drinks available later. She said it would be starting early and going late, and that the pool area was being set up with music and lights. When we were shown to our rooms, BK and I agreed to meet at eight thirty for the start of dinner.

Before leaving Jagdalpur, I had packed everything I possessed in India, which didn't amount to much. Now, I dug out the cleanest and nicest clothes I could find. That still left me underdressed compared to most of the other guests, but no one seemed to mind as I wandered about the expansive hotel and its sweeping courtyard, passing time until evening.

During dinner with BK later, his phone would not stop ringing. He was taking phone calls from friends and family all over India, and his deep, booming laughter filled the restaurant, drowning out the nonstop chatter of the other diners who filled the room. Spirits were high and getting higher. When we were finished with our meal I held up my whiskey and toasted BK, wished him a Happy New Year, then stood up to peruse the scene around the decorated pool area.

He still had the phone stuck to his ear, but toasted me back with his glass of cola. Covering the mouthpiece, he said, "Happy New Year, Cap'n. You like me ta' come with you?"

"Sure, bud," I said. "I'm gonna relax outdoors for a while, maybe put on my dancing shoes."

"Yes! Dancing, Captain! Tonight is a night for dancing!" His baritone laughter shook the drinking glasses.

The hotel had tables and chairs set up around the pool area, and we found a table, sat down, and sipped our drinks. BK continued jabbering on his phone with half of India while I vowed to have only a couple of drinks; we had our final leg to fly in the morning.

Having only a couple of drinks was vastly shy of my past New Year celebrations. I thought back to the year before, when I had been on the helideck of a pitching and rolling tuna boat, celebrating New Year's Eve in the middle of the South Pacific with Cager and the deck hands. Cager and I had been perched on the float of the helicopter, our noses into the breeze over the bow, while the deck hands took up positions on the helideck, sitting cross-legged. The seas were not violent, but still we had to use the helicopter tie-down straps from time to time to hold steady, and holding steady became quite difficult as more of the oily, black night slipped by.

We had passed amongst ourselves what was apparently an endless supply of Korean Soju—because try as we might, we couldn't drink it all—and chased it down with Budweiser while watching a thousand stars bob up and down on the invisible horizon. We spent all night up on the helideck, nearly losing a couple of deckhands overboard when they went to relieve themselves off the side of the boat; the helideck had no safety rails. Although Cager and I talked about it, we never did get around to doing a head count the next morning.

Only when the Pacific's eastern sky began to change color from black to gray to a light pale did we creep down off the helideck and drop face-first into our bunks, pain free; but we did not stay there long. A few hours later, we rendezvoused and tied up with a resupply ship in the middle of the ocean. The ship brought spare parts, food and fuel, and then, the last item we wanted to see during that brutal morning: our replacement stock of beer and booze.

We were not in top shape, to say the least, and dropping the newly arrived hooch over the side was discussed. More than one deckhand spent time arched over the rail of the main deck in loud wretchedness. I felt near to death and swore myself off alcohol. Even tough and grizzled old Cager, who had a stomach of cast iron, had to evacuate his guts twice. Regardless, we hauled it aboard.

"Oh gaawwd," Cager doubled over and moaned, holding his gut with one hand and gripping the rail with his other gnarled-up and liver-spotted crab hook. "Jus' fuckin' t'row me over da side... I'd do it myself, but too weak."

Digging out a cigarette, he lit up and inhaled deeply. Blowing the smoke out in a spluttering, lung murdering cough, he croaked, "Oh yeah, jus' what da doctor ordered."

Scuttling my seafaring ruminations, I received a text message from Anika, who'd been partying with her sister and friends in Bhubaneswar. They had gone to a concert at one of the colleges and, for the New Year stroke of midnight itself, were celebrating at a high-flying restaurant. I called her, but the conversation was short.

"Hello Michael! Happy New Year!" she screamed, the music, shouting and laughter from her end registering on the Richter scale.

"Hello, my dear! Happy New Year to you!"

"Where are you, Captain? Are you in Mumbai?"

"No, not yet! We had to stop in Aurangabad!" I shouted back into the phone, a few bystanders raising their eyebrows at my increased decibels.

Someone near her was shouting loudly in Hindi, and the volume of her ferocious reply back at them made me pull the phone away from my ear. Then she was shouting to me: "Aurang-what? I can't hear you, Michael, I'll call you back later! Sorry!"

With a click, she was gone.

My hotel's own music had begun thumping, and the Bollywood beat combined with alcohol had the younger men in attendance yelping and dancing on the grass of the courtyard near the pool. Dancing? Perhaps, but there was probably a better word to describe what they were doing, as their flailing about resembled more of a medical condition than an art form.

With my eardrums getting hammered, I stuck it out until the big countdown, searching for a New Year's kiss from an Indian angel that would never come. I retired to my room shortly after and prepared for the flight into Mumbai.

Planning for an eight o'clock departure the next day had me in the Aurangabad airport tower at seven, too early for the aforementioned airport fee collector. BK was at the helicopter doing his preflight; we had refueled the day before, wanting to avoid any delays from that particular task. It was just a matter of paying the landing and overnight parking fees, then we could be on our way.

Once again, something I had eaten was not sitting well in my stomach, and I had been awake earlier than I wanted to be, assuming the familiar position in the bathroom. It wasn't the whiskey, I'm sure. That had amounted to less than three shots. Perhaps it was the stale vada-donut the dazzling receptionist had offered upon check-in the evening before. Whatever the cause, the air inside the control tower was stuffy and warm, and the smell of someone's spicy breakfast wafted around the room. I wanted to be away.

Finally getting the payment and receipt handled, I barreled down the long stairwell to the tarmac. As I gained speed down the first flight of stairs, one of the controllers shouted down after me, "Captain, if you could wait five minutes, we can give you a ride to your aircraft!"

Our Astar was parked over 400 yards from the tower, but I was in the mood for a walk and fresh air. Without stopping my downward descent, I yelled back, "No thanks, I'm walking!"

"But Captain, only five minutes!" I let his last words go unanswered, echoing up and down the narrow stairwell. Five minutes could mean five, or it could mean fifty. Reaching the bottom, I swung open the door and walked out to BK and our helicopter in the quiet, wide open space and peaceful morning that only a small airport with little air traffic can provide.

Our flight out of Aurangabad first crossed mile after mile of agricultural fields: not only rice paddies, which was the predominant farm crop back in Chhattisgarh, but other crops, such as corn and sugar cane. In fact, rice paddies became more scarce the farther west into Maharashtra we flew. About halfway through the 150 mile flight to Mumbai, the terrain below began to rise and became more rugged and hilly. I would hesitate to say it was mountainous, but at sixty miles inbound to the big city, the terrain was getting steeper and topped out over four thousand feet.

By that time, I had Mumbai's Approach Control frequency dialed in on the radio and heard that the controller was a busy man. I had never flown into Mumbai before and hoped for a smooth flight. I searched my notes and information, most of what I had received from Chatterjee, but could not find any alternate, less busy frequency.

Knowing that one of our company hangars was in Mumbai and that flying there was a possibility, Chatterjee, in his thorough role as mentor all those many months ago, had explained in detail what to expect if I was to fly there. And because VFR charts were rare, he even sketched a few maps for guidance. At the time, I was bored stiff while he droned on and on with that info, but when flying farther and farther into Mumbai airspace, I was scouring every detail he had written and was hopeful we would end up in Mumbai and not Karachi.

57.

Mumbai

Waiting for just the tiniest of breaks in the radio exchange between the airliners and Mumbai Approach Control, I keyed my radio and called the controller, rattling off who I was, where I was and where I wanted to go. There was a moment's hesitation from his end while he switched gears and thought processes. From the usual, heavily scheduled IFR (Instrument Flight Rules) airliners that he was directing for landing at Mumbai International, he had to stop and consider me—one lone and unscheduled VFR helicopter, flying inbound from Aurangabad and landing at Mumbai Juhu Aerodrome.

He fired back an acknowledgement and followed that quickly with a transponder squawk code and several sentences of altitude and location restrictions, along with his clearance to the next reporting point. I was able to satisfactorily read back his instructions and clearances, evidently, as having no objections, he was done with me. With barely a breath, he was on to the next Boeing or Airbus filling up his radar screen.

BK had been crew chief on many flights into Juhu and was familiar with the landmarks around Mumbai. With his eyeballs looking out the left side of the helicopter and mine looking out the right, together with Chatterjee's detailed notes, we had no problem finding our way. Given the proximity of Juhu to the busy international airport—the departure end of runway 27 was less than a mile away—it was quite critical that the pilot knew where he or she was. Overshooting Juhu could put them in the path of a departing jet.

Unless the pilot was distracted or a complete screw up, it was quite straightforward when flying from the northeast as we were. There were two guiding terrain features that would lead directly to Juhu, the first being an obvious set of north-to-south running railroad tracks. If you happened to miss them, in another few miles you would hit the coast and the Arabian Sea; turn south there, and soon you would see Juhu's runway 08-26 jutting out onto to Juhu beach. Of course, a good aviation GPS will tell you everything you need to know, too, if properly set-up.

Approach Control eventually handed me off to Juhu Tower, who warned me of two taxiing helicopters. Besides that, there was no other traffic, and he cleared me to land. As there were many hangars spread across the old airfield, BK pointed out our immense hangar, and I hover-taxied over to it, coming to a stop in front of a gathered crowd from our company.

I shut down while BK jumped out and began greeting his old acquaintances and colleagues; it was the return of a prodigal son. There must have been close to fifty people, including Chandru, Mumbai's lead mechanic, and Babeesh, who had left Jagdalpur days before and reached Mumbai by railroad.

The main rotor coming to a halt, I switched off the battery, climbed down and was greeted like Charles Lindbergh crossing the Atlantic—if you subtract 150 thousand people. Old faces and new, all were happy to have us and thrilled to get the party started.

Chandru shook my hand, surrounded by smiling colleagues, and said, "Happy New Year, Captain. Welcome to Mumbai."

"Thank you, Chandru." Getting cheap chuckles, I said, "Now someone show me the way to Bollywood, I need to see my agent."

Juhu Aerodrome was built in 1928 as India's first civil aviation airport and served as Mumbai's airport up to and during World War Two. After the war, commercial operations were moved to the nearby and much larger British Royal Air Force airfield, then known as Santacruz, which later became what it is today: Mumbai International.

Juhu Aerodrome still had a lot of commercial traffic, but little if any of the fixed-wing variety. The oldest flying club in India, the Bombay Flying Club, still had meetings and a couple of airplanes at the airport, but due to the congested airspace, most of their flights and training were held elsewhere. There were about a hundred helicopters based there, though, most of those used for offshore oil and gas missions; Pawan Hans Helicopters and Global Vectra Helicopters were two of the biggest companies, although there were a few smaller outfits.

After handshakes, introductions and "Namastes" were passed around, the maintenance crew attached the wheels to the Astar and rolled it into our gargantuan hangar. With the addition of my aircraft, the hangar held four helicopters: two Astars, one MD600 and one well-experienced Hiller UH12. Chatterjee was flying the Mi17 up in Shimla, but even if that beast of a helicopter had been inside, there would have been plenty of room left over for a barn dance.

For the rest of the morning and up until lunchtime, I was shown around and introduced at the various offices. The chairman's wife liked dogs and kept several charity cases around and inside the hangar, including one poor old soul that had cancer. Another one, Bruno, a yellow lab that carried an empty water bottle wherever he went, was instantly my friend after a short game of fetch. He rarely left my side during my stay in Mumbai.

Inside the hangar, staff had set up tables and chairs with a buffet-style lunch of masala, aloo gobi and other bowls of food, varying in shades of gooey color from orange to yellow to brown. It wasn't long before someone found a boom box and Bollywood music echoed off the metal siding of the building. When lunch wrapped up, glasses of whiskey were passed around and, as the afternoon oozed into evening, I asked Boppi, the cook, to show me to my quarters. Activities were getting loud and wild out on the hangar floor disco, and again, there were a few too many men dancing together. After I was rambunctiously asked to dance for the fourth time, I could tell conditions and brain-cell counts were deteriorating.

As Boppi grabbed one of my bags, I asked, "Have I seen you before? You look familiar, Boppi. Are you related to Beebu in Jagdalpur?"

"Jee, saa, Beebu's my brotha', saa," he replied. "Banda in Bhubaneswar, he my brotha' too."

"Oh yeah," I chuckled, remembering the time Banda wet himself.

"Banda's told me 'bout you, saa," he smiled. "You climb walls like Spiderman!"

The company's hangar was more than an aircraft hangar; the first and second floors consisted of offices, while the third and fourth floors were guest rooms; I was billeted on the third floor with, apparently, every mosquito traveling through Mumbai. After a year in India, I still had not learned to carry a mosquito net wherever I went, and I paid the price that first night. I cursed India's builders and architects all night long for not being able to construct mosquito-proof buildings, even in the twenty-first century. Turning the air conditioning way down low and the ceiling fan way up high, I wrapped myself in a bed sheet like a mummy, again, and fell over onto the bed. The whole night through, I tossed and turned, sweated and slapped, and if parts of my body became exposed to the hungry devils, scratched.

It took a day for the maintenance team to recover enough from their disco fever to start gathering around my Astar again. Slowly but steadily, aircraft panels were pulled off and laid out of the way. The aftermarket air-conditioning unit had arrived from the USA but was trapped in Mumbai's Himalayan Mountains of red tape at Customs, awaiting inspection.

Chandru and BK were seated in chairs next to the helicopter, supervising their underlings while they went about disassembling the aircraft. "How goes it, gents?" I asked. "Did we lose anyone to the dance troupe the other night?"

They chuckled, and BK said, "No saa, don' haf to worry 'bout dat happenin."

"Well, good... What's the latest news with the aircraft?"

"Good news and bad news," said Chandru. "The good news, our air conditioning should clear Customs in a week."

"So that means three weeks, India time," I said, grinning and ever the smart ass.

Mumbai

"Yep, you're right," he said, smiling tolerantly. "The bad news, though, is we're waiting for a section of the engine to come from France, and it's on hold at the factory."

In a phone conversation with Sami, he had mentioned the issue. He was hoping it would be a minor delay. Now it appeared the helicopter might be grounded longer than they anticipated, and my chances of taking leave back in the USA were improving.

"Alright, let me know when you hear something, or if you need anything from me," I said. "I'll be in touch with Sami, and I'm gonna push for leave time."

The days went by too slowly while I waited for Sami and the rest of the head office to get sorted and decide on my leave. In the meantime, I ventured south from Juhu to see such sights as the Gateway to India, Marine Drive and Chowpatty Beach. In a true sign of desperation, I even spent time inside a shopping mall.

I meant to check out Juhu beach as well, it was nearby and within walking distance from our hangar. I asked Chandru for directions.

"We used to be able to access the beach easily through the airport entrance on the west side," he said. "The beach is right off the end of runway 26, but the entrance was closed after the terrorist attacks. The only way now is to go out the east gate and hire a rickshaw."

"Can I walk there? Is it close enough?"

"Yeah, I suppose... But hire a rickshaw. It's only like thirty rupees."

"I'd like to walk and see what I could see."

"If you wanna walk," he said, "just take two left turns, one outside the gate, and the next left will take you directly to the beach."

"Got it," I said, and walked the half-mile to the gate.

Showing my identification at the airport exit and guard shack, I turned left and headed down the street. It was busy and noisy, with the usual horns of thousands of vehicles blaring away senselessly, and after walking for what I thought was a far-enough distance, saw a road headed west, left. I figured it must be the way. It looked smaller than the street I'd been following. *But hey, Chandru said the next left.*

I veered onto it without much hesitation, thinking I was on the correct heading, and continued walking. But after fifty yards, I felt that something was not right. It didn't look like a commercial street, and there was no traffic. A man dressed in dusty robes and turban noticed me, and his eyes bugged out. He was standing next to a tall, paint-flaked gate in front of an old, equally paint-flaked, dilapidated building. He rushed out on the road to overtake me. "Whe' you go? Whe' you go? You shou'n be heeya'." He pointed back the way I had come.

"The beach, Juhu beach," I said, "It's down this way, yes?"

"No, no, go back... and dat way," he pointed again and made shooing gestures, as if I were a large fly, "Fun'ral, fun'ral... Go now."

His accent was difficult, but I thought he said funeral. As I turned back, I hoped he didn't mean my funeral. Walking to where I had errantly made my turn, I glanced back at him, and he gestured wildly to keep moving. With great luck, I did.

I turned and left the man's forbidden road just as a surging crowd swung into it. They were in obvious mourning; women and men crying, children being rushed along with looks of confusion. There was the usual loud traffic noise, but over that I could hear howling and shrieking from the swarming mob that was now headed down the quiet lane I had barely vacated. I saw a coffin, but not really a coffin—it was a body wrapped in sheets being carried aloft in the middle of the mob, a few of the bearded chaps who were in the lead of the mournful procession looked my way and glared. I rounded the corner and picked up my pace, desiring distance.

58.

I.N.D.I.A.

Finding my correct left turn on a street that I hoped did not contain a dead body or a swarming mob, I continued walking until the pungent fragrance of sea air filled my nostrils and eradicated the smell of exhaust fumes and other filth that lined the street. The beach came into view and it was packed with Mumbaikar beachcombers, and as it was late afternoon, the relentless, blinding sun of the day was fading into a friendly orange balloon floating down toward the horizon.

Stopping at the Marriott, I considered a cold beer, but then wanting an atmosphere with a more local flavor, headed further down the beach. It was an enchanting sandy scene, albeit without bikinis and bare skin; everyone was dressed in their street clothes. I had on jeans and a pocket t-shirt and was quite underdressed compared to the fashionable button-down-dress-shirts-tucked-into-dress-pants look that many local gentlemen favored for beachwear. The surf was light, and the water shallow, which tempted more than a few daring teenagers to wade in up to their waists, splashing around and frolicking in the highly polluted water.

Although I had ridden the waves of the Arabian Sea during my US Navy years, I hadn't approached it from this angle, and I generally made it a point to touch every new sea I encountered, just out of a wayfarer's principle. Figuring this body of water should be no different, I walked close but not too far, and let a bit of the surf splash over my unbecoming jungle boots while dipping in a finger. Pulling my exploratory digit back for examination, there wasn't any stinging, or mutant organisms, and I surmised I would survive the encounter.

Continuing my walk down the beach, I found a cozy-looking open-air restaurant in front of a faded sign belonging to the Sea View Hotel. A plump, cheerful waiter loudly singing in Hindi showed me to a table overlooking the beach that was perfect for people watching and sunset critiquing. Ordering beer nuts, Budweiser and a plate of chicken, I made myself comfortable. There were twenty tables covered with blue and white checkered table cloths, half of them filled with Indian couples, although a foursome of older tourists with Australian accents sipped on beers a couple of tables away.

Crunching on the peanuts and pouring a mouthful of beer down my throat, I called my friends in Delhi. Sami answered, "Captaaiin! How are you?"

"Sami, I'm doing great. I have a cold beer in front of me, chicken on the grill and a great view of the sunset."

"Any women, Captaaiin?" he asked, his voice rising to a squeak.

"Yes and no," I said. "There are women everywhere, but they're all avoiding this foreigner. I'm at Juhu beach, my friend."

"You need to find a good Indian bride and settle down!" he laughed. "Captaaiin, I've been meaning to call you today. I have bad news, bro."

"Bad news?" My heart sank. I feared my leave was in peril. "What is it, Sami?"

"There's been further delay from France. Not until after the end of the month will we receive our engine parts."

"That is bad news," I lied.

"Captaaiin, what do you think about going on leave for a short time?"

"Paid leave?" I asked.

"Yes, oh yes, you are still an employee and part of the team, part of the family!" With his usual energy, he shouted that last phrase, making me pull the phone from my ear. Then he continued, "We feel this time will be better for you at home, and once the helicopter is ready, you can return fresh and strong to your job as King of the Jungle."

I.N.D.I.A.

This moniker for me, King of the Jungle, had been created by Sami months ago. At first, he used it to feed my ego when trying to persuade me to agree to his malarkey, but the title stuck and was used in nearly every conversation lately.

"Sami, paid vacation will be hard to take, but I'll give it a shot."

"Yeah, right, I knew you'd like that part," he said. "Listen, bro, I'll call you tomorrow once I have the travel arrangements hammered out. Be ready to move in the next couple of days."

After disconnecting with Sami, I leaned back in my chair and took another sip of beer. My chicken had arrived, still smoking and hot. On the beach nearby, a barefoot merchant was pushing his cart of coconuts toward what he hoped were his next customers—a young family whose four-year-old was pointing at the coconut drinks and trying to get his mother's attention. Just as common as the coconuts were the numerous carts of panipuri vendors. An unwritten rule must have been observed as the mini-merchants all remained evenly spaced out along the beach and did not encroach on one another's turf.

A couple of entrepreneurs had set up a miniature Ferris wheel and merry-go-round, offering rides to youngsters. Their Ferris wheel held four small benches in its circular frame and was no taller than six feet; the occupants were not much older than three or four years—any older or larger, and they wouldn't fit. The contraptions appeared to be safe enough; the fact that they were powered by the skinny arms of the proprietors ensured that the seated toddler occupants would not be propelled through the air at anything approaching takeoff velocity.

Families were sitting on the sand with blankets, others without, sharing a snack and enjoying the carefree mood a sandy beach at sunset provides. The sun was beginning to touch the far western horizon and becoming larger the lower it dropped. People were posing in front of the distant reddish-orange ball, taking snaps, or *clicks* as the Indian vernacular went, and I bothered the waiter to take a few of me with the fading, luminous sphere on my shoulder.

I have been lucky enough to see hundreds of beautiful sunsets, and a few stand out memorably. There was one on Beau Vallon Beach in the Seychelles, when the beauty of the moment combined with the company I shared it with seared a lasting, lifelong image in my mind. Another on Tanjung Aru beach in Borneo, a sheer explosion of color across the western sky caused everyone around to hush themselves and stand, with hands on hips, gaping in silent awe at the departing day, only the parrots squawking their approval from the trees.

That evening on Juhu Beach, my first and possibly only year in India drawing to a close, became another. I wasn't with a gorgeous member of the opposite sex, nor was I with a partying group of friends, but hundreds of strangers on a beach tainted with toxic seawater. I would've loved to have company, but I was content. It was the peculiarity and uniqueness of the scene that made the aloneness forgettable and the hazy sunset memorable.

A joke among expats who gave India a try was that I.N.D.I.A. is an acronym for I'll Never Do It Again. That once you have been there, tasted the tikka and sat on a toilet all night, or endured the hundreds of other infamous quirks about India, once was enough. If you'd been there, done that, and escaped with your life and sanity, you would never do it again. For me, I had sufficiently good reasons.

One of the biggest was that the food and hygiene did not agree with me. I had gone through my stash of loperamide within the first six weeks of being in-country. The months after that, I just dealt with it—the anti-diarrheal medicine seemed to have little effect on the treacherous bacteria that would invade my guts routinely anyway.

India, for the most part, was not keen on keeping clean. My initial exposure to that was at the first guesthouse I stayed at in Delhi after arriving a year earlier. Out of all the rooms within, the most disgusting was the kitchen, and that was not to be an isolated observation. I stayed in perhaps two dozen of these guesthouses. Most were run by my company at different locations, and others were run by the local government, or the

IPS and CRPF that I flew for, and every one of them would qualify for barnyard status.

Spilled and decaying old food, garbage, fruit and vegetable peelings left for days, cockroaches, ants, rats—I would sometimes even find snakes in the kitchens. I would like to think the hotels I was fortunate enough to stay at were held to a higher degree of hygiene, but I doubt it. It was the accepted culture. I can't speak for all of India, not having traveled to all corners of the country, but from Delhi to Mumbai, Bhubaneswar to Bangalore, Nagpur, Raipur and the jungles of Chhattisgarh, those places I came to know well, and cleanliness was not high on the list of priorities. The exception being the general's house and two or three others.

The cultural differences were colossal. The endless organized chaos that Indians lived with every day was hard to adjust to or ignore. I was raised in a developed country with law and order taken for granted; step outside the line, and there were consequences. I was raised in a family that stressed the importance of a strong work ethic. Seeing the half-assed and laissez faire attitudes spiked my blood pressure daily.

It was dangerous work. On the hangar wall in Mumbai hung my tailrotor driveshaft that was machine-gunned over Kistaram. I cheated death once that I know of; I wondered how many other times my Astar was in a bad guy's gun sights. Did I want to risk it again?

A couple of days later, Sami had an airline ticket in my inbox. He routed me through Amsterdam and arranged for a nice layover there before I would continue on to the frozen tundra near Minneapolis. I was eager to see friends and family, the midwinter cold not so much.

At the airport, I stood in line for my Immigration stamp, being harried and harassed, asking myself, *Why put up with it anymore?* When leaving Mumbai, I had mixed feelings; while I enjoyed flying for the IPS, CRPF and other paramilitaries, and enjoyed my position as "King of the Jungle," the culture of chaos left me wary.

The opportunity to continue with my exotic Indian experience won out. Although the decision wasn't easy and I was tempted by a job offer in Guatemala along with other pilot jobs closer to home in the USA, I wasn't ready to come home. I'd been working overseas for a few years by that point and had discovered so much more about the world than what cable news or the World Wide Web provided. I was curious to learn more. Not only about India, but any other majestic or not so majestic land where I could get my passport stamped, and get paid for doing it.

Once I hit the deck in a foreign land on my own terms—non-military, that is—there was no stopping. I would, of course, get home from time to time, but wanderlust always pulled me back to the airline check-in counter. What was I missing out there?

A quote from Mark Twain says, "Travel is fatal to prejudice, bigotry and narrow-mindedness." With the finite time we are given in this world, I should've started sooner.

Blasting off from Mumbai on a homeward bound Boeing marked the end of my first year in India, but the beginning of another three years of adventure when I returned.

Author's Note

Amassing vast fortune may be an elusive dream for many of us. I feel privileged to have met—and continue to meet—good friends, acquaintances and characters through aviation while seeing the world, and its people. That ranks close enough for me.

Michael Sobotta
Bangkok, Thailand
2015

www.ingramcontent.com/pod-product-compliance
Lightning Source LLC
Chambersburg PA
CBHW031404290426
44110CB00011B/259